AF560279

Farm Animals and Their Management

Farm Animals and Their Management

Dr. Poonam Lodhi

RANDOM PUBLICATIONS
NEW DELHI (INDIA)

Farm Animals and Their Management

ISBN 978-93-5111-377-5

Published in 2014 in India by

RANDOM PUBLICATIONS

4376-A/4B, Gali Murari Lal, Ansari Road
New Delhi-110 002
Phone : +91-11-43580356, +91-11-23289044
e-mail: randomexports@gmail.com, sales@randompublications.com,
info@randompublications.com

Type Setting by : Keystoneprintads, Delhi-110051
Digitally Printed at : Replika Press Pvt. Ltd.

Preface

Farm animals and their management, making and implementing of the decisions involved in organizing and operating a farm for maximum production and profit. Farm management draws on agricultural economics for information on prices, markets, agricultural policy, and economic institutions such as leasing and credit. It also draws on plant and animal sciences for information on soils, seed, and fertilizer, on control of weeds, insects, and disease, and on rations and breeding; on agricultural engineering for information on farm buildings, machinery, irrigation, crop drying, drainage, and erosion control systems; and on psychology and sociology for information on human behaviour. In making his decisions, a farm manager thus integrates information from the biological, physical, and social sciences.

Because farms differ widely, the significant concern in farm management is the specific individual farm; the plan most satisfactory for one farm may be most unsatisfactory for another. Farm management problems range from those of the small, near-subsistence and family-operated farms to those of large-scale commercial farms where trained managers use the latest technological advances, and from farms administered by single proprietors to farms managed by the state.

In Southeast Asia the manager of the typical small farm with ample labour, limited capital, and only four to eight acres (1.6-3.2 hectares) of land, often fragmented and dispersed, faces an acute capital-land management problem. Use of early maturing crop varieties; efficient scheduling of the sequence of land preparation, planting, and harvesting; use of seedbeds and transplanting operations for intensive land use through multiple cropping; efficient use of irrigation and commercial fertilizer; and selection of chemicals to control insects, diseases, and weeds-all of these are possible measures for increasing production and income from each unit of land.

In western Europe the typical family farmer has less land than is economical with modern machinery, equipment, and levels of education and training, and so must select from the products of an emerging stream of technology the elements that promise improved crop and livestock yields at low cost; adjust his choice of products as relative prices and costs change; and acquire more land as farm labour is attracted by nonfarm employment opportunities and farm numbers decline.

On a typical 400-acre (160-hectare) corn-belt farm in the United States with a labour force equivalent to two full-time men, physical conditions and available technologies allow a wide range of options in farming systems. To reach a satisfactory income requires operating on an increasing scale of output and increasing specialization. Corn and soybean cash-crop farming systems have increased in number along with corn-hog-fattening farms and corn-beef-fattening farms. Thus, the choice of a farming system, the degree of specialization to be chosen, the size of operation, and the method of financing are top concerns of management.

The objective of the book is to provide delegates with sufficient information and knowledge to be able to identify and understand modern animal production systems and their impact on animal health and welfare. It provides a vital insight into the current and recent issues facing the livestock production industries and highlights management practices and basic scientific principles.

I thank all members of my team who have helped in the preparation of the book. My special thanks go to "Random Publications" who have published the book.

– Dr. Poonam Lodhi

Contents

1

Introduction

Ever since the beginning of civilization, humans have depended on animals for many requirements, such as that of food (milk, meat and egg), clothing (hide or wool), labour (pulling, carrying load) and security etc. The development of desirable qualities in all such animal species, through creating better breeds, has been an important human achievement. For this, humans have consistently tried to improve the breeds of domesticated animals to make them more useful for them. As suggested, learn about the common breeds of such animals, their uses and some methods of improving their breeds.

UNDERSTANDING THE ANIMAL HUSBANDRY

The branch of science, which deals with the study of various breeds of domesticated animals and their management for obtaining better products and services from them is known as *Animal Husbandry*. The term husbandry derives from the word "husband" which means 'one who takes care'. When it incorporates the study of proper utilisation of economically important domestic animals, it is called *Livestock Management*.

DIFFERENT CATEGORIES OF ANIMALS

- *Wild*: Those that breed better where they are free than they do when they are captivated. They have no common use for humans. Example Lion, Tiger, Rhinoceres, Deer etc.
- *Tamed*: Those, which are caught from the wild and trained to be useful to humans in some way. Elephant, Chimpanzee, Gorilla, Yak etc.
- *Domesticated*: Those that are of use at home and are easily bred and looked after by humans. Common domesticated animals are dog, horse, cow, sheep, buffalo, fowl etc.

IMPORTANCE OF DOMESTIC ANIMALS

On the basis of utility, domestic animals are categorised into the following functional groups.

- Milk giving animals:
  - Cattle,
  - Buffalo,
  - Goat,
  - Sheep etc.
- Draught (used for load bearing) animals:
  - Bullock,
  - Horse,
  - Donkey,
  - Mule,
  - Camel,
  - Elephant,
  - Yak etc.
- Fibre, hide and skin yielding:
  - Sheep,
  - Goat,
  - Cattle,
  - Buffalo,
  - Camel etc.
- Meat and egg yielding animals:
  - Fowl (hen) and duck,
  - Goat,
  - Buffalo,
  - Pig etc.

MILK AND MEAT YIELDING ANIMALS

Depending upon the availability and regional considerations different animals are reared for the purposes of yielding milk and meat in India. India is the world's largest producer of milk. The majority of the milk consumed is also in liquid form in India. Over 53 per cent of milk produced in India is from the water buffalo and a majority of milk processing plants in the country depend upon buffalo milk. The *National Dairy Development Board (NDDB)* is the main agency behind the cooperative movement in India. India is now seeking joint ventures and financial participation from the private sector including foreign investment for production of milk and milk products in India.

CATTLE

Cattle mainly include cow, bull, oxen, goat, sheep etc. The females of the species provide milk, which in turn contribute animals protein to the diet of people. While the female species of these cattle are used for milk, the male species play an important role in the agricultural economy by providing labour, meat and hide. Milk itself is taken in many forms like ghee, curd, butter and cheese etc. The excreta of these animals (dung) is used as manure, in biogas and as fuel. There are several important breeds of cattle in India and abroad.

MILK YIELDING ANIMALS

What is a Breed

A breed is a group of one species of animals, which have the same descent and are similar in body shape, size and structure.

Categories of Important Breeds

There is following three categories:

1. Indian breeds
2. Exotic Breeds
3. Improved breeds

Indian Breeds

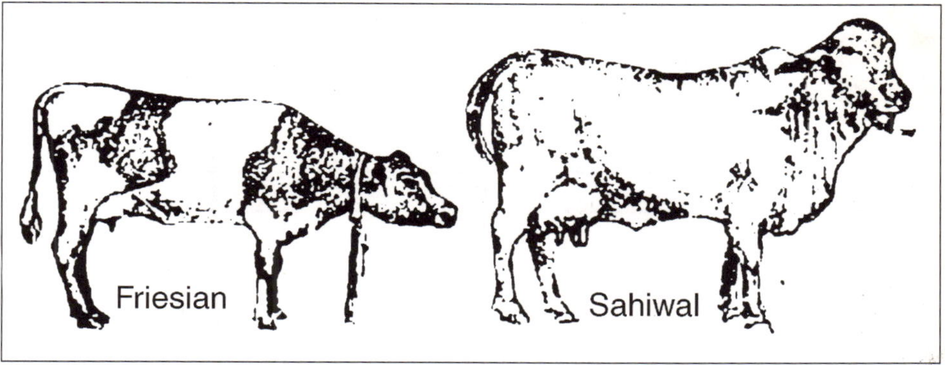

Fig. Indian Breeds of High Milk Yielding

Gir, Sahiwal, Red Sindhi, Thararkar, Kankrej etc. are some high yielding varieties of Indian cattle.

Exotic Breeds (Imported Breeds)

Hilstein, Friesian, Jersey, Swiss etc. are some of the high yielding varieties that have been imported from abroad and reared widely in India.

Improved breeds of Indian cattle

Certain improved breeds have been developed by making a cross between two desired breeds. A cross between Sahiwal and Friesian varieties has been named as Friewal, Karan Swiss is another improved breed for milk production in large quantities. Table shows some indian breeds, their milk yield and distribution.

Table. Some Indian Breeds and their Milk Yield

Breed	Milk Yield (litres) per Lactation Period	Distribution
Gir	1200-2200	Gujarat, Rajasthan, Maharastra
Red Sindhi	700-2200	Andhra Pradesh, all part of
world including		India and Pakistan
Sahiwal	1100-3100	Haryana, Punjab. Uttar
Pradesh		
Kankrej	1400	Gujarat
Tharparkar	700-2200	Rajasthan
Mewati	1100	Rajasthan
Ongole	700	Andhra Pradesh
Hariana	500	Gujarat, Rajasthan
Hallikar	227-1134 litres	South India
Kangayam	665 litres	Tamil Nadu
Murrah	20-22 litre/day	Punajb, Haryana, Uttar
Pradesh		

Lactation Period is the period of milk production between birth of a young one and the next pregnancy and it usually lasts about 300 days.

Table. Breeds of Buffaloes

Breed	Distribution
Murrah	Haryana and Punjab
Bhadawari	Uttar Pradesh and Madhya Pradesh
Jaffarabadi	Gujarat
Surti	Gujarat
Mehsana	Gujarat (cross breed between Surti and Murrah)
Nagpuri	Maharastra
Nill Ravi	Punjab
Porlakmedi	Orissa

Table Contd...

CATTLE FEED

The main feed of cows and buffaloes are grass but this does not provide them all the nourishment. They require balanced diet in the form of roughage which is fibrous food containing large amount of fibres such as hay fodder, leguminous plants-soyabeans, peas and cereals like maize, jowar etc. The diet of cattle mainly consists of roughage (dry or green fodder or fibrous food) and concentrates like grains, oil cakes and seeds, mineral salts and vitamins.

DAIRY PRODUCTS

Milk as drawn from the animals is known as full cream milk. When the cream is separated and the remaining milk is called toned milk. This milk contains no fat and is known as skimmed milk.

On the basis of fat contents the various milk product are as follows:

- *Cream*: It is prepared by churning milk, the fat comes on the top which is separated by draining out the liquid. It is known as cream with 10-70 per cent fat contents.
- *Curd*: Milk is converted to curd due to bacterial activities.
- *Butter Milk*: It is the left over liquid after removal of butter.
- *Ghee*: After heating butter, the water evaporates and fat contents are almost 100 per cent.
- *Condensed Milk*: Milk is concentrated by removing water contents with or without adding sugar. It has 31 per cent milk solids with 9 per cent fats.
- *Powdered Milk*: It is the powdered form of milk.
- *Cheese*: It is coagulated milk protein-casein with fat and water.
- *Khoya*: A desicated milk product prepared by evaporating water contents and reducing the bulk to about 70-75 per cent.
- *Cattle Dung*: Cattle dung is mainly used to make dung cakes for burning as fuels. It is used mainly in villages of India. The farmers also use cattle dung to produce bio gas and the leftover residue as manure.

Biogas Plant (Gobar Gas Plant)

Bio gas plant is a chamber where animal excreta (Cow dung, buffalo dung etc) and some anaerobic bacteria are fed into airtight biogas chamber. Decomposition of excreta produces methane gas used as a smoke free gas for cooking. This gas can also be utilized for lighting. The left over solid residue serves as a good manure.

MEAT YIELDING ANIMALS

Sheep

Sheep is the second largest species reared by mankind and it provides wool, meat, milk and hide. Their droppings form good manure. Important breeds of sheep in India are as follows:

Table. Breeds of Sheep

Breed	Distribution
Chokla	Rajasthan
Nial	Rajasthan and Haryana
Marwari	Rajasthan and Gujarat

Magra	Rajasthan
Jaisalmeri	Rajasthan
Pugul	Bikaner (Rajasthan)
Malpura	Rajasthan
Potanwadi	Uttar Pradesh and Delhi
Muzaffararanagari	Haryana
Hissardale	Himachal Pradesh and Haryana
Nellore	Andhra Pradesh
Bellary, Hassan, Mandya	Karnataka
Mecheri, Kalikarsal, Vembur	Tamil Nadu

Exotic Breeds

The main exotic breeds of sheep are Toggenberg, Saanen, French, Alpine and Nuibian and Angora.

Feeding of Sheep

They feed on green grasses and other wild plants. When sheep are reared for a particular purpose, they are given protein, minerals and vitamin rich food.

The main constituents of their food are as follows:

- *Leguminous Fodder*: Urad, mung, berseem etc.
- *Oil Cakes*: Groundnut, seasame cake, (rich in proteins)
- *Grains*: Maize, barley, oats and jowar.
- *Lime, Common Salt*: Sterilised bone meal (rich in mineral salts)

Goat

Important breeds of goats used for milk, meat and hide. There are about 19 well known Indian breeds, apart from a number of local non-descript breeds that are scattered throughout the country.

Himalayan Region (hilly track):

- *Cham, Gadd*: Kashmir, Himachal Pradesh,
- *Jammu and Kashmir Pashmina*: Himachal Pradesh, Ladakh,
- *Lahul and Spiti Valley Chegu*: Kashmir

Northern Region:

- *Jamunaparu*: Uttar Pradesh, Madhya Pradesh
- *Beetal*: Punjab
- *Barhari*: Delhi, Uttar Pradesh, Haryana

Central Region:

- *Marwari, Mehsana and Zelwadi*: Rajasthan, Gujarat and Madhya Pradesh
- *Kathiawar*: Gujarat and Rajasthan

Southern Region:

- *Surti*: Gujarat

- *Deccani, Osmanabadi*: Andhra Pradesh, Tamilnadu
- *Malabari*: Kerala

Eastern Region:

- *Bengali*: West Bengal, Assam and Tripura

Feeding of goat:

The goats are fed on open fields with enough green. They can be only given cereal and grain products. Sometimes however, a milk goat requires a balanced feed with 4-5 kg of fodder and a mixture of crushed grains such as yellow maize, jowar and other cereals and ground nut or linseed oil meal or steamed bone meal.

Pig

Pig farming is gaining importance in India. Pigs provide only 8 per cent of total meat production in our country. Pig skin, fat and hair are required for leather, soap, oil, hair-brush industry respectively. Pig manure is rich in nitrogen, phosporus and potassium. Pigs contribute about 5 per cent of total meat production in India, and constitute a rich source of animal protein available at low cost. The calorific value of Pork (pig's meat) is much more than the other edible meats. Pigs can feed on farm waste, garbage and spoiled grains.

Breeds of Pigs

Breed	Distribution
Large white Yorkshire	England, India
Middle white Yorkshire	England, India
Landrace	Denmark
Essex saddleback	Hempshire
Tamworth	England
Bershile	England

DRAUGHT ANIMALS

Draught animals are animals need for carrying load. From time immemorial a number of animal species have been used for special purposes by humans, utilising their mechanical strength, endurance and speed. These include horse for riding and swift running; elephant for riding, strength and heavy load lifting, camel for riding in sandy desert and ability to survive without water for long duration, donkey and mule (a hybrid of male donkey and female horse) for carrying load. Most of the draught animals are herbivorous and survive on leaves of trees, shrubs and bushes. While raising them, they are also fed on grains, beans, cottonseeds, maize and bran besides dry/green fodder. In Rajasthan, camel is used for yielding milk also.

HORSE

The horse has fast movement, great stamina and endurance. Its body is suited for ride, load pulling, mountain climbing and forest travelling. So the horse is an important draught or work animal. They learn fast and can be maintained easily in various climatic conditions. Due to their ability to move swiftly in rough areas, they are still useful in hills and in the deserts. Common Indian breeds and their distribution are as follows-

Breed	Region
Kathiawari or kaunchi	Rajasthan and Gujarat
Marwari or malvi	Rajasthan
Bhutia	Tarai belt of Himalayan region (Punjab-
Bhutan)	
Manipuri Pony	Eastern hill region
Sipti Pony	Himachal Pradesh

FIBRE, HIDE AND SKIN YIELDING ANIMALS

Besides providing meat, milk and transport, livestock provide many commercially useful products such as fibre, skin and hide. Generally sheep and goat provide fibres for making of products like wollen strings, ropes, carpets, clothing and brushes etc.

EGG YIELDING ANIMALS

This category consists of egg producing animals whose eggs are used as food by mankind to provide proteins. Poultry farming is defined as a term for rearing and keeping of birds such as fowl, duck and hen for egg and meat. Poultry farming has become popular because it is comparatively easy to start and maintain. It gives quick return within one to six month of investments, , is easily manageable and requires less space and labour. Poultry birds and their eggs are a rich source of nutrients. Figure gives a comparative account of the composition of fowl meat and that of eggs.

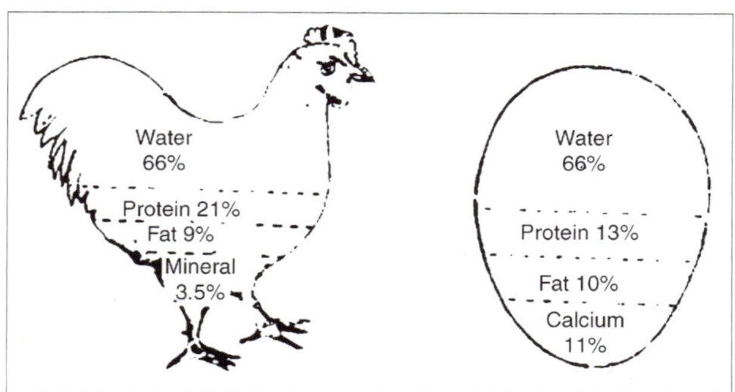

Fig. Composition of Chicken and Egg

COMMON BREEDS OF POULTRY BIRDS

Indian poultry breeds provide good quality meat but produces small sized eggs. They have natural immunity against common diseases as compared to exotic varieties bred abroad which require greater protection and immunisation.

The chicken is commonly classified on the basis of its origin:

- American,
- Asiatic,
- Mediterranean and
- English
- Plymouth Rock, Rhode Island Red, New Hampshire-American
- Brahma, Cochin, Langshan-Asiatic
- Leg horn, Minoxa-Mediterranean
- Cornish, Australorp-English

INDIGENOUS BREEDS

- *Aseel*: Rajasthan, Andhra Pradesh, Uttar Pradesh
- *Busra*: Gujarat and Maharastra
- *Chittagong*: Eastern India
- *Karaknath*: Madhya Pradesh

Indian Breeds

The Indian breeds of hen include Aseel, Chittagaog, Ghagus and Basra. Their egg laying capacity is around 200 eggs per year.

Exotic Breeds

These breeds are important from other countries and include White leghorn, Minorca, Rhode Island red. These birds have high egg laying capacity but carry less flesh as compared to Indian birds.

Upgraded Variety

Some improved varieties have been developed in India by hybridisation such as B 77, ILS 82 etc. They grow fast and also have as high an egg laying capacity as the exotic varieties and are better suited to the Indian climate.

Poultry Feed

Depending upon the requirement of meat or egg production, poultry feed mainly consists of maize, rice, wheat bran, ground nut cake, fish meal, lime stones, bone meal, common salt, vitamins and minerals.

GENETIC IMPROVEMENT IN ANIMALS

The application of laws of animal health and reproduction genetics has contributed towards increase in milk, egg and meat productivity. The increase in egg production brought about the silver revolution in the area of animal husbandry. The methods being widely used are artificial insemination and embryo transplant.

ARTIFICIAL INSEMINATION

Artificial insemination involves collection of semen from a healthy bull of the desired breed, its storage at low temperatures and introduction into the females of cattle of other breeds for bringing about fertilisation using sterilised (germ free) equipment.

Advantages of this method are:

- Up to 3000 females can be fertilised from semen collected from one bull.
- The semen can be stored for a long period and transported over long distances.
- Economical and high success rates of fertilisation.

EMBRYO TRANSPLANT

This method of breed improvement has been quite successful in sheep and goat. In this method, embryos (depending on their period of development) from superior breeds are removed during the early stages of pregnancy and are transferred to the other female with inferior characters, in whose body the gestation period is completed. By this technique, quality and productivity in the livestock can be improved. Unlike artificial insemination, this method has low success rate due to greater chances of contamination.

COMMON DISEASES OF ANIMALS

Domestic animals often suffer from various diseases caused due to infection by bacteria, viruses, fungi, protozoa and worms.

CATTLE

Category of Pathogen	Disease	Symptoms
Bacteria	Anthrax	Swelling on the body reduced yield of milk
	Tuberculosis	Dry husky cough, Lungs are affected.
Virus	Foot and Mouth disease	Excessive salivation, Lameness and fever
	Rinder pest	Blood stained high fever diarrhoea
Protozoa	Trypanosomiasis	Intermittent fever and death
Fungus	Ringwork	Rounded scabs on head and neck.

POULTRY DISEASE

Rearing of poultry birds requires properly ventilated place and vaccination of new born chicks. Poultry diseases can be classified as infectious or non-infectious. Noninfectious diseases are caused by faulty management, faulty feed preparation and inadequate diet or nutritionally deficient disease.

Infectious diseases are classified according to the type of disease causing organisms and are as follows:

- Parasitic (external)–
  - Lice,
  - Mites,
  - Tick and
  - Fleas
- Parasitic (internal)–
  - Round worms,
  - Tapeworm and
  - Hexamitiasis
- Protozoan–
  - Coccidiosis in chicken,
  - Leucocytozoonosis
- Bacterial–
  - Pullorum,
  - Typhoid,
  - Paratyphoid,
  - Fowl cholera
- Viral–
  - Ranikhet disease,
  - Fowl pox,
  - Infectious bronchitis,
  - Infection bursitis,
  - Avian encephalomycytis,
  - Marek disease,
  - Leukosis,
  - Chronic respiratory disease,
  - Hepatitis etc.
- Fungal–
  - Aspergillosis,
  - Moniliasis

2

Ammonia Emissions fromAnimal Husbandry

OVERVIEW

Almost 5 million tons a year of ammonia are emitted nationally and as shown in Figure animal husbandry is the largest contributor to ammonia emissions nationally.

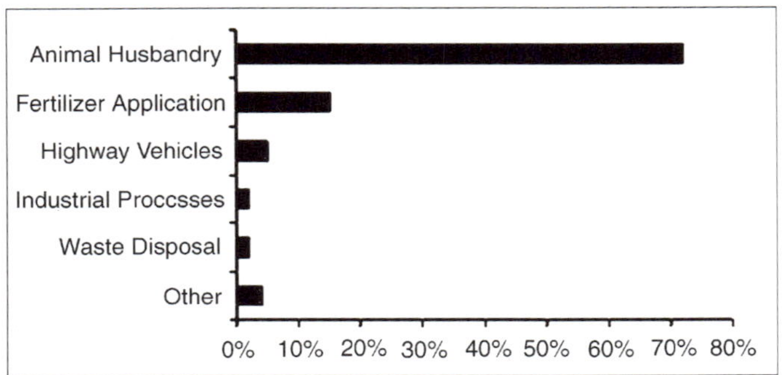

In addition to being the largest contributor to ammonia emissions nationally, it is important to address ammonia emissions from animal husbandry because inverse modeling suggests that ammonia emissions may be overestimated. Inverse modeling involves doing a complete chemical transformation and transport modeling of an area and accounting for all of the ammonia through transformation and deposition processes.

Comparing these results to the ammonia that has been found in the ambient air indicates that ammonia may be overestimated nationally. The interim improvements described in Section 8.2 below address many of these shortcomings. Additionally, problems with the old NEI have been identified. For example, there are probable errors in the emission factor selections, especially for beef.

Also, the NEI does not use information on variability of emissions due to different manure handling practices within a given animal industry, nor does it make total use of the National Agricultural Statistic Service (NASS) data on different animal populations by weight. The NEI also does not take temperature into account, which would greatly increase the temporal variation in ammonia emissions. Moreover, EPA's water emission effluent guidelines project has provided some new information on animal production and waste handling practices. Also, the National Academy of Sciences, at the behest of the agricultural community, has reviewed EPA's inventory work, and recommended a longterm data-gathering effort.

IMPROVING THE NEI

EPA has recently prepared a report that provides a basis for making interim improvements to the NEI. It provides improved data on populations, practices, and emissions. It is the beginning of a switch-over to a processbased framework that is a consistent and transparent way of estimating emissions that would allow for partial updating as better data becomes available.

This technique provides a lot of motivation and a structure for making data-collection improvements. It also provides an opportunity to educate users about the data limitations and the proper use of the data. The goal is for the higher animal production states to begin to adopt and offer improvements to the NEI using this new method. Table lists the six steps that comprise this new methodology for estimating ammonia emissions from animal husbandry operations.

Table. Overview of New Estimation Methodology

Step 1	Estimate Animal Populations
Step 2	Identify Manure Management Trains (MMT)
Step 3	Estimate Amount of Nitrogen Excreted
Step 4	Identify Emission Factors
Step 5	Estimate Ammonia Emissions
Step 6	Estimate Future Ammonia Emissions

STEP 1

The first step in this process is estimating average animal populations by animal group, state, and county. This step uses the 2002 NASS data for statelevel populations, and the 1997 census of agricultural to apportion the statelevel NASS data to the county level. However, there are some privacy issues with regard to animal populations. For example, a county with only one large facility would create an industrial privacy issue since that facility will not want their competition to know how many animals they are raising.

STEP 2

The second step is using Manure Management Trains (MMT) for each animal group to estimate the distribution of the animal population. Fifteen manure management trains have been identified. Figure shows an advanced manure management train, one of several such trains for the dairy industry. This manure management train begins with the amount of nitrogen excreted by dairy cows.

The train traces the manure through the different handling options and shows how much is handled in different ways. The train also shows the nitrogen and ammonia emissions at the various handling points. For example, there is nitrogen loss in the flush barn and the lagoon, and ammonia loss in the dry lot. There are other trains that provide similar information for other farm industries. These trains characterize a type of industry, and the general way that manure would be handled in a facility.

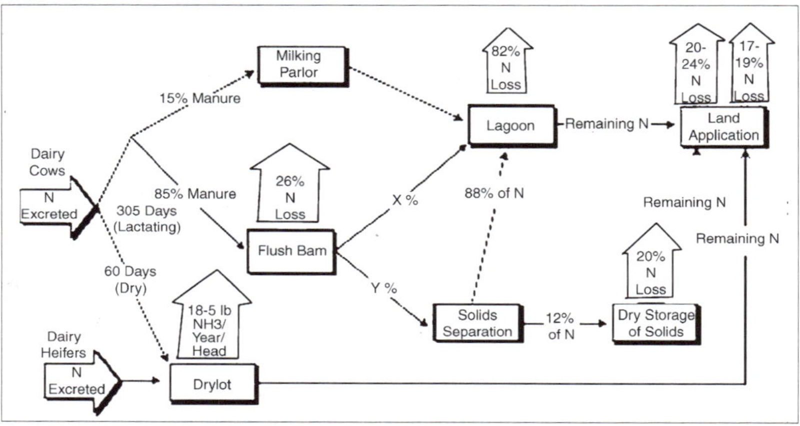

Fig. NH3: Example Manure Management Train

Some of the variables that affect the different trains include the way the animals are housed, the waste storage methods, and the land application methods that are used. For example, the non-feedlot outdoor confinement (*e.g.*, pasture) is one of the trains for swine, dairy, and beef. The MMTs represent different pathways for the escape of ammonia into the air.

In applying the MMT approach to estimate the 2002 ammonia inventory, the mix of MMTs is assumed to vary by state, but not within a state. Animal population is allocated among the applicable trains. For example, in a given state 20 per cent of the hogs may be handled using manure management train 3, another 60 per cent may be using manure management train 7, and the rest of them may be using manure management train 14. Finally, it should be noted that the final stage on every train is land application.

STEP 3

The third step is estimating the amount of nitrogen excreted from the animals using each type of MMT. This step involves looking at typical animal weights and data on the amount of nitrogen per thousand kilos of live weight.

Another useful source of information is land grant university researchers and local agricultural extension agents. It is important to include experts in the agricultural industry in the inventory development efforts.

STEP 4

Step four involves identifying or developing the emission factors for each component of each manure management train. Some of these factors are in pounds per animal, and some are per cent air release of the input ammonia. These factors are used to determine the amount of ammonia that goes to the next stage of the manure train process. Under this approach, the air emissions could never be higher than the original manure content. Also, using this approach sets the stage for applying temporal profiles and process-related variables such as moisture and rainfall.

STEP 5

The next step involves applying this methodology to estimate annual ammonia emissions from each animal group by MMT. This includes tracking the ammonia release through each manure management train for each animal type for each county and calculating ammonia releases to the air and transfers to the next stage. This whole process assumes no air emission controls at this time, but control assumptions could be added later. Emissions are summed up to animal type and county, but the database is preserved with full detail for transparency so that changes and improvements can be made.

STEP 6

The last step involves estimating ammonia emissions for future years. Other improvements that are being made to the NEI for animal husbandry operations are to incorporate emission estimates for sheep, ducks, goats, and horses. Additional data sources are being examined to provide recently available data on manure production and excretion rates by animal type and weight.

Finally, EPA is examining ways to better address special, seasonal, and regional differences in emissions. Carnegie Mellon University has prepared a model for estimating ammonia emissions from agricultural activities, humans, wastewater treatment, wildfires, domestic and wild animals, transportation sources, industrial activities, and soils. The Carnegie Mellon model includes an improved methodology for fertilizer application when compared to the methodology used in previous versions of the NEI. EPA is evaluating the methodologies used for other source categories in the Carnegie Mellon model.

COMPARISON OF THE 1999 AND 2002 AMMONIA NEIS

A comparison of the 1999 NEI version 3 with the 2002 NEI version 1 shows that there are some significant differences in the ammonia emissions. As shown on this chart, about half of the emissions from all animals come from calves and cattle. Also, total ammonia emissions from animal husbandry operations decreased significantly from 3.4 million in 1999 to 2.3 million in 2002.

Table. NH3: Comparison of '99 and '02 NEIs

Animal	**1999 NEI**			**2002 NEI**	
Group **Emission** **Tons/Year** **Head/Yr**	**Population** **Emissions**	**Emission** **Factor** **lb/Head/Yr**	**Emissions** **Tons/Year**	**Population**	**Factor** **lb/**
Cattle and 1,205,493 Calves Composite	100,126,106	50.5	2,476,333	100,939,728	23.90
Hogs and 429,468 Pigs Composite	63,095,955	20.3	640,100	59,987,850	14.32
Poultry and 664,238 Chickens Composite	1,754,482,225	0.394	345,325	2,201,945,253	0.60
Total 2,299,199	1,917,704,286	N/A	3,461,758	2,362,863,831	N/A

3

Care and Use of Agricultural Animals

AGRICULTURAL ANIMAL HEALTH CARE

Agricultural animal health care involves proper management and husbandry as well as veterinary care. Proper management is essential for the well-being of animals, the validity and effectiveness of research and teaching activities, and the health and safety of animal care personnel. Sound animal husbandry programmes provide systems of care that permit the animals to grow, mature, reproduce, express some species-specific behaviour, and be healthy. Specific operating procedures depend on factors that are unique to individual institutions. Well-trained and motivated personnel can often achieve high-quality animal care with less than ideal physical plants and equipment.

ANIMAL PROCUREMENT

When an institution acquires new animals, attention must be paid to applicable international, federal, and state regulations and institutional procedures, particularly those dealing with transportation and animal health. All animals must be obtained and transported legally. The attending veterinarian, in conjunction with the principal scientist, should formulate written procedures to assess the health status of a herd or flock obtained from a vendor before acquiring animals.

The institution should develop a mechanism and process of control for animal acquisition that ensures coordination of resources that will preclude the arrival of animals in advance of preparation of adequate housing and appropriate veterinary quarantine procedures. Quality control for vendors and knowledge of the history of purchased animals is part of an adequate institutional veterinary care programme.

Animals of unknown origin or from stockyards should only be used if necessary; such animals may pose significant unknown health risks compared with animals of known origin and therefore should be handled appropriately. Newly acquired animals should undergo a quarantine and acclimation period, including preventive and clinical treatments as appropriate for their health status.

ACCLIMATION AND STABILIZATION

Newly arrived animals require a period of acclimation. Acclimation refers to a stabilization period, before animal use, which permits physiological and behavioural adaptation to the new environment. The attending veterinarian should establish general acclimation guidelines for each species. Any modifications to the general programme should be discussed with the attending veterinarian before animals are shipped. In some cases, animals may require an extended acclimation period because of their history or health status. On the other hand, some studies, such as comparisons of metaphylactic treatments for shipping fever, need to begin as soon as animals arrive. Such exemptions from the acclimation period must be scientifically justified and approved by the Institutional Animal Care and Use Committee (IACUC).

QUARANTINE

Quarantine is the separation of newly received animals from those already in the facility or on the premises until the health of the new animals has been evaluated and found to be acceptable. The attending veterinarian should ensure that quarantine facilities or locations are appropriate and that quarantine procedures are consistent with current veterinary practices and applicable regulations. The quarantine period should be long enough to observe signs of infectious disease or obtain diagnostic evidence of infection status.

Quarantine and testing of animals before introduction is especially important for herds or flocks that have attained specific-pathogen-free status, but these additions should be discouraged. If the health history of newly received animals is unknown, the quarantine programme should be more comprehensive and sufficiently long to allow expression or detection of diseases present in the early incubation stage. Exceptions to quarantine practices should be approved by the attending veterinarian in advance of shipment of the animals.

The attending veterinarian, or skilled personnel under the direction of the attending veterinarian, should perform an initial examination and subsequent daily observations for newly arrived animals. Animals should be observed in quarantine until they are cleared for introduction into a herd or facility. During the quarantine period, animals should be vaccinated and treated for diseases and parasites as appropriate to protect their health and maintain the health of animals in the home facility. In addition to having adequate quarantine procedures, research facilities and animal use protocols should be designed to minimize the risk of introducing or transmitting disease agents.

VETERINARY CARE

ATTENDING VETERINARIAN

The agricultural animal health care programme is the responsibility of the attending veterinarian. The Institute for Laboratory Animal Research (ILAR), National Research Council *Guide for the Care and Use of Laboratory Animals* defines the attending veterinarian as "a veterinarian who has direct or delegated authority" and who "should give research personnel advice that ensures that humane needs are met and are compatible with scientific requirements."

Animal Welfare Act regulations and the Public Health Service policy require that the attending veterinarian have the authority to oversee the adequacy of other aspects of animal care and use, including animal husbandry and nutrition, sanitation practices, zoonoses control, and hazard containment. Research and teaching institutions must provide investigators and instructors with access to a veterinarian who has experience in the care of agricultural animals. The veterinarian can be full-time or part-time and must have authority to ensure that the provisions of the programme are met. The attending veterinarian must be provided access to all research and teaching animals and to any related documents including health care records.

The attending veterinarian also must be involved in the development and oversight of the veterinary care programme, as well as in other aspects of animal care and use such as protocol review, establishment of anesthetic and analgesic guidelines, study removal criteria, training of animal users, and responsible conduct of research activities. Veterinary involvement in these activities helps to ensure animal health and well-being.

The attending veterinarian is not required to be the sole provider of veterinary care and can delegate authority to another qualified veterinarian. However, the attending veterinarian must communicate with, and oversee veterinary care provided by, other veterinarians. When necessary, the attending veterinarian should utilize the expertise of other professionals when making determinations about agricultural animal care. Trained nonveterinary staff may administer treatments according to standard operating procedures approved by the attending veterinarian.

PREVENTIVE MEDICINE

Adequate agricultural animal health care in research and teaching involves a written and implemented programme for disease prevention, surveillance, diagnosis, treatment, and endpoint resolution. The objectives of such a programme are to ensure animal health and wellbeing, minimize pain and distress, maintain animal production, prevent zoonoses, provide assistance to investigators on study-related animal health issues, and avoid contaminants or residues in animal products.

The programme should include training for animal users regarding animal behaviour, humane restraint, anesthesia, analgesia, surgical and postsurgical care, and euthanasia. A mechanism for direct, frequent, and regular communication must be established among personnel who are responsible for daily animal care and observation, animal users, and the attending veterinarian. This will help ensure that timely and accurate animal health information is effectively communicated.

SICK, INJURED, AND DEAD ANIMALS

Animal care personnel must be trained to recognize signs of illness and injury. In general, sick and injured animals should be segregated from the main group to protect them and the other animals, observed at least once daily, and provided with veterinary care as appropriate. When animals are separated, a mechanism should be in place to communicate to staff the status of the animals and to ensure proper daily, weekend, holiday, and emergency care.

In some circumstances, segregation is not feasible or may disrupt the social hierarchy, cause additional stress to the animal, or adversely affect research. The advantages of segregation should be weighed against its disadvantages, especially for mild illnesses or injuries that can be easily managed. Care should be taken to minimize spread of pathogens from ill animals to healthy animals by observing appropriate biocontainment measures. Incurably ill animals or ill or injured animals with unrelievable pain or distress should be humanely killed as soon as possible.

Unexpected deaths should be reported to the attending veterinarian. Dead animals are potential sources of infection and should be disposed of promptly by a commercial rendering service or other appropriate means following applicable state and local ordinances and regulations.

Postmortem examination of fresh or well-preserved animals may provide important animal health information and aid in preventing further losses. When warranted, waste and bedding that have been removed from a site occupied by an animal that has died should be moved to an area that is inaccessible to other animals and the site appropriately disinfected.

MEDICAL RECORDS

An important component of an agricultural animal health programme is maintaining records that can be used to monitor animal health events, both physical and behavioural health events, as well as outcomes and levels of production. Medical records should comply with the American College of Laboratory Animal Medicine (ACLAM) statement on medical records.

Group health records may be appropriate for animals that are kept as cohorts, particularly when animals undergo periodic evaluation by means of examining several representative individuals of the group. The institution, under the guidance of the attending veterinarian, should determine the method(s) by which medical records are maintained. Oversight of medical records is the responsibility of the attending veterinarian and the IACUC.

When institutional representatives determine that a medical record should be created, the record typically contains the following information:

- Identification of the animal(s) or group(s);
- Clinical information, such as the animal's behaviour, results of physical examinations, and observed abnormalities, illnesses, and/ or injuries;
- Immunizations and other prophylactic treatments and procedures;
- Documentation and interpretation of diagnostic tests;
- Documentation of research interventions;
- Treatments prescribed and administered;
- Clinical response and follow up information;
- Descriptions of surgical procedures, anesthesia, analgesia, and perioperative care;
- Methods used to control pain and distress;
- Documentation of resolution;
- Documentation of euthanasia or other disposition; and
- Necropsy findings if necropsy is indicated.

The record system must be structured so that information is easily collected, gathered, analysed, summarized, and available to the veterinarian, the principal scientist, and the IACUC.

The ACLAM statement on *Medical Records for Animals used in Research Teaching and Testing* suggests that:

- Notations in the medical record should be made by individuals who have administered treatments, or made direct observations or evaluations of the animal(s) or their diagnostic results, or their designee. Individuals typically responsible for making notations in the record include veterinary staff, animal husbandry staff, and research staff. All entries in the record should be dated, indicate the originator of the entry and be legible to someone other than the writer.

SURGERY

MULTIPLE MAJOR SURGICAL PROCEDURES

The ILAR Guide differentiates major from minor surgery as follows: "Major survival surgery penetrates and exposes a body cavity or produces substantial impairment of physical or physiologic functions. Minor survival surgery does not expose a body cavity and causes little or no physical impairment." Minimally invasive surgery such as laparoscopy may benefit the animal relative to traditional surgical techniques.

Performance of more than one major survival surgical procedure on a single animal is discouraged but may be necessary to ensure or maintain the health of the animal. Long-lived animals may undergo multiple major surgeries, such as a cow that requires surgery for correction of displaced abomasum and cesarean section for therapeutic purposes. Multiple major survival surgeries performed for nontherapeutic reasons should be performed only when justified and must be reviewed and approved by the IACUC. Multiple major surgeries that produce minor physiologic or physical impairment and reduce overall animal use, such as multiple endoscopic laparotomies in sheep for reproductive purposes, might be appropriate. Likewise, multiple surgical procedures might be justified when they are related components of the same project.

ANESTHESIA AND ANALGESIA

Certain animal husbandry-related procedures may be conducted without anesthesia after consideration and approval by the IACUC. These procedures should be performed early in the life of the animal in accordance with accepted veterinary practices. When surgery is performed on older animals, appropriate anesthesia and sterile instruments should be used, trauma minimized, and hemorrhage controlled. It is important that husbandry practices be established to minimize stress, prevent infection, and ensure the comfort of the animals during the recovery period.

Specific recommendations for each species are provided in subsequent chapters. The attending veterinarian should advise investigators about the choice and use of analgesics and/or anesthetics or any other pain-or distress-relieving measure, including recommended times for withholding of food and water.

After being trained and subsequently supervised by a qualified scientist or veterinarian, technical personnel may administer anesthetics and analgesics as part of a research or teaching protocol. If a painful or distressful experimental procedure must be conducted without the use of an anesthetic or analgesic because such use would prevent collection of useful data, this must be scientifically documented in the animal care and use protocol and approved by the IACUC. Paralytic drugs are not anesthetics. They must not be used unless animals are in a surgical plane of anesthesia and thus unconscious.

Use of paralytic agents must be justified in the animal use protocol and appropriate monitoring for depth of anesthesia described. Tranquilizers are psychotropic substances that alter mental processes or behaviour but do not produce anesthesia. These medications can reduce the dose of anesthetic required. When used alone, tranquilizers should only be used to allay fear and anxiety. Their use may render restraint less stressful and enable animals to adapt more easily to novel situations.

SURGERY PERSONNEL

Inappropriately performed surgical techniques or inadequate postoperative care will result in unnecessary pain and distress. Experimental surgery on agricultural animals should be performed or supervised by an experienced veterinarian or his/her designee in accordance with established protocols approved by an IACUC. Institutions must provide basic surgical training and opportunities to upgrade surgical skills for persons who will conduct or assist with experimental surgery. The training programme must be reviewed by the IACUC and under the direction of the attending veterinarian or his/her designee. Training provided must be documented and the competency of personnel assured.

SURGICAL FACILITIES AND ASEPTIC TECHNIQUE

Major survival surgeries should be performed in facilities designed and prepared to accommodate surgery whenever possible, and appropriate aseptic surgical procedures should be employed. Good surgical practice includes the use of surgical caps, masks, gowns, and gloves, as well as aseptic surgical site preparation and draping. Sterile instruments must be used.

Manufacturers' recommendations must be followed for chemical sterilants. For nonsurvival surgeries, during which the animal is euthanized before recovery from anesthesia, it may not be necessary to follow all aseptic techniques, but the instruments and surrounding area should be clean. Minor surgical procedures that do not penetrate a body cavity or produce substantial impairment may be performed under less stringent conditions if performed in accord with standard veterinary practices. Therapeutic and emergency surgeries may sometimes need to be performed in agricultural settings that are not conducive to rigid asepsis.

However, every effort should be made to conduct such surgeries in a sanitary or aseptic manner and to use anesthetics and analgesics commensurate with the risks to the animal's well-being. Research protocols that carry a high likelihood of the need for emergency surgery should contain provisions for handling anticipated cases. Surgical packs and equipment for such events should be prepared and be readily available for emergency use.

POSTSURGICAL CARE

Appropriate facilities should be available for animals that are recovering from general anesthesia and major surgery.

The following are required:

- Segregation from other animals until recovery from anesthesia;
- Clean and sanitary recovery area;
- Adequate space, with consideration for physical comfort and well-being of the animal, in a place suitable for recovery from anesthesia without injury;
- Environmental controls sufficient to ensure maintenance of environmental temperature within the thermoneutral zone and animal temperature within the normal range during postsurgical recovery; and

- Trained personnel for postsurgical observation to help to ensure a safe recovery.
- Postsurgical observation should be provided until the animal is fully recovered from anesthesia, ambulatory, and able to safely return to its original housing location.

SIGNS OF PAIN AND DISTRESS

Pain is a sensation of discomfort that may lead to distress and feelings of urgency. Although pain and distress in animals can often be detected by an experienced observer, these conditions can sometimes be unapparent, especially in stoic animals. When unanticipated pain and distress are detected, animal-care attendants or research staff should take immediate ameliorative action as necessary and contact the attending veterinarian.

Pain can be one of the earliest signs of disease or injury. Animals in pain may become less active, restless, may continually get up and down, and refuse to stay in one place, reduce feed consumption, grind their teeth, or vocalize. Some animals become less active, whereas others appear frightened or agitated. Animals in pain may resist handling or favour the painful area by adopting an abnormal stance or abnormal behaviour. In some cases, pain may not be noticed until a physiological act is induced such as swallowing, coughing, chewing, or defecating.

The observer should try to determine whether pain appears to be constant or associated with a provoking act. Sudden, severe pain is often associated with fractures, rupture or torsion of visceral organs, or acute inflammatory processes and should be considered an emergency. Relief of pain and/or distress in agricultural animals involves removing or correcting the inciting cause when possible, administering appropriate analgesics, and taking steps to reduce stimulation of pain receptors.

Relief of pain should be one of the first tasks of the attending veterinarian, adhering to the following principles:

- Relief of pain is a humane act;
- Relief of pain must be initiated promptly once it is deemed necessary;
- It may be necessary to protect animals in pain from self-injury.

The attending veterinarian must be familiar with analgesics labeled for use in agricultural animals and must be able to prescribe and establish withdrawal times for extra-label use of analgesics when indicated. Animals with severe or chronic pain that cannot be alleviated must be euthanized.

ZOONOSES

For the purposes of this guide, zoonotic diseases are defined as infectious diseases in agricultural animals used in research and teaching that can be transmitted to humans and a natural reservoir for the infectious agent is an agricultural animal. Zoonotic pathogens, mode of transmission, disease signs in ruminants, and disease signs and symptoms in humans. A current list and incidence of notifiable diseases such as Q-fever may be obtained from the US Centers for Disease Control and Prevention. The attending veterinarian, working with the animal scientists, should establish appropriate preventive medicine programmes and husbandry practices to decrease the likelihood of transmission of zoonotic agents. Each institution must have an appropriate occupational health and safety programme for evaluating the human health risks associated with animal contact and must take steps to ensure that health risks for each individual are assessed and managed to an acceptable level.

RESIDUE AVOIDANCE

Residues of 3 groups of chemicals must be prevented from occurring in research animals if those animals, or their products, are going into the human food chain.

These are:

1) Approved drugs used according to directions on the label,
2) Drugs used in an extra-label fashion, and
3) Other chemicals such as herbicides, pesticides, and wood preservatives.

The Food Animal Residue Avoidance Database is a project sponsored by the USDA Cooperative State Research, Education and Extension Service. The FARAD *Compendium of FDA Approved Drugs* provides information about drugs that are available for treating animal diseases, the withholding times for milk and eggs, and preslaughter withdrawal times for meat. Information about the drugs approved for use in food animals in the United States is included in this online database.

The FARAD compendium allows selection of over-the-counter products that satisfy particular needs as well as alerts to the need for veterinary assistance with prescription drugs; FARAD also supplies estimated meat and milk withdrawal times for extra-label use of drugs. Drug administration to animals destined to enter the food chain requires special consideration.

Before animals may be slaughtered for human or animal food purposes, time must be allowed for medications, drugs approved by the Food and Drug Administration (FDA), or substances allowed by the FDA for experimental testing under the Investigational New Animal Drug (INAD) exemption to be depleted from the tissues. Such use is only permitted when it adheres to the regulations in the Animal Medicinal Drug Use Clarification Act of 1994, Public Law 103-396. A record of the product used, dose, route of administration, duration of treatment, and period of withdrawal must be maintained. Adherence to proper withdrawal times must be ensured before animals are transported to the auction, market, or abattoir.

DRUG STORAGE AND CONTROL

Pharmaceuticals intended for use in food-producing animals must be managed responsibly. Storage should be in an area that is clean and dry and that offers protection from changes in temperature, sunlight, dust, moisture, and vermin. The manufacturer's labeling should be consulted for specific information regarding appropriate storage conditions and product shelf-life. In addition, the integrity of product containers should be periodically evaluated to assess for potential leakage or contamination of the stored product.

Products in damaged containers or with missing or illegible labels should be disposed of properly. To minimize the potential for treatment errors, products should be physically segregated according to indicated use, with special attention to separate drugs that are intended only for animals of a certain age or production state.

For large inventories, separate storage cabinets for each group of products will further reduce the opportunity for errors in selection and use. When necessary, lockable storage units should be used to prevent access by unauthorized persons.

RECORD KEEPING

Records of all potentially harmful products used in the facility, their storage, their use, and their disposal should be maintained. Such record keeping should be similar to the quality assurance programmes used by responsible farmers in the food animal industry. If used in accord with the label and with allowance for the correct withdrawal time, approved drugs should not result in violative residues. Record-keeping and management should be audited and should confirm that drugs are not outdated and that the directions on the label have been followed. Records should be maintained for at least 3 months or in timelines consistent with state and federal requirements as they apply.

QUALITY ASSURANCE PROGRAMMES

The food animal industries have developed several quality assurance programmes such as:

- The Milk and Dairy Beef Quality Assurance Programme,
- The Beef Quality Assurance Programme,
- The United Egg Producers Five Star Quality Assurance Programme,
- The Pork Quality Assurance Programme, and
- The Veal Producer Quality Assurance Programme.

Agricultural research or teaching programmes using animals that may be slaughtered for human consumption must institute quality assurance programmes that are equivalent or superior to those used in the food animal industries. Many food animal industries, private corporations, and humane organizations have also developed animal welfare assurance programmes that should be referenced.

REGULATORY OVERSIGHT

In the event that animals are given a new animal drug for investigational purposes, no meat, eggs, or milk from those animals may be processed for human food, unless authorization has been granted by the FDA or the USDA, and an appropriate INAD exemption from the FDA has been obtained for use of the investigational drug. In such cases, the investigator must follow specifications outlined in the INAD.

The authorization to process meat, eggs, or milk from such animals for human food will depend on the development of data to show that the consumption of food from animals so treated is consistent with public health considerations and that the food does not contain the residues of harmful drugs or their metabolites.

In the event that animals are given a new animal drug, no meat, eggs, or milk from those animals may be processed for human food consumption under any circumstances. Proper methods of disposal of such meat, eggs, and milk may include incineration, burial, or other procedures ensuring safety, sanitation, and avoidance of the human food supply.

EXTRA-LABEL USE

The use of different dosages, formulations, or routes of administration, or the treatment of animals for conditions not specifically mentioned on the product label, constitutes extra-label use. Such use may be considered by licensed veterinarians when the health of the animal is immediately threatened and when suffering or death would result from failure to treat the affected animal. Such use is only permitted when it adheres to the regulations promulgated by the FDA under the Animal Medicinal Drug Use Clarification Act (AMDUCA) of 1994, Public Law 103-396.

The major principles guiding such use are that:

- There must be a valid relationship between veterinarian, client, and patient, and
- There must be an adequate safety margin in the withdrawal time that is based on the most complete pharmacokinetic data available.

The FDA should be contacted whenever guidance is needed.

ORGANIC FARMING

Some institutions have organic farming components. The US National Organic Standards state that "producers must not withhold medical treatment from a sick animal to maintain its organic status. All appropriate medications and treatments must be used to restore an animal to health when methods acceptable to organic production standards fail." It is important that research animals managed under organic standards be provided prompt and adequate health care as necessary even if the animal will, as a result, be removed from organic production.

HAZARDOUS CHEMICALS

There are many chemicals used on farms and in agricultural research establishments that could potentially result in residues in the meat, milk, or eggs of animals exposed to these chemicals. Examples are pesticides for insect control, herbicides, poisons for rodent control, wood preservatives, and disinfectants. Harmful products should be properly labeled and stored, a record of their purchase and expiration dates should be kept, and personnel must be informed of potential hazards and wear appropriate protective equipment. Chemicals must be stored, used, and disposed of in a manner that prevents contamination of animals and residues in milk, meat, or eggs.

RESTRAINT

Brief physical restraint of agricultural animals for examination, collection of samples, and a variety of other experimental and clinical manipulations can be accomplished manually or with devices such as stocks, head gates, stanchions, or squeeze chutes. It is important that such devices be suitable in size and design for the animal being held and be operated properly to minimize stress and avoid pain and injury. Personnel should be trained on the use of hydraulically operated restraint devices to prevent potential injury. Extended physical restraint should be reviewed and approved by the IACUC.

TRANSGENIC AND GENETICALLY ENGINEERED AND CLONED ANIMALS

Recent years have seen a growing interest in the development and use of transgenic and genetically modified agricultural animals for agricultural and human therapeutic purposes. A transgenic animal is one that carries a foreign gene that has been deliberately inserted into its genome. Genetically engineered animal models require deliberate modification of the animal genome by moving a desired trait into the genome.

These modifications are accomplished by microinjection, retroviral transfection, and a variety of other techniques. It is important not to confuse genetically engineered animals with cloned animals. Genetically engineered animals may be produced by cloning as well. The progeny of cloned animals are not properly termed "cloned animals." It is also important to distinguish between research and commercial application of cloning techniques.

Cloning technology has been reviewed by the FDA and is one of several commercially available assisted reproductive technologies including in vitro fertilization and embryo transfer. As advancements in research continue and new technologies are developed, specific considerations may need to be made for the care and use of agricultural animals.

Both transgenic and genetically engineered animal models may have physiologic or phenotypic problems including abortions, large offspring, enlarged umbilicus, retained placenta, hydrops, multiple births, and placenta deformities. The scientist is responsible for identifying physiologic and phenotypic changes and must have a plan to address changes that affect animal health to facilitate and ensure animal welfare. The US FDA is responsible for approving the use of genetically modified foods in the United States under the Food, Drug, and Cosmetic Act of 1992.

EUTHANASIA

Protocols for euthanasia should follow current guidelines established by the American Veterinary Medical Association and copies of the protocols should be made available to all personnel who euthanize animals. The agents and methods of euthanasia appropriate for agricultural animals are available in the AVMA Guidelines for Euthanasia or subsequent revisions of that document. Euthanasia is the procedure of killing an animal rapidly, painlessly, and without distress.

Euthanasia must be carried out by trained personnel using acceptable techniques in accordance with applicable regulations and policies. The method used should not interfere with postmortem evaluations. Proper euthanasia involves skilled personnel to help ensure that the technique is performed humanely and effectively and to minimize risk of injury to people.

Personnel who perform euthanasia must have training and experience with the techniques to be used. This training and experience must include familiarity with the normal behaviour of agricultural animals and how handling and restraint affect their behaviour.

The equipment and materials required to perform euthanasia should be readily available, and the attending veterinarian or a qualified animal scientist should ensure that all personnel performing euthanasia have demonstrated proficiency in the use of the techniques selected. Acceptable methods of euthanasia are those that initially depress the central nervous system to ensure insensitivity to pain.

Euthanasia techniques should result in rapid unconsciousness followed by cardiac or respiratory arrest and the ultimate loss of brain function. In addition, the technique used should minimize any stress and anxiety experienced by the animal before unconsciousness. For this reason, anesthetic agents are generally acceptable, and animals of most species can be quickly and humanely euthanized with the appropriate injection of an overdose of a barbiturate.

Certain other methods may be used for euthanasia of anesthetized animals because the major criterion has been fulfilled. Physical methods of euthanasia may be used. Every attempt should be made to minimize stress to the animal before euthanasia. Personnel must be trained on the proper use of the captive bolt per species, and the captive bolt device must be appropriately maintained. Electrocution is an acceptable means of euthanasia if the electrodes are placed so that the current travels through the brain and through the heart.

Methods in which the current is directed through the heart only are not acceptable. It is imperative to ensure that the animal is indeed dead. Techniques that apply electric current from head to tail, head to foot, or head to moistened metal plates on which the animal is standing are unacceptable. Agents that result in tissue residues cannot be used for euthanasia of animals intended for human or animal food unless those agents are approved by the FDA.

Carbon dioxide is the only chemical currently used for euthanasia of food animals that does not lead to tissue residues. The carcasses of animals euthanized by barbiturates may contain potentially harmful residues and should be disposed of in a manner that prevents them from being consumed by human beings or animals. No matter what method of euthanasia is performed, personnel must ensure that death has occurred. Assurance of death may include ascertaining the absence of heartbeat and respiration, lack of corneal or other reflexes, and lack of physical movement. Personnel should be trained on how to assure death in animals.

HUMANE SLAUGHTER

Slaughter of animals entering the human food chain must be accomplished in compliance with regulations promulgated under the federal Humane Methods of Slaughter Act. These regulations outline the requirements for the humane treatment of livestock before and during slaughter. The Food Safety and Inspection Service is the agency within the USDA responsible for ensuring compliance with this Act.

When stunning is used during slaughter, stunning must be done appropriately and effectively. All equipment for stunning must be properly maintained, and personnel performing stunning must be properly trained, including instruction in assessing insensibility. The use of carbon dioxide alone or in combination with other gaseous inhalants remains controversial.

4

Environmental Enrichment

Environmental enrichment involves the enhancement of an animal's physical or social environment. Environmental enrichment is increasingly viewed as a significant component of refinement efforts for animals used in research and teaching, and should be considered where opportunities for social interactions are not available or where the animals' physical environment is restricted or lacking in complexity.

Environmental enrichment has been shown to have wide-ranging physiological and behavioural effects on a variety of species of animals and can be particularly effective in the research setting to reduce the incidence or severity of undesirable or abnormal behaviours. Abnormal behaviours observed in farm animals include locomotor stereotypies such as weaving, pacing, and route-tracing and mouth-based behaviours such as wool-eating by sheep, feather pecking and cannibalism by poultry, bar biting by pigs, tongue rolling by cattle, and wind-sucking by horses.

These behaviours can cause injury to the animal performing them or to other animals in the social group and are most commonly observed in situations in which the quality or quantity of space provided to the animal is inadequate. Environmental enrichment may reduce the frequency or severity of these behaviours, or even prevent them from developing in the first place.

Unfortunately, the term "environmental enrichment" does not have a precise definition and is used inconsistently often referring simply to changes that involve adding one or more objects to an animal's enclosure rather than specifying the desired endpoints of these changes. Newberry suggested a useful concept: the endpoint of enrichment should be to improve the biological functioning of the animal.

Therefore, goals of enrichment programmes include:

- Increasing the number and range of normal behaviours shown by the animal;
- Preventing the development of abnormal behaviours or reducing their frequency or severity;

- Increasing positive utilization of the environment; and
- Increasing the animal's ability to cope with behavioural and physiological challenges such as exposure to humans, experimental manipulation, or environmental variation.

To accomplish these goals, enrichment strategies should be based on an understanding of speciesspecific behaviour and physiology, and the enrichments provided should not only be attractive to the animals but also result in interest that is sufficiently sustained to achieve the desired performance outcomes.

Bloomsmith et al. provided a useful categorization of enrichment types:

- Social enrichment, which can involve either direct or indirect contact with conspecifics or humans.
- Occupational enrichment, which encompasses both psychological enrichment and enrichment that encourages exercise.
- Physical enrichment, which can involve altering the size or complexity of the animal's enclosure or adding accessories to the enclosure such as objects, substrate, or permanent structures.
- Sensory enrichment, or stimuli that are visual, auditory or in other modalities.
- Nutritional enrichment, which can involve either presenting varied or novel food types or changing the method of food delivery.

All of these types of enrichment have been assessed for use with agricultural animals. Validated or potential enrichments for each species are discussed as appropriate. All agricultural animals are social, and social behaviour and management of social groups are covered in the respective species chapters; in this chapter, the focus is on indirect contact or contact with humans as substitutes for conspecific contact in situations in which animals must be individually housed. Genetic differences between breeds, lines, or strains of agricultural animals may be present that affect their use of, or responses to, enrichment.

CATTLE

SOCIAL ENRICHMENT

If the experimental protocol dictates individual housing for cattle, visual and auditory contact with conspecifics is desirable. Research on cattle–human interactions indicates that humans may serve as a substitute for conspecific contact if social contact is not possible.

Gentle and confident handlers benefit animals and may result in improved milk production. For example, when humans stroke body parts commonly groomed by other cattle such as the neck, cattle are more likely to approach humans, indicating that appropriate and gentle contact with humans can improve human–animal interactions. Conversely, rough handing is stressful for cattle. Cattle recognize individual people and become frightened of those who handle them aggressively. Shouting, hitting, and use of the cattle prod are frightening and cattle should not be handled in this way. Indeed, cattle will show more vigilance behaviour when exposed to a human who has handled them roughly compared with a gentle or unfamiliar handler.

OCCUPATIONAL ENRICHMENT

Tied dairy cattle should have daily exercise in a yard. Exercise provides numerous health benefits; for example, cattle given daily exercise had fewer illnesses requiring veterinary attention and fewer hock injuries. Cattle provided with such exercise use this time to groom parts of the body that they cannot reach while tied. Indeed, loose-housed cattle increase grooming when provided a mechanical brush and will use these brushes to groom hard-to-reach areas, such as the hindquarters. Scratching/ribbing devices were used more frequently and for longer by cattle compared with other types of enrichment devices tested.

NUTRITIONAL ENRICHMENT

Weather permitting, access to well-managed pasture is beneficial and recommended for all cattle. Dairy cows with access to pasture have fewer health problems such as mastitis. Cattle also do not exhibit stereotypic tongue rolling while at pasture. Indeed, provision of exercise adequate roughage, and group housing calves have all been found to reduce stereotypic tongue rolling in cattle.

SENSORY ENRICHMENT

Noise is a possible stressor within cattle housing environments and during routine management practices such as handling, milking, and transport. Beef cattle exposed to either human shouting or noise of metal clanging move more while restrained in the chute; thus, quiet environments facilitate animal handling and well being. Quiet environments may be even more important for dairy cattle, as they are more reactive to sound than beef cattle.

Although music and noise can serve as a cue that will synchronize attendance at an automatic milking machine, cows will avoid noise, such as a radio or sounds of a milking machine, associated with milking when given the choice. Olfactory enrichment may also be important for cattle; feedlot cattle are reported to be more attracted to scented enrichment devices than to unscented devices. Feedlot cattle will spend time scratching their skin against brushes which may act as a form of tactile enrichment.

HORSES

SOCIAL ENRICHMENT

As prey species, horses are highly motivated to interact with individuals of their own species for comfort, play, access to food and shelter resources, and as an antipredator strategy. During fearful situations and when separated from closely bonded companions, restlessness, pacing, and vocalizations occur and suggest experiences of acute anxiety and distress. Horses housed singly display greater activity and reduced foraging compared with horses kept in pairs or groups. Horses housed singly also display more aggression towards human handlers and learn new tasks more slowly than horses housed in groups.

Confining horses for long periods may produce behavioural problems that sometimes progress to the exhibition of stereotypies, commonly referred to as vices. Examples include stall weaving, cribbing, or wind sucking. Management efforts to minimize stereotypies include companionship, exercise, environmental enrichment objects, or increasing dietary fibre by pasture grazing, availability of hay, or providing multiple forage types. In feral and wild situations, horses maintain longterm relationships.

Stallions and mares stay together year-round over multiple breeding seasons, whereas colts and fillies emigrate from the natal herd when they are juveniles. Mare–mare bonds are very stable and persist for years, although social interactions decrease markedly during the postparturient period when mares direct social behaviour towards their foals. For mares and fillies, social bonds are likely to develop between individuals that are familiar, closely related, and similar in social rank.

Social relationships between females are characterized by mutual grooming and maintaining close proximity. In the absence of these factors, social bonds are directed towards unfamiliar individuals that have the same coat colour as the filly's dam. Mutual grooming is directed towards the withers and neck region and is associated with reduced heart rate suggesting a role in reducing anxiety. Mutual grooming is rarely performed by stallions, except following periods of social deprivation.

In contrast, colts and gelding are highly motivated to play with each other. When housed in extensive conditions, colts perform hourly play bouts, such as mock fighting, whereas mares do not typically engage in this behaviour. Because aggression and play can result in injuries, stallions are typically housed singly. Aggression is influenced by reproductive status, with greater aggression in established groups occurring in the breeding and foaling season.

In mixed groups, mares display more aggression in the postparturient period, primarily in the form of interventions to protect foals from barren mares and geldings. Similarly during feeding trials, yearling females perform significantly more agonistic interactions than geldings of the same age, likely because of circulating steroid levels at estrus. When horses are housed singly or in isolation facilities, distress associated with social deprivation can be alleviated by providing visual contact with other equids.

Weaving and head-nodding stereotypies, which are associated with frustration are significantly reduced when horses can see other equids through grilled side windows or when mirrors or life-sized poster images of a horse's face are placed in the stalls. Lateral visual contact appears to be important, because weaving is significantly more likely to occur when stalls are arranged face-to-face than side-by-side. In the absence of equids, horses readily form social relationships with other species, such as goats, dogs, and humans.

Intensively managed horses detect and respond to subtle indicators of emotional state and confidence in their human handlers, eliciting both fearfulness and calmness. Horses accept being groomed by humans; reductions in heart rate that occur when horses perform mutual grooming are also observed when humans brush or scratch the withers and neck regions. However, this positive association with tactile stimulation by humans appears to be learned rather than innate and in the absence of positive interactions, foals begin to avoid humans at 3 wk of age.

PHYSICAL ENRICHMENT

Horses provided access to paddocks or pasture can alleviate foraging motivation through grazing, but horses also benefit from opportunities to exercise, with activity positively associated with paddock size. Horses appear to be motivated to perform exercise in its own right, with motivation building up and compensatory activity performed after periods of deprivation.

Furthermore, horses provided with turn-out display more varied rolling behaviour, which is believed to be associated with comfort. In a study of racing horses, benefits of regular turn-out also included less aggression directed towards handlers and superior race and career performance.

OCCUPATIONAL ENRICHMENT

In the absence of turning out in paddocks or pastures, horses can direct play behaviour towards "toys" placed in the stall. Several commercially available products such as the large durable balls designed to be used with stabled horses can be provided, as well as home-made devices such as plastic jugs hanging on ropes. Scientific evidence regarding the efficacy of these products is lacking.

SENSORY ENRICHMENT

In many stables, it is common for background noise to be provided by a radio, with the assumption that this provides a calming effect on the horses and alleviates boredom. However, the presence or type of music was not found to significantly affect the behaviour of ponies subjected to short-term isolation distress. These authors speculate that background music may indirectly affect equine behaviour through the attitudes of their human caretakers. Conversely, a synthetic Equine Appeasement Pheromone product is commercially available, and there is minimal evidence that this product effectively reduces behavioural and physiologic fear responses of horses subjected to a stressful situation.

NUTRITIONAL ENRICHMENT

Opportunities to forage provide significant enrichment for stabled horses. Horses typically spend 10 to 12 h grazing per day and lactating mares spend 70 per cent of their time grazing on pasture. In the absence of foraging material, horses frequently may direct foraging towards the stall bedding or stall surfaces or may display oral stereotypies such as crib-biting, wind-sucking, sham chewing, hair eating, and wood chewing/licking. Undesirable oral behaviour can be addressed by providing at least 6.8 kg of hay per day, providing multiple forages, and dividing concentrate feed into smaller and more frequent meals throughout the day.

Horses provided with straw bedding perform less stereotypic behaviour than those bedded on paper or shavings. Several food toys are commercially available, which horses manipulate to obtain high-fibre food pellets. These food-balls result in increased foraging time and reduced stereotypic behaviour. Toys with round or polyhedral designs are most effective. These toys can be provided in the manger to prevent horses from ingesting pathogens and nonnutritive materials from the stall bedding.

POULTRY

SOCIAL ENRICHMENT

Socialization of poultry with humans can be carried out with relative ease by frequent exposure to kind, gentle care. Even brief periods of handling, beginning at the youngest possible age, confer advantages for ease of later handling of birds and increase feed efficiency, body weights, and antibody responses. In addition, Gross and Siegel found that positively socialized chickens had reduced responses to stressors and that resistance to most diseases tested was better than that of birds that had not been socialized.

OCCUPATIONAL ENRICHMENT

A primary method for promoting exercise in poultry is the provision of perches or other elevated areas that encourage the use of vertical space in the enclosure. Egg-laying strains of chickens are highly motivated to use perches at night and the entire flock will utilize perches at night if sufficient perch space is provided. When hens are housed in floor pens, perches allow them to roost comfortably with a minimum of disturbance and provide them with an opportunity to seek refuge from other birds to avoid cannibalistic pecking.

Perches can also minimize bird flightiness and fearfulness and the exercise facilitated by vertical movement can improve bone strength. Early exposure to perches during rearing facilitates perching behaviour in adult birds. Poults and young broiler chickens also use perches but use tends to decrease when the birds are older. At later stages of the production cycle, perches are used much less frequently by broilers and turkeys than by laying hens.

Because of their body size and conformation, older turkeys and broiler chickens need to be provided with lower perches of a shape and size that allow them to easily access the perches and to balance properly when perching. For older turkeys it advisable to locate the perches high enough that turkeys on the ground cannot peck and pull the feathers of perching birds; ramps can be installed in front of these higher perches to facilitate access.

Straw bales can also be added to pens to provide an elevated surface for broilers and turkeys but again ramps may need to be installed so that older birds can easily access these. Because straw is also used as a foraging substrate, however, the bales may be rapidly pecked apart and scattered.

In general, perches should be free of sharp edges, of a size that can be readily gripped by the claws but large enough in diameter that the bird's toenails do not damage its footpad, and made of a material that is nonslip but that can be cleaned.

Perches soiled with feces are a major contributing factor to the development of a painful foot condition, bumblefoot, in floor-housed poultry, so it is important that perches be properly designed to minimize this problem. In addition, hens may develop deviated keel bones from resting on perches, although it is unknown if this condition is painful. Laying hens prefer high perches.

However, hens tend to develop osteoporosis and this makes perch placement critical to ensure that the hens can navigate the perches without breaking bones during landings. Ducks will swim if water of sufficient depth is provided. If swimming water is made available to ducklings, the water should be very shallow so that the ducklings do not drown, and care must be taken until their waterproof feathers emerge to ensure that they do not become soaked and chilled.

PHYSICAL ENRICHMENT

NESTBOXES

The most important physical enrichment for laying hens is a nestbox. Egg laying involves a complex sequence of behaviours, including searching for a suitable site in which to lay an egg and then preparing that site by pecking, treading, and molding the substrate to create a nest. Laying hens that are not provided with a nest site may show agitated pacing behaviour during the nest-seeking phase, which has been interpreted as evidence of frustration. Hens place a high value on accessing nests, and their motivation for nest use increases greatly as the time of oviposition approaches. Even hens without prior exposure to nests show a strong motivation to use nests for egg laying. Laying hens also generally prefer enclosed nesting sites to ones that are more open. Providing an appropriate substrate in the nestbox is also important to allow for nest-building behaviour. There have been few experimental studies of prelaying behaviour or nest-site selection in either ducks or turkeys.

However, it is likely that they have a similarly strong motivation to lay their eggs in a nest box. There are many different types of nestboxes available commercially and most have been used successfully in both industry and research settings for ducks and turkeys, suggesting that the important features of a nest to these species, as for laying hens, are fairly simple.

SUBSTRATE

The provision of suitable substrate, such as friable litter material for turkeys and fowl and both water and friable material for ducks, facilitates both foraging and grooming behaviour. Poultry would normally spend a large part of their day foraging, and increasing foraging opportunities can help to reduce the incidence of two abnormal behaviours, feather pecking and cannibalism.

These behaviours are not related to aggression but, like aggression, are directed towards other birds in the flock. Feather pecking can consist of gentle pecking that does not result in the removal of feathers from the pecked bird or more severe pecking that results in feather loss. Having a feather removed is painful, and severe feather pecking can lead to birds having denuded areas that expose the skin to injury and impair thermoregulation. These denuded areas may also attract tissue pecking and cannibalism by other birds.

Cannibalism involves the pecking and tearing of skin, underlying tissues, and organs. Cannibalistic pecking is most often directed towards the toes, tail, vent area, or emerging primary feathers on the wings and can cause high flock injury and mortality if birds are not beak-or bill-trimmed. Outbreaks of feather pecking and cannibalism are difficult to control once started because these behaviours are socially transmitted among birds in the flock, so it is best to prevent their occurrence through early intervention.

Other factors such as nutritional deficiencies or environmental or management variables can contribute to outbreaks of feather pecking and cannibalism. There are also strong genetic effects, and these behaviours are more difficult to control in some species or strains than in others. For example, Muscovy ducks are much more likely to engage in cannibalistic behaviour than Pekin ducks and providing Muscovy ducks with a variety of water-and food-based foraging enrichments was found to be ineffective in preventing cannibalism.

Aggressive behaviours in turkeys can be reduced by the provision of foraging materials. Martrenchar *et al.* provided growing turkeys with straw and hanging chains and found reduced pecking injuries in both toms and hens. Sherwin *et al.* reared turkeys with a variety of pecking substrates and found that this reduced injuries due to wing and tail-pecking. These types of items can be effective in reducing behaviour problems, even in cage environments.

For example, chickens are attracted to and manipulate hanging strings, and providing these in cages was found to reduce feather damage, presumably because of reduced feather pecking, in caged laying hens. If an appropriate substrate is provided, chickens and turkeys will dustbathe in long bouts on most days, particularly in sunny or bright locations in their enclosure. During dustbathing, loose particles are worked through the feathers and then shaken out. This improves feather condition by dispersing lipids and possibly serves to remove ectoparasites.

Chickens will dustbathe in different types of loose material, but prefer litter with smaller diameter particles to litter with larger diameter particles; smaller particles are also more effective in penetrating the feathers. Ducks maintain good plumage condition by water bathing.

If swimming water is not provided for practical or hygienic reasons, providing a source of water that is at least deep enough for the ducks to immerse their heads and shake water over their body can help them to maintain good plumage, nostril, and eye condition, as can providing them with an overhead shower Bedding material can become contaminated with feces and produce unacceptable levels of atmospheric ammonia if not well maintained.

Wet or contaminated bedding can also cause foot and leg problems such as footpad dermatitis. Certain types of litter can also become aerosolized, creating excessive dust. When water is provided as a swimming, foraging, or grooming substrate for ducks, it must be changed frequently to prevent it from becoming contaminated. The resulting moisture in the environment can also lead to unacceptable levels of ammonia, and contact with feed and bedding that has become moldy because of excess moisture in the atmosphere predisposes ducks to infection with Aspergillosis.

COVER

Providing floor-housed chickens with cover in the form of overhead vertical panels has been shown to improve pen usage, increase resting and preening behaviours, and decrease the number of times that birds disturb one another. Striped panels providing 67 per cent cover are effective, and are preferred by the chickens to solid, transparent, or less fully striped panels.

OBJECTS

Several studies have investigated whether providing novel objects can decrease fear in poultry. Chicks provided with such objects were less fearful during several standardized tests, although the birds were not tested as adults to determine whether this effect persisted. Reed *et al.* reported that exposing laying hen chicks to novel objects, a radio playing a human voice, and human handling resulted in less fearfulness to novel stimuli and decreased injury from handling when the hens were adults.

In contrast, Nicol and Scott found no reduction in fear in broiler chickens exposed to human handling and auditory and novel object enrichment, and Nicol actually found that novel object enrichment could increase fearfulness in broilers. Although chickens do show interest in exploring semi-unfamiliar environments, novel objects and food can themselves cause fear reactions and so should be introduced cautiously to older birds.

SENSORY ENRICHMENT

The effects of 3 forms of sensory enrichment on chickens have been reviewed by Jones. Both chicks and hens are attracted to video images shown outside of their enclosures. Bright, colored, complex, and moving video images are more attractive to the birds than dull, still, greytone, and simple images. Regular exposure of chicks to video stimulation reduced their fear of a novel place.

Fear responses in a novel environment were also found to be reduced in chicks if the environment contained an odour with which the chicks had been reared, and the chicks also showed less fear of novel food and consumed that food sooner if it was associated with the familiar odour. Playing music has also been advocated to reduce fear responses in chickens, but claims about its efficacy are not based on empirical studies.

NUTRITIONAL ENRICHMENT

The provision of appropriate substrate, such as wood-shavings litter for fowl or water for ducks, also facilitates foraging behaviour. Other methods of increasing foraging time include scattering feed in the litter when birds are housed on substrate, and placing rocks, edible items, or other objects in water containers for ducks or in the feed troughs of chickens.

If scatter feeding or water feeding are used, body weight should be monitored to ensure that birds are maintaining adequate feed intake. There has been only limited research on the effects of providing varied food items to poultry, but chickens are able to self-select among various ingredients to create a nutritionally balanced diet. Several guidelines recommend providing poultry with brassicas or similar foods to stimulate foraging and to vary the feeding regimen.

SHEEP AND GOATS

SOCIAL ENRICHMENT

Validation of enrichment devices and procedures for sheep is extremely limited. However, sheep are highly social animals, and if social contact must be limited it may be beneficial to provide the sheep with visual contact with other sheep through fencing or other transparent materials. It has also been suggested that a mirror or an inanimate object covered with animal skin could serve as a social surrogate. Mirrors can reduce but do not abolish the physiological stress response to social isolation in sheep. However, because sheep appear to treat their own reflection as a strange individual it is also possible that a mirror image could cause social stress.

NUTRITIONAL ENRICHMENT

Devices that provide feed supplements when manipulated by licking or pushing with the head may occupy the animals' attention. However, care must be taken to keep these objects clean, as they quickly become contaminated with manure.

OCCUPATIONAL AND PHYSICAL ENRICHMENT

An undesirable behaviour called wool biting may develop in confined sheep. Wool-biting sheep take bites of and eat wool from other sheep. This may compromise the health and well-being of the sheep that are "victimized," and may alter the nutritional status of the sheep performing the wool biting. Wool biting seems to be a redirected behaviour of confined sheep, and lack of environmental stimulation and diet may contribute to the onset of wool biting.

Strategies that have been used to prevent or stop wool biting include hanging chains above the surface of the pen, adding objects to the pen playing music, and altering the diet. Increasing the roughage content of the diet may reduce the incidence of wool biting, although definitive methods for preventing or reducing this behaviour have not been reported.

Goats will climb a variety of objects such as tables, empty cable spools, or even elaborate jungle gyms. These structures will be used throughout the day. An enriched environment has been shown to increase feed consumption and reduce aggression in goats in feedlots. Care must be taken to provide appropriate climbing space that is ample for the number of animals in the group, as dominant animals will displace subordinates. Also, climbing devices should be placed in such a manner as to prevent the goats from vaulting out of the enclosure.

SWINE

An enriched environment contributes to pig wellbeing in numerous ways, as indicated by increased behavioural diversity, adaptability to novelty, and learning ability, coupled with reduced aggression, fearfulness, stereotyped behaviour, belly nosing, and tail and ear biting. An extensive enrichment programme would provide sufficient environmental complexity to enable pigs to express a wide range of normal behaviour and to exercise a degree of control and choice in their environment, but also needs to promote pig health and be practical to employ.

SOCIAL ENRICHMENT

Housing pigs in stable social groups with ample space and environmental complexity enables them to adjust their proximity to different individuals according to their social relationships and current state. Alternative housing systems that minimize regrouping and social stress are available and may be of use for certain research and teaching protocols or in certain herds.

When pigs must be isolated from conspecifics for experimental purposes, friendly social contact with familiar caretakers could be especially important. Pigs recognize familiar caretakers using visual as well as vocal and olfactory cues. Caretakers can develop positive social contact with pigs by moving slowly and calmly, crouching to reduce apparent body size, avoiding aversive or inconsistent handling, and stroking or scratching pigs that approach.

When pigs have a positive attitude towards caretakers, they will approach confidently and seek interaction, which may have positive implications for handling strategies. Providing companionship from familiar pen-mates and a warm, artificial udder with flexible nipples can decrease distress in piglets that must be weaned at an early age for experimental reasons.

OCCUPATIONAL ENRICHMENT

Occupational enrichment is achieved by allowing and promoting physical exercise, foraging, exploration, nest-building, playing, and manipulative and cognitive activities. Access to pasture, soil, straw, peat, mushroom compost, hay, bark, branches, logs, and other malleable materials helps to satisfy these urges. These materials provide an outlet for exploration, sniffing, biting, rooting, and chewing activities, reducing the likelihood that these behaviours will be redirected towards the bodies of pen-mates or pen fixtures.

Such enrichment materials can lower the risk of injuries and harassment from tail biting, ear chewing, and belly nosing, as well as reducing aggressive behaviour and wear and tear on housing fixtures. Pigs are initially attracted to materials that are odorous, deformable, and chewable, but for sustained occupational enrichment, the best materials are complex, changeable, manipulatable, destructible, and are ingestible or contain sparsely distributed edible parts. Thus, pigs prefer to root in and manipulate materials such as corn silage mixed with straw, compost, turf, peat, forest soil, beets, spruce chips, and fir branches.

Although somewhat less preferred than these materials, long straw is a useful enrichment material, being more effective than chopped straw, sand, or ropes, and much more effective than indestructible objects such as hoses, chains, and tires. Unattached objects presented at floor level may be more attractive to pigs than hanging objects but lose their attractiveness when soiled with excreta. Most research on enrichment materials has focused on straw. The amount of behaviour directed towards long straw rather than towards pen-mates is proportional to the amount of straw provided.

Although providing straw only after tail biting has started can reduce the behaviour, it does not act as a complete curative. Providing straw from an early age helps to prevent tail biting, lowers aggression, and maintains normal activity. However, the risk of tail biting is elevated, and activity is depressed, if pigs initially reared with straw are subsequently housed without straw. These findings highlight the importance of continuing an enrichment programme once it has started.

Slatted floors and liquid-manure systems usually preclude the provision of ample amounts of long straw and other particulate foraging materials. In this situation, offering small amounts of such materials in racks or troughs, and replenishing the supply frequently, stimulates sniffing, rooting, and chewing while maintaining a degree of novelty that is important for sustaining the interest of curious pigs. When particulate materials cannot be used, hanging ropes with unraveled ends that can be pulled, shaken, chewed, and torn apart are the next best option.

Less-destructible novel hanging objects can offer short-term enrichment by attracting exploration and stimulating play but they need to be changed frequently because pigs rapidly lose interest in such objects when they are no longer novel. Enrichment materials and objects should be monitored to ensure that they do not cause health problems or compromise food safety. Supplying ample free access to preferred enrichment materials and objects will minimize aggressive competition for these resources. Offering opportunities for pigs to respond to environmental cues to find occasional food rewards and to work for access to foraging materials and hidden food treats can be rewarding. This form of enrichment has been found to speed wound healing.

At least 24 h before farrowing, provision of an earth or sand substrate along with straw, branches, or other nesting materials enables sows to address their strong motivation to engage in nest-building behaviour, which, under natural conditions, involves digging a shallow depression with the snout and then gathering nesting materials such as long grass, twigs, and branches, carrying them to the nest site in the mouth, and arranging them into a nest. Providing nest materials can contribute to early piglet survival although results are variable. Long straw is preferred over cloth tassels as a nesting material although the latter may have some benefit in liquid-manure systems that preclude the use of straw.

PHYSICAL ENRICHMENT

Pigs show spatial separation of different behaviours such as lying, feeding, and excretion. Providing ample space or appropriate subdivision of the enclosure area enables the establishment of separate functional areas. For example, Simonsen subdivided pens into areas with straw bedding, a pig-operated shower, straw racks, and logs hung on chains, and Stolba and Wood-Gush subdivided enclosures into areas for nesting, feeding, rooting, and excretion.

Two-level pens also subdivide the pen space, thereby encouraging exercise, making handling and herding of pigs easier, and allowing pigs to exercise choice of thermal environment. Habituation to ramps and alleys in the housing environment reduces novelty-induced fear when pigs are subsequently handled. Allowing pigs daily access to enriched areas that are not accessible full time can stimulate anticipation and play.

To avoid overcrowding and competition in one area of a subdivided or multi-level pen, calculation of stocking density and feeder space should take into account variations in the distribution of pigs across different areas of the pen. Providing visual barriers helps pigs to avoid aggressive pen-mates. This can be achieved by installing solid partitions between feeding spaces, boxes, or holes in the wall where pigs can hide their heads, straw bales, dividers between different functional areas, or an upper pen level accessed by a ramp.

In outdoor pens, bushes, trees, and varied terrain can serve to create visually discrete areas. Loose housing of sows allows freedom of movement leading to a shorter farrowing duration and lower stress at parturition relative to confinement in crates, and the risk of injuries can be reduced by secure footing and well-managed bedding. Pens with stalls along with communal activity and resting areas allow gestating sows in groups to move freely and rest together while enabling temporary separation in stalls for feeding or experimental purposes.

In addition to providing occupational enrichment, bedding gives thermal comfort in cool weather as well as cushioning the body against hard surfaces. Only good-quality bedding should be used to avoid introduction of mycotoxin molds, and bedding must be managed to avoid wet litter and high ammonia emissions. Certain types of artificial lying mats may also contribute to lying comfort.

In outdoor pens, huts or kennels supplied with straw create suitable lying areas in cold weather. In hot weather, wallows, snout coolers, or snout-operated showers aid thermoregulation. An earth substrate allows pigs to dig a simple depression in the ground for nesting. Shade may be needed to protect outdoor pigs from heat stress and sunburn.

SENSORY ENRICHMENT

Pigs can learn to associate olfactory, vocal, and colour cues with a food reward. For example, pigs use the odour of dimethyl sulfide to locate buried truffles, a highly desired food item that has a musky garlic/mushroom flavour and contains the boar sex pheromone 5-α-androstenol. Pigs also seek opportunities to interact with materials that provide tactile stimulation of different areas of their snout and mouth. Sensory cues paired with rewards, including access to enrichment materials, can be used to stimulate anticipatory excitement and play.

Habituation to a wide array of nonharmful sensory stimuli when young may reduce fear in novel situations when older, and exposure to sensory stimuli that evoke comforting associations may be helpful at times of unavoidable stress. Decisions about cleaning regimens should take into account that pigs communicate through odours. It is important to avoid disruptive cleaning routines during the first week after farrowing, which is an important time for social attachment between the sow and her piglets and the establishment of the teat order.

Although moderate levels of ammonia do not appear to be highly aversive and do not disrupt social recognition, keeping ammonia to a minimum should facilitate exploration of diverse environmental odours. Enrichment materials with noticeable odours attract exploration, and pigs show preferences for foods with certain odours or flavours, whereas materials soiled by excreta are aversive.

Providing chewable tubes offering flavoured water may not be sufficient to prevent tail biting. To facilitate vocal communication between pigs, continuous loud noise should be avoided. This is especially important in the farrowing area because vocalizations between sows and piglets are important for social bonding and effective nursing, and masking these vocalizations with high levels of ambient sound can disrupt suckling behaviour.

Piglets should be handled in a manner that minimizes loud vocalizations that signal piglet distress and disturb the sows. Consideration should be given to handling piglets outside the hearing range of sows if loud calling by piglets is unavoidable. Silence is more effective in quieting piglets separated from the sow than playback of meditation music, white noise, or vocalizations of unfamiliar piglets.

Furthermore, pigs are not especially attracted to enrichment materials that produce sound when manipulated. On the other hand, habituation to a variety of environmental sounds should help to reduce fear when pigs are moved to new environments, and playing a radio may be useful for masking sounds on occasions when sudden, unpredictable, loud noises are anticipated, such as those generated during construction.

NUTRITIONAL ENRICHMENT

When feeding concentrated diets, feed restriction is usually needed during pregnancy to prevent excessive weight gain, which may result in later difficulties during farrowing and lactation. Although the ration fulfills their nutrient requirements, the sows eat it quickly and are hungry for much of the day. The sows' normal response is to forage for additional food. When sows are housed in an environment with no outlet for diverse foraging behaviours, aggression may increase, foraging behaviour may be channeled into a few elements performed repetitively in stereotyped sequences or abnormal amounts of water may be consumed.

These behaviours are reduced by providing straw and other ingestible foraging substrates that occupy the sows in diverse foraging activities and by feeding a diet high in fermentable nonstarch polysaccharides to increase satiety. Although increasing the fibre content of the diet does not always influence stereotyped oral-nasal-facial behaviours, the incidence of gastric lesions may be reduced in pigs given straw compared with those lacking access to roughage.

Chewable and destructible but inedible substrates and objects such as ropes and cloth tassels are less satisfying to sows than straw or other fibrous materials but are better than hard, indestructible objects such as chains and stones towards which sows direct stereotypic behaviour. Incorporating a nutritional reward in a rootable or chewable object increases its attractiveness over objects that do not provide food reinforcement.

Although stereotyped behaviour peaks in the period immediately following a meal suggesting that limit-fed sows should be given concentrated feed in a single daily meal rather than multiple smaller meals, provision of small food rewards does not appear to cause stereotypic behaviour when combined with loose housing in straw-bedded pens.

Under these conditions, limit-fed sows can be extensively occupied by provision of food in devices that require work to extract it. It is important to make sure that there are sufficient nutritional enrichment devices to avoid aggressive competition. In general, the benefits of environmental enrichment for pigs are likely to be greatest when multiple forms of enrichment are supplied.

GENERAL CONSIDERATIONS

When providing animals with environmental enrichment, it is critical to assess outcomes to ensure that the enrichment programme is effectively meeting the intended goals. Observations of animal behaviour, health, performance characteristics, and use of the enrichments are important components of such an assessment. Behavioural observations might include assessments of the frequency of normal behaviours, the frequency and severity of stereotypies and injurious behaviours, and the frequency and severity of undesirable behaviours such as excessive fearfulness or aggression.

For outcomes to be assessed adequately, it is important that the individuals who are making the observations be appropriately trained in sampling methods and that these methods are standardized across raters. These types of observations are often made by the animal caretakers, because they are typically the individuals with the most day-to-day contact with the animals.

As Nelson and Mandrell point out, caretakers should therefore be "encouraged to become knowledgeable about the behaviour of individual animals, to be active participants in the implementation of the enrichment programmes, and to be made aware of the special role they play in communicating the successes and failures of enrichment strategies".

These individuals should also be encouraged to be creative in developing environmental enrichment programmes for agricultural animals. Books and articles about farm animal behaviour are useful resources. In addition, Young provides helpful information about designing and analysing enrichment studies as well as a list of sources of general information about various environmental enrichment methods.

There are important practical considerations involved in providing animals with enrichments, including those related to safety. Animals are periodically reported to sustain injuries from environmental enrichment; for example, intestinal obstruction due to the provision of foraging enrichments or items that can be chewed and ingested.

Young lists several considerations that should be taken into account when evaluating the safety characteristics of potential enrichment devices:

- Does the enrichment have sharp edges?
- Can the animal's limbs or other parts of the animal's body become trapped in any part of the enrichment?
- Can the enrichment be broken or dismantled by the animal, and if so, would the fragments or constituent parts pose a safety risk?
- Can the enrichment or any part of it be gnawed and swallowed?
- Is the enrichment made of nontoxic material?
- Can the enrichment be cleaned adequately or sterilized to prevent disease transmission?
- Could the animal use the enrichment to damage its cage or pen-mates or its enclosure?

In addition, close monitoring is required when objects are introduced into social housing environments because aggression may increase if the animals compete for access to the resource. Other constraints on enrichment are related to facility design, cost, sanitation, ease of management and potential effects on research outcomes. Input should, therefore, be sought from the IACUC, veterinarians, researchers, and the caretakers who will be responsible for the day-to-day implementation of the enrichment programme.

5

Animal Handling and Transport

Handling refers to how agricultural animals are touched, moved, and interacted with during husbandry procedures. Transport means when agricultural animals are moved by vehicles or vessel from one place to another. Performance standards during handling include careful, considerate, respectful, calm, human interactions with animals in as positive a manner as is possible. Animals handled in a respectful manner will be calmer and easier to handle than animals handled in a rough or disrespectful manner.

Whenever possible, animals should be moved at a normal walking speed, and acclimating the animals to handling and close contact with people will reduce stress. Research clearly shows that animals that are handled in a negative manner and fear humans have lower weight gains, fewer piglets, and give less milk and reduced egg production.

Cattle that become agitated during restraint in a squeeze chute or exit from the squeeze chute rapidly have lower weight gains, poorer meat quality, and higher cortisol levels compared with calmer animals. Socialization of agricultural animals with humans should be done when feasible when small numbers of animals are used for research.

Socialization and gentling can be carried out with relative ease by frequent exposure to kind, gentle care. Even brief periods of handling, beginning at the youngest possible age, confer advantages for ease of handling of birds and increase feed efficiency, body weight, and antibody responses to red blood cell antigens.

For example, Gross and Siegel and Jones and Hughes found that positively socialized chickens had reduced responses to stressors and that resistance to most diseases tested was better than that of birds that had not been socialized. When large numbers of animals are housed under commercial conditions, socialization may not be possible, but the flightiness can be reduced if a person either walks through the flock herds or groups of animals or walks by their cages on a daily basis.

Calm animals will also provide more accurate research results that are less confounded by handling stress. Handling and restraint stresses can significantly alter physiological measurements. Beef cattle not accustomed to handling had significantly higher cortisol levels after restraint compared with dairy cattle that were accustomed to handling. Prolonged 6-h restraint of sheep where they could not move resulted in extremely high cortisol levels of >110 ng/mL.

Aggressive handling should never be used for farm animals. Multiple shocks with an electrical prod more than doubled the levels of lactate and glucose in pigs compared with careful handling without electric prods. Transportation performance standards include movement of animals with minimal risk of injury or death to animal or handler.

Transportation is only performed when necessary. Making the transport experience more comfortable for each species should be a priority for animal handlers.

BIOMEDICAL VERSUS AGRICULTURAL RESEARCH REQUIREMENTS

For research results to be applicable to commercial agriculture, the animals have to be handled and housed in conditions similar to those on commercial farms. In these situations, many of the animals may not be accustomed to close contact with people, and commercial handling equipment such as cattle squeeze chutes and other specialized equipment will be required.

In another type of research, an agricultural animal may be used for biomedical research and housed in small indoor pens that are not similar to commercial conditions. Biomedical researchers have conditioned and trained animals to cooperate with injections, restraint, and other procedures. Primates, pigs, and sheep can be easily trained to voluntarily enter a restraint device or hold out a limb for various procedures.

Hutson reported that providing food rewards to sheep made them more willing to move through a handling facility in the future. Training animals to cooperate greatly improves welfare, and removes some effects of restraint stress on physiological data.

Low levels of cortisol and glucose were obtained from unsedated antelopes that had been conditioned to enter a restraint box and voluntarily stand still for blood tests. Training animals to voluntarily cooperate with injections, blood sampling, and other procedures is definitely recommended for biomedical settings where a few animals are used for medical experiments. However, it is often not practical for agricultural research in which large numbers of animals are handled.

FLIGHT ZONE AND BEHAVIOUR PRINCIPLES

People who are handling cattle, bison, sheep, horses, and other grazing animals should have knowledge of flight zone principles.

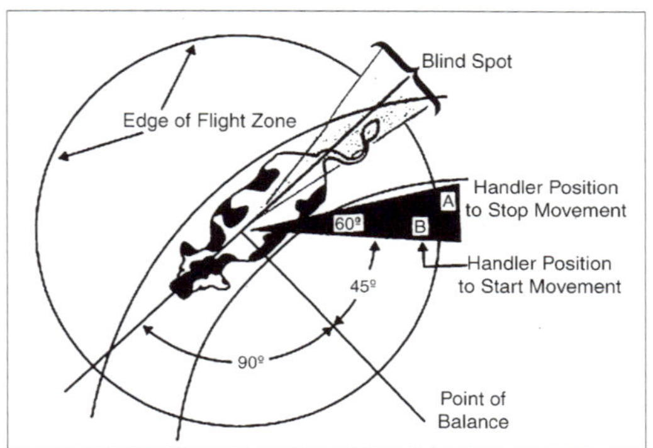

Fig. Flight Zone Diagram Showing the Most Effective Handle Positions for Moving an Animal Forward. Reproduced with Permission of T. Grandin.

The flight zone concept does not apply to animals that are trained to lead with a halter or otherwise conditioned to close human handling. The flight zone varies depending on whether cattle or other livestock have been extensively or intensively raised. Extensively raised cattle may have flight zones up to 50 m, but intensively raised cattle may have flight zones only 2 to 8 m.

The size of an alley can change flight zones. Sheep in a 2-m wide alley had a smaller flight zone than sheep in a 4-m wide alley. An approximation of the flight zone can be made by approaching the animal and noting at what distance the animal moves away. When the handler is outside of the flight zone, cattle will turn and face the handler. Flight zones can be exploited by handlers to move cattle and other livestock efficiently and quietly.

For example, handlers should be positioned at the edge of the flight zone and behind the point of balance to move cattle forward. A common mistake made by many handlers is to stand in front of the shoulder and attempt to make an animal go forward by poking its rear. This gives the animal conflicting signals. To move the animal forward, the handler should be behind the point of balance; Figure presents the concept of flight zone and point of balance.

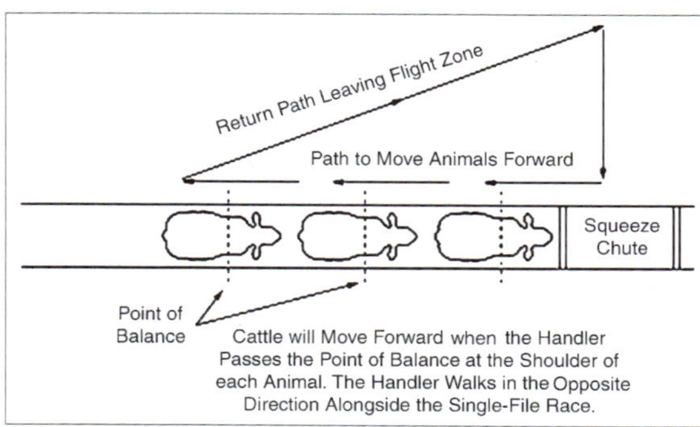

Fig. Handler Movement Pattern to Induce Cattle to Move Forward in a Race. Reproduced with Permission of T. Grandin.

Figure shows how to move an animal forward in a chute by walking quickly past the point of balance at the shoulder in the opposite direction of desired movement. To cause cattle to stop or back up, handlers should be positioned ahead of the point of balance. Too deep a penetration of the flight zone may cause extensively raised cattle to bolt or run away or rear up in a chute. Animals will often stop rearing if the handler backs up and gets out of the flight zone.

Personnel working with cattle should be trained to use flight zones correctly. Extensively raised grazing animals that arrive at a research facility may have a large flight zone. The size of the flight zone will gradually diminish if they are handled calmly and have frequent contact with people. Farm animals are social and a lone animal separated from its herdmate often becomes severely agitated. Many injuries to both people and animals occur when a single lone animal runs into a fence or charges.

An agitated lone animal can be calmed by putting some other animals in with it. Cattle and sheep will follow a leader. When one of the animals starts to move, the others will follow. Natural following behaviour can be used to facilitate calm movement of animals. If animals are calmly moving in the desired direction, the handler should back up and stop putting pressure on the flight zone. Continuous pressure on the flight zone may cause animals to start running, which is undesirable.

AIDS FOR MOVING ANIMALS

Animals in properly designed facilities may be moved using their natural behaviour and without the use of any aids. The goals of movement should be to minimize stress to each individual animal, reduce fear, and maintain calmness in all animals. All handlers should be trained in the natural behaviour of the species including their flight zone and in proper handler movement and interaction, and be able to recognize any signs of distress, anxiety, or behaviours that may result in injury or stress to the animals.

When necessary, nonelectrical driving aids such as paddles, flags, and panels may be an adjunct with the use of natural behaviour and handling skills. Handlers should be trained in the proper and effective use of each driving aid, which is appropriate to the species. An electric prod should only be picked up and used in a specific situation where it is needed and then put away.

Handlers have a better attitude towards the animals when electric shocks are not used. Data collected at meat plants indicate that most cattle and pigs could be moved throughout an entire handling system without electric prods. On a ranch or feedlot, the use of electric prods should be limited to 10 per cent or less of the cattle. When an electric prod needs to be used, it should be applied to the hindquarters of the animal. Usually 1 to 3 brief shocks are needed.

If the animal does not respond, the use of the electric prod should be discontinued immediately. It should never be applied to sensitive areas of the animal such as the eyes, ears, genitals, udder, or anus. Battery-operated prods are recommended because they administer a localized shock between 2 prongs. Electric prods should not be used on newborn animals, debilitated weak animals, nonambulatory downed animals, or emaciated animals. Electric prods are highly stressful to pigs. Repeated shocks greatly increased the percentage of nonambulatory pigs. Multiple shocks and aggressive handling significantly increased blood lactate and other indicators of metabolic stress compared with gentle handling. Pigs that become nonambulatory because of fatigue or porcine stress syndrome should not have electric prods used on them.

Some examples of the use of an electric prod as a last resort or if human or animal safety is in jeopardy are listed below:

- To move an animal after repeated attempts with nonelectrified driving aids such as a plastic bag on the end of a stick, flags, slappers, rattle paddles, or streamers tied to the end of a stick have failed; the use of an electric prod is preferable to beating, ragging, pushing, or hard tail twisting of animals. If excessive slapping or electric prodding is required routinely, then the personnel involved may be too anxious or inadequately trained in proper animal handling or the facility may need modifications. Smaller animals may be gently lifted or rolled onto a transport mechanism.
- To get a downed animal in a truck that is located at a truck stop on the side of a highway. In this situation, opening up the truck gates or unloading the animals is not possible. 3 For cattle that are choking in a head stanchion or headgate or become jammed in a chute or other equipment.

ANIMAL PERCEPTION

Hearing

All species of grazing animals have sensitive hearing. Cattle and horses have hearing that is more sensitive compared with humans to high-pitched sounds. The human ear is most sensitive at 1000 to 3000 Hz and cattle are most sensitive to 8000 Hz. Handlers should not yell or shout at cattle because shouting may be just as aversive as an electric prod. In another experiment, the sounds of people yelling caused a greater increase in heart rate than the sounds of gates clanging. Intermittent or high-pitched sounds caused greater behavioural reactions and increased heart rate in pigs compared with steady or low-pitched sounds. Intermittent sounds and rapid movements are also more likely to cause cattle to react. Handlers should be observant of the position of an animal's ears. Horses and cattle will point their ears directly towards things that attract their attention.

Vision

Cattle, sheep, and horses have wide-angle vision and they can see all around themselves without turning their heads. Grazing animals have depth perception when they are standing still with their heads down. Depth perception is probably poor when the animals are moving with their heads up. This explains why they stop and put their heads down when they see a shadow on the floor. Grazing animals are dichromats. The retinas of cattle, sheep, and goats are most sensitive to yellowish-green; and bluish-purple light.

The dichromatic vision of the horse is most sensitive at 428 and 539 nm. Dichromatic vision and the absence of a retina receptor for red may explain why livestock are so sensitive to sharp contrasts of light and dark such as shadows or shiny reflections on handling equipment. Poultry appear to have excellent vision. Chickens and turkeys possess 4 cone-cell types in the retina giving them tetrachromatic colour vision, compared with the human trichromatic vision based on 3 cone-cell types.

Moreover, the spectral sensitivity of chickens is greater than that of humans from 320 to 480 nm and 580 to 700 nm. Their maximum sensitivity is in a similar range to humans. The broader spectral sensitivity of poultry may make them perceive many light sources as being brighter than a human would see. Poultry may be more docile during handling in blue light spectra. Lighting conditions have a large effect on chicken behaviour when the birds are shackled for slaughter. During handling of poultry, the occurrence of flapping should be minimized. Changes in lighting may be used as one tool to keep birds calmer during handling.

EFFECTS OF VISUAL DISTRACTIONS AND HANDLING

Livestock of all species will often refuse to move through a chute or other handling facility if they see distractions such as shadows, reflections, or people ahead of them. Removing distractions that cause animals to balk and stop will facilitate animal movement. A calm animal will stand and point its eyes and ears towards distractions that attract its attention. If the leader is allowed to stop and look at a distraction, it will often move forward and the other animals will follow. If the animals are rushed, they may turn back and refuse to move forward when they see a distraction. Distractions are most likely to cause balking or other handling problems if the animals are not familiar with the facility. Experienced dairy cows will often ignore a distraction such as a floor drain, but new, inexperienced heifers will balk at it.

Visual Distractions that may Cause Animals to Balk and Refuse to Move:

- Sudden changes in floor structure or surface such as drain grates, objects on the floor or change in flooring material.
- Shadows, puddles, and shafts of light; seeing light through a slatted floor.

- Animals may refuse to enter a dark place. Use indirect lighting to facilitate movement towards the light. Animals tend to move from a darker place to a more brightly illuminated place, but they will not move into blinding light.
- Reflections on a wet floor or shiny metal. Move lights to eliminate the reflection or use non-reflective surfaces.
- Moving people in front of approaching animals. People should stand where approaching animals do not see them.
- Jiggling chains, coats on a fence, flapping plastic, or swinging ropes. Remove these distractions.
- Animals see people, moving objects such as vehicles or objects with high colour contrasts outside of the chute. Improve movement by installing solid sides.

Table contains a list of distractions that may cause animals to balk and refuse to move. This list can be used as a guide for modifying handling facilities where excessive use of electric prods is occurring. In facilities where animals move easily and quietly and electric prods are seldom used, removal of distractions may not be needed.

FACILITY DESIGN PRINCIPLES FOR ALL SPECIES

Flooring

For all species, nonslip flooring is essential. Animals often become agitated when they start slipping. Handling and restraint will be safer and animals will remain calm if animals have nonslip flooring. Handling facilities should have nonslip floors and good drainage.

Equipment Maintenance

Surfaces that contact the animals must be smooth and free of sharp edges that could injure animals. Sharp edges will cause bruises and injury. Managers should routinely inspect equipment and have a programme of regular maintenance based on use. Special attention should be paid to latches on restraint devices.

Sanitation

Managers should regularly inspect facilities to ensure cleanliness. When new facilities are being designed, ease of cleaning is an important part of the design. Concrete curbs can be used to direct manure to a drain. Hoses, shovels, and other tools that are needed for cleaning should be readily available. Sanitation equipment should be removed after routine cleaning.

Animal handling facilities should be regularly cleaned after use and maintained in good working condition. Injuries and accidents can happen to animals and handlers from equipment lockup or other problems that can occur with build-up of filth, breakage, or wear and tear. Managers should routinely inspect the facilities to ensure cleanliness and to maintain a regular maintenance schedule based on use.

GENERAL PRINCIPLES OF RESTRAINT AND HANDLING

Training of animal care personnel in handling procedures should include consideration of the well-being of the animals. During the handling and restraint of animals, care should be exercised to prevent injury to animals or personnel. Animals should be handled quietly but firmly. Properly designed and maintained facilities operated by trained personnel greatly facilitate efficient movement of animals. Prolonged restraint of any animal must be avoided unless such restraint is essential to research or teaching objectives.

The following are important guidelines for the use of animal restraint equipment:

- Animals to be placed in restraint equipment ordinarily should be conditioned to such equipment before initiation of the project, unless the preconditioning itself would increase the stress to the animals.
- The period of restraint should be the minimum required to accomplish the research or teaching objectives.
- Electrical immobilization must not be used as a method of restraint. It is highly aversive to cattle and sheep. Electrical immobilization must not be confused with electrical stunning that causes instantaneous insensibility or electric prod use that does not immobilize animals.
- Restraint devices should not be considered normal methods of housing, although they may be required for specific research and teaching objectives.
- Attention should be paid to the possible development of lesions or illness associated with restraint, including contusions, knee or hock abrasions, decubital ulcers, dependent edema, and weight loss. Health care should be provided if these or other serious problems occur, and, if necessary, the animal should be removed either temporarily or permanently from the restraint device. Animals should be handled and restrained in facilities and by equipment appropriate for the species and procedure.

Some aggressive behaviours of larger farm animals pose a risk to the health and well-being of both herdmates and human handlers. These behaviours may be modified or their impact reduced by several acceptable restraint devices and practices. Only the minimum restraint necessary to control the animal and to ensure the safety of attendants should be used. Care should be exercised when mixing animals to minimize fighting, especially when animals are grouped together for the first time. Animals should be handled and restrained in facilities and by equipment appropriate for the species and procedure. For cattle, for example, a chute facility should be available. Unless they are very young or tame, calves restrained for routine procedures should be handled by means of a calf chute equipped with a calf cradle.

PRINCIPLES TO PREVENT BEHAVIOURAL AGITATION DURING RESTRAINT FOR ALL SPECIES

The following guidance is provided to prevent behavioural agitation:

- Nonslip flooring should be provided. Repeated small rapid slips may cause agitation.
- Avoid sudden jerky motion of either people or equipment. Smooth movements will keep animals calmer.
- When an animal is raised off the ground, during restraint, it will usually remain calmer if its body is fully supported.
- Even pressure over a wide area of the body has a calming effect. The Panepinto sling for small pigs and cattle squeeze chutes use this principle.
- A calm, confident tone of voice will help keep livestock calmer.
- *Optimum Pressure*: Not too loose and not too tight. An animal needs to be held tight enough to feel the feeling of restraint, but not so tight that it feels pain. Excessive pressure will cause struggling.
- *Blocking Vision:* Using a blindfold made from a completely opaque material will often keep cattle and horses with a large flight zone calmer. Solid sides on cattle chutes or a fully enclosed dark box have a calming effect.

RECOMMENDATIONS FOR EACH SPECIES

BEEF CATTLE HANDLING

Animals that are extensively raised and have large flight zones may become agitated if people stand close to the chutes and pens in the handling facility. If this occurs, solid fences may need to be installed so the animals do not see the people that are deep in their flight zone. Further information on facility design is in Grandin and Grandin and Deesing. There are many different designs of restraining chutes. Squeeze chutes should permit all animals to stand in a balanced position and the squeeze sides are applied evenly on both sides.

Squeeze chutes may be hydraulic or manual models. Settings of pressure relief valves for hydraulic restraint chutes should be adjusted to prevent excessive pressure from being applied. The chute should automatically stop squeezing at a reasonable pressure even if the operator continues to pull on the squeeze lever. A separate pressure control is required on chutes that have a hydraulic device for restraining the head. To avoid animal injury, this device must be set at a lighter pressure than other parts of the chute.

Pressure should be applied slowly to avoid exciting the animal. Excessive pressure can cause injury and incite cattle to fight the restraint. If cattle bellow the moment pressure is applied by a hydraulic device, this is an indicator of excessive pressure. Bellowing during restraint is associated with higher cortisol levels. Cattle should be able to breathe normally during restraint. The head gate can be self-catching or manually operated.

Self-catching head gates are generally not recommended for use with horned cattle unless they are operated manually. Unless they are very young or tame, calves restrained for routine procedures should be handled by means of a calf chute equipped with a calf cradle. Roping of cattle is necessary under certain conditions. However, roping should be performed by trained and experienced personnel and in a manner that minimizes stress to both the individual and the total herd. For head restraint of cattle in a squeeze chute, a properly fitted rope halter is recommended.

Nose tongs may be used on fractious animals in conjunction with other means of cattle restraint but nose tongs can slip and tear out of the nose, causing injury to both animal and personnel, and therefore are not recommended as a sole means of restraint. Nose tongs are aversive and cattle may resist the attachment of the tongs in the future. For repeated procedures that require head restraint, a rope halter is strongly recommended.

Electroimmobilization must not be used as a method of animal restraint; cattle and sheep find this procedure very aversive. Plastic streamers or a grocery bag tied to the end of a stick is an effective device for moving cattle and changing their direction. Cattle temperaments vary among individuals and among breeds. Handling should be adjusted for genetic and phenotypic differences.

DAIRY CATTLE HANDLING

Mature milking dairy cows can be handled in head stanchions or a management rail. A complete squeeze chute is not required. Diagrams and pictures in Sheldon *et al.* illustrate methods for restraining tame dairy cows when they are held in a head stanchion. Young dairy heifers that are not accustomed to close contact with people are often handled most efficiently and safely in beeftype facilities with a squeeze chute. Disturbances by veterinarians and other visitors can reduce milk yield.

If the cows are accustomed to many people walking through the milking parlor, there may be no effect because the frequent visitors have become part of their normal routine. Dairy animals are able to discriminate between people who have handled them in a negative manner and people who handled them in a positive manner. They were most likely to avoid the negative handler when he was seen in the same location where the aversive events occurred. Dairy bulls are usually more dangerous than beef bulls. Bull attacks are a major cause of fatalities when people are working with livestock. One of the reasons beef bulls are safer is that they are reared in a social group on a cow. Price and Wallach found that beef bulls attacked more often when they were raised in individual pens. A dairy bull calf raised to maturity alone in a pen is more likely to be dangerous than a bull that was always kept with other animals.

If a bull is going to become dangerous, he is most likely to show aggression towards people at 18 to 24 mo. Handlers must learn to recognize signs of aggression that precede an attack such as the broadside threat. The bull will turn sideways to show how big he is before he attacks. Good descriptions are in Albright and Arave and Albright and Fulwider. Bulls that show aggressive tendencies towards people should be culled or transferred to a secure facility.

HORSE HANDLING

Teaching and research horses are usually handled using halters and lead ropes, and extra control may be achieved by using the chain of a lead shank placed over the horse's nose. Only trained horses should be tied and only to solid objects that will not give way if the horse pulls back. Lead ropes attached to the halter should be tied with quick release knot. Horses should never be tied with a chain looped across the top of the nose.

Cross-ties attached to each side of the halter should be equipped with panic-snaps or safety releases. A twitch may be applied to the horse's upper lip as a short-term restraint procedure. The movement of a horse may be restrained in stocks and chutes. An equine stock or chute may be as simple as a rectangular structure with a nonslip floor.

Other methods of restraint that may be applied by experienced individuals include front foot hobbles, sideline or breeding hobbles, or leg straps, but should be carefully considered depending on the training of the individual horse and the degree of restraint necessary. Chemical restraint can be effective and should be administered by a qualified person. With some drugs, an apparently sedated horse may react suddenly and forcefully to painful stimuli. General or local anesthesia should be administered by a qualified person, preferably a veterinarian, for painful procedures such as castration.

SWINE HANDLING

Snaring by the nose is a common method for holding swine for blood testing and other procedures. Good descriptions are in Battaglia and Sheldon. Snaring is probably stressful for pigs because they will attempt to avoid the snare after they have experienced snaring. For biomedical research, small pigs can be trained to enter the Panepinto sling. The animal is fully supported in a sling and its legs protrude out through leg holes. A panel is the best device for moving pigs. Nonelectric driving aids such as cattle paddles and flags can also be used by properly trained people. Guidelines on electric prod use are in the section on driving aids. Previous experiences with handling and the amount of contact with people will affect the ease of pig movement. Pigs with previous experiences of being calmly moved may be easier to move in the future. Calm, nonthreatening movements of people will reduce stress levels in pigs and make them more willing to approach people.

SHEEP AND GOAT HANDLING

Sheep and goats show strong flocking behaviour in pens as well as on pasture. Breed, stocking rate, topography, vegetation, shelter, and distance to water may influence flocking behaviours. Isolation of individual sheep or goats usually brings about signs of anxiety. Separations from the flock, herd, or social companions are important factors that cause sheep and goats to try to escape. Sheep and goats tend to follow one another even in activities such as grazing, bedding down, reacting to obstacles, and feeding.

When handling sheep and goats, these characteristic behaviours should be considered and used advantageously and, more importantly, for the best interest of the animal's health and welfare. Transportation of sheep and goats should take into consideration the climatic conditions and productive stage of the animals. Care should be exercised in the transport of animals, and special consideration should be given during conditions of temperature extremes and high humidity.

Measures such as increasing the supply of nutrients immediately before long-distance transport that may reduce the risk of pregnancy toxemia and transport tetany in sheep and goats should be considered. Except for short distances when hauling is less physically taxing than trailing, transportation of ewes and does during late gestation should be avoided. When possible, animals should be gated off into smaller groups during transport to prevent pileups and death losses. Additionally, temperature extremes or exposures should be considered and adequate and appropriate crating provided. Preventative or prophylactic medicinal agents may also be administered in an effort to minimize diseases that are associated with shipping. Sheep can be easily trained to enter a squeeze tilt table. The Panepinto sling can also be used for sheep.

Some restraint devices are more aversive than others. Welldesigned restrainers support the animal's body and do not have sharp pressure points. Both sheep and goats can be easily trained to enter head stanchions. Sheldon and Battaglia have illustrated guides on manual methods for holding sheep and goats. Designs for sheep races and corrals can be found in Barber and Freeman and American Sheep Industry Association.

POULTRY HANDLING

Poultry are handled in many experimental and teaching situations. Examples include wing-or leg-banding, immunization by intramuscular and subcutaneous injections, intranasal or intraocular application of drops and wing-web puncture, and removing or placing birds in different groups, cages, or holding and transportation crates. Injured, diseased or birds for transport should be euthanized on the farm. They should not be placed in transportation crates. People handling birds should be adequately trained so that stress to birds is minimal.

Poultry that are not familiarized to humans tend to struggle vigourously when caught. They can easily be injured if grasped improperly or subjected to excessive force. All poultry tend to flap their wings when caught, inverted, or caused to struggle for balance or footing. This tendency leads to risk of joint dislocation, bone fracture, or bruises when wings strike objects or other birds. The risk is particularly great for modern varieties of market-weight meat-type birds, which have powerful breast muscles but relatively weak joints due to their youth, or for caged light hybrid laying hens, which have fragile wing bones.

Poultry should be handled in ways that minimize wing-flapping or its harmful consequences. Care should be taken to prevent birds from striking their wings on door edges when placing them into or pulling them from cages or compartments. Particular care should be exercised in handling caged laying hens, which are prone to osteoporosis. To minimize the risk of bone fracture, hens should be held by both legs when removing them from the cage.

The manner in which a bird is carried can affect its fearfulness and stress. Broilers carried even briefly in the inverted position by the legs show a greater corticosterone response than do birds carried in an upright position, and the response lasts for about 3h. Therefore, birds should be carried upright whenever possible. Birds struggle less if they have been socialized, the body is fully supported in an upright position with wings restrained, the environment is relatively quiet, and the lighting is subdued.

Poultry should not be picked up or moved by one wing unless the wing is grasped near the base of the wing close to the body. They should quickly be released from such a hold, as when transferring birds from a coop to a floor pen. They should be shifted to a hold that firmly grasps both wings at their bases or that supports the body to minimize struggle and chance of a limb injury.

Ducks should not be caught by the leg because they are prone to leg injury if handled in this way. Large, strong birds such as turkey toms can be difficult to control by grasping a limb. They can also deliver punishing blows with their wings when struggling against capture.

To pick up a very large turkey such as breeder tom, grasp one wing near the base of the body and then grasp the leg on the opposite side and set the bird's breast on the floor. Finally, proceed with restraining the bird by grasping both legs. For intermediate-sized turkeys, the base of the wing and then both legs can be grasped simultaneously while lifting the turkey off the floor. Turkeys and ducks can be driven, so catching and handling of individual birds can be minimized by judicious use of alleys, ramps, and driving techniques when flocks must be relocated.

However, some birds such as older turkeys will not walk on different surfaces and therefore may have to be moved by individual handling. In many experimental and teaching situations, newly hatched birds or relatively small numbers of older birds need to be handled. In those cases, individuals can be easily caught and manipulated. Examples included wing-or leg-banding; immunization by intranasal or intra-ocular application of drops and wing-web puncture; and removing or placing birds in different groups, cages, and holding crates.

Trained and experienced scientists and caretakers know that birds struggle less if they have been socialized, if the environment is relatively quiet, and if the body is fully supported in an upright position. More complex procedures; for example, obtaining blood samples, intraperitoneal and venous puncture, and artificial insemination, often require at least 2 experienced persons. Skilled operators should adequately train personnel in such handling procedures so that stress to birds is minimal. Particular care should be exercised in handling caged layers to minimize the risk of bone fractures. When large numbers of birds housed under commercial conditions are to be moved or treated, handling methods need to be compatible with the housing systems involved.

A source of major concern should be the manner in which individual birds are caught, carried, and placed in new quarters or crates. In many situations, birds are at risk of injury because they are caught and moved by grasping a single wing with subsequent exertion of excessive force in moving the bird. No types of poultry should be picked up by one wing.

Gregory and Wilkins found that when laying hens were caught by one leg and removed from cages at the end of lay, the incidence of broken bones was 12.7 per cent; the incidence was only 4.6 per cent when both legs were used in removing hens from the cages. On commercial broiler farms, the chickens are usually picked up by a single leg. Leg breakage can be reduced if the birds are carried a short distance to the transport cage. When research is done under commercial broiler farm conditions, it is acceptable to pickup broiler chickens in this manner.

TRANSPORT

The transport of livestock involves a complex series of operations including handling, loading and unloading, unfamiliar environments, and, in some cases, isolation, social disruption, confinement, loss of balance, fluctuations in environmental temperature and humidity, exposure to pollutants, feed and water deprivation, and other factors. Hence, it is often difficult to determine with precision which component or combination of components is most responsible for transportation stress. Therefore, it becomes important to pay attention to all components and the potential for cumulative effects on the well-being of the animals to be transported. In-depth reviews and research on space allowances for each species of livestock have been published for cattle, sheep, pigs, and horses.

In addition, the National Academy of Sciences published recommendations for the transport of research animals that include space requirements during transport that are consistent with the guide. In the absence of data supporting specific space requirements of farm animals during transport, formulae from ILAR Transportation Guide may be useful in determining space allowances during transport. The minimum areas per animal for animals of different weights when shipped in groups.

The safety and comfort of the animal should be the primary concerns in the transportation of any animal. Nonambulatory or weak, debilitated animals must not be loaded or transported unless necessary for medical attention. Animals that are nearing the time of parturition should not be transported. The only exception to this is when moving an animal a short distance to the place where it will give birth or to a hospital facility.

If ani mals become injured or nonambulatory during the course of transport, appropriate steps should be taken immediately to segregate such animals and attend to their needs. Specialized carts and sleds, canvas tarpaulins, or slide boards are recommended for offloading nonambulatory animals. Animals must not be dragged, hoisted, or dropped from transport vehicles. If the animal cannot be removed with the use of recommended devices, then the animal should be euthanized by trained personnel using acceptable methods established by the AVMA.

Non-ambulatory animals in research and teaching facilities must be euthanized using approved procedures unless they are receiving medical treatment before removal. If young or newborn calves are to be transported, individual care and colostrum should be provided within 2 to 3 hours after birth. Calves should always have a dry hair coat, dry navel cord, and be able to walk easily without assistance before being transported.

They only exception to this recommendation is when calves are transported a short distance to a specialized calf rearing facility. In all species, weak newborns, emaciated animals, animals with severe injuries or animals that have great difficulty walking must never be transported to livestock auctions or markets. When animals are transported, they should be provided with proper ventilation and a floor surface that minimizes slipping. When possible, animals should be shipped in groups of uniform weight, sex, and species. Stocking densities affect stress-related plasma constituents and carcass bruising as well as behavioural parameters of cattle. Similar results have been found for swine and sheep. Animal injuries, bruises, and carcass damage can result from improper handling of animals during transport.

Grandin identified rough handling, mixing of animals of different sexes, horned animals, and poorly designed, maintained, and broken equipment as major causes of carcass damage in cattle. Recommendations for facility design, loading and unloading trucks, restraint of animals, and animal handling in abattoirs have been published. Good driving practices such as smooth acceleration and no sudden stops will help reduce injuries from animals being thrown off balance.

THERMAL ENVIRONMENT ON THE VEHICLE

Transport and handling stresses can be aggravated greatly by adverse weather conditions, especially during rapid weather changes. Hot weather is a time for particular caution. The Livestock Weather Safety Index is used as the basis for handling and shipping decisions for swine during periods of weather extremes. The values for cattle are conservative especially for heat-tolerant Brahman and Brahman crosses.

Animals should be protected from heat stress while in transit. For all species, heat will build up rapidly in a stationary vehicle unless it has mechanical ventilation. Arriving vehicles should be promptly unloaded and vehicles should start moving promptly after loading. If a loaded truck has to be parked during hot weather, fans or water misters should be provided to keep animals cool. Chickens and pigs are especially prone to heat stress. Banks of fans beside which a loaded truck can park are used extensively in the pork and poultry industries. Further information on the thermal environment can be found in the National Research Council's *Guidelines for Humane Transportation of Research Animals.*

The thermal neutral zones for different animals can be found in Robertshaw. Means of protection include shading, wetting, and bedding with wet sand or shavings when livestock are at high density and air speed is low during hot weather. During transportation, animals should also be protected from cold stress. Wind protections should be provided when the effective temperature in the animal's microenvironment is expected to drop below the lower critical level. Recommendations for protecting animals from cold stress are in Grandin and the National Pork Board *Trucker Quality Assurance.*

Table. Truck Set-up Procedures During Temperature Extremes for Pigs

		Side Slats	
Air temperature, °C (°F)	**Bedding**	**Closed,%**	**Open,%**
<–12 (<10)	Heavy	90	10

–12 to–7 (10 to 20) 25	Medium	75
–7 to 4 (20 to 40) 50	Medium	50
4 to 10 (40 to 50) 75	Light	25
>10 (>50) 100	Light	0

Adequate ventilation is always necessary. During cold weather, trucks transporting livestock should be bedded with a material having high thermal insulative properties if the animals will spend more than a few minutes in the transport vehicle. This is especially important for pigs to reduce death losses. Currently there are no trucking quality assurance recommendations for space allowance of weaned pigs during transport in the United States.

A space allowance of 0.06 and 0.07 was preferable to 0.05 m^2/pig when transporting weaned pigs between 60 and 112 min in summer and winter based on neutrophil: lymphocyte ratio and behaviour. However, the effect of space allowance on the welfare of weaned pigs may differ when for transport durations longer than 112 min. Sufficient bedding must be provided so that it stays dry.

VEHICLE RECOMMENDATIONS

Truck beds for livestock transport should be clean, dry, and equipped with a well-bedded, nonslippery floor. Animals should be loaded and unloaded easily and promptly. Chutes should be well designed for the animals being handled. Animals should be transported at appropriate densities to reduce the chances of injury. The type of transport vehicle is also important with regard to differences between and within species of livestock. For example, depending on breed type, horses often have special transport requirements.

Livestock should not be transported on trucks that do not have sufficient clearance to accommodate their height, as would be the case for horses transported on doubled-decked cattle trucks. Many teaching and research activities require the frequent transport of animals for short distances. Careful loading and unloading will reduce stress. On short trips, loading and unloading is the most stressful part of the journey. On short trips, pigs remain standing and they can be stocked at a higher density than on longer trips where the animals will need more space to lie down.

For heavy pigs, increasing the floor spaces from 0.39 to 0.48 m2/pig reduced transport deaths from 0.88 to 0.36 per cent on trips lasting approximately 3h. Vehicles should be of adequate size and strength for the animals carried and have adequate ventilation. Stock trailers and pickup truck beds fitted with stock racks are the most frequently used vehicles for short-distance transport.

The inside walls and lining of the vehicles should have no sharp edges or protrusions that would be likely to cause injury. Animals may be transported either loose in these vehicles or may be haltered and tied in the case of cattle, sheep, and horses. Only animals that have been previously trained to a halter and that are of a quiet disposition should be tied when transported.

Animals should be tied with a quick-release knot to the side of the vehicle at a height that is approximately even with the top of the shoulder. The tie should be short enough so that animals cannot step over the lead. The condition of the animals should be checked periodically during transit. Drivers should start and stop the vehicle smoothly and slow down for curves and corners.

LOADING AND UNLOADING RAMPS FOR LIVESTOCK

A ramp is not required when the animals are transported in a low stock trailer. A well-maintained ramp with a nonslip surface is essential for loading animals onto trucks with beds taller than an animal's ability to step up onto the vehicle. Loading ramps must provide nonslip footing to prevent slipping and falling or damage to the dew claws. On concrete ramps, stair steps provide good footing. For cattle, each step should be 10 cm high with a 30 cm tread width. For all species, if the animals are not completely tame, the ramp should have solid sides.

HORSE TRANSPORT

The typical vehicles designed to transport horses by road are vans, trailers, and trucks. The capacity of these vehicles ranges from transporting a single horse or multiple horses. During transportation, attempts should be made to minimize the trauma and anxiety of the horse. Considerations include the loading procedures, manner of driving, interior space, footing, ventilation, noise, lighting, duration of transit, mixing of unfamiliar or aggressive horses, fitness to travel, and handling.

Horses are sometimes transported in small groups, and sorting horses for compatibility is important to minimize stress and injuries. Considerations for sorting may include size, sex, and behaviour. Horses should not be placed in double-deck conveyances designed for cattle because these trailers are too limited in the height from floor to ceiling for most horses and injuries are prevalent.

All vehicles should be examined before each trip for safety and maintenance. The floor planking and metal floor braces should be of sufficient strength to bear twice the weight of any horse being transported. Door latches, tiers, and hitches should be inspected before the start of the trip and repaired if needed because these deteriorate with use and exposure.

Trailers

The required dimensions of a trailer depend on the size of the horses being hauled.

Table. Recommended Dimensions of Transportation Accommodations for Horses and Ponies Used in Agricultural Research and Teaching

Trailer or Van Dimension	(m)	(ft)
Ceiling for horse height		
Up to 1. 5 m (15 hands[1])	1.7–2.0	5.6–6.5
1. 5–1. 6 m (15 to 16 hands)	2.0–2.2	6.5–7.0
Width		
Single or tandem	1.2	4
	1.7–2 ×	5.6–6.6 ×
Two horses abreast	1.8–3.1	5.9–10.2

Note:

[1]One hand is about 10 cm (4 in).

Horse trailers with individual stalls should have a butt chain or bar to prevent the exiting of a horse from the trailer. The rear doors may either be hinged or have a loading ramp, or both, with a strong fastening device to prevent the doors from opening during transit. In horse vans, full, solid partitions are often used between horses to form small box stalls. A partial partition located at the height of the middle of the horse's body should be used to separate horses in trailers and between cross-tied horses in vans.

These partial partitions allow the horse to spread its legs enough to achieve proper balance in a limited area. The flooring should not be slippery. Sand, bedding, or rubber matting may provide better footing, which reduces anxiety and potential injuries. Legs wraps, tail wraps, bell boots, or padded halters are not necessary, but may be beneficial in preventing or minimizing injuries for some horses during transit. Lighting at night in the trailer and loading areas facilitates safe handling and loading of horses.

Horses traveling together in small groups are usually not tied during transport and may exhibit limited movement depending on the loading density within the compartment. Excessive movement of horses during transit may indicate a problem and should be assessed by the driver. Horses in trailers and vans may be tied in transit to prevent turning around and interaction with other horses and should be tied using either a quick-release knot or panic-snaps.

Tying horses limits the movement of the head and neck. The elevation of the horse's head above the withers during transit compromises the immune system and may predispose the horse to respiratory disorders. Respiratory problems can be avoided by ensuring the head is not elevated above the point of the shoulder at least every 12 h, usually by feeding hay below chest level during transit or by taking breaks to allow the horse to lower its head.

Horses may need to be watered during the trip, preferably every 12 h and more often during hot weather conditions. Many horses traveling in trailers or vans are provided with hay while in transit. Horses without access to feed during transit should be fed at least every 24 h. Horses should not be expected to travel more than 24 h at one time without experiencing fatigue and dehydration, especially in extreme environmental conditions.

Regulation of air movement through the transport vehicle is essential to avoid thermal stress or excessive exposure to exhaust fumes. Adequate ventilation is especially crucial during extremely hot or cold weather. In hot weather, horses should not be left in parked trailers because heat stroke is likely; in cold weather, horses in moving trailers may need to be provided with blankets, especially if air flow cannot be controlled.

POULTRY TRANSPORT

Unlike the loading ramp and chute system used for livestock, poultry on commercial farms are caught manually and loaded into transport crates that are then stacked on an open bed truck. Special attention to developing skilled staff for the catching, loading, and transport of poultry is important. Increased fear, leg breakage, and mortality have been associated with poor catching and loading techniques.

Also, poorly feathered birds have greater body heat loss than well-feathered birds. The thermal neutral zone ranges from 8 to 18°C and 24 to 28°C for well-feathered chickens and poorly feathered chickens, respectively, under typical transit conditions of low air movement and high humidity. Increased time in transit, feed and water deprivation, and fatigue can cause increased death loss and stress. Therefore, these factors should be minimized.

TRANSPORT DISTANCE AND DURATION

Most of the animals transported for use in research and teaching will be transported short distances for durations less than 6h. In these situations, the amount of time on a transport vehicle does not become a welfare issue. A high percentage of the animals will be transported for less than 2h. United States regulations specify that livestock have to be unloaded, fed, and watered after 28 h on a vehicle without food or water during interstate transport.

The US *Humane Slaughter Act* requires that livestock in the lairage of a slaughter plant must have access to water in all of the holding pens. People who use agricultural animals in research and teaching need to keep the time that livestock or poultry are on vehicles as short as possible. There may be situations where research has to be conducted on a commercial farm, feedlot, or slaughterhouse when the researcher has no control over the transport conditions.

REGULATORY REQUIREMENTS FOR TRANSPORT

Transporters must comply with all county, state, and federal animal health regulations and identification requirements before transporting livestock and poultry. When animals are transported across state lines or from foreign countries, federal regulations for vaccinations, veterinary inspections, and health certificates must be complied with. There are different regulations for each species, and each state may also have regulations for health certificates.

State animal health laws apply to all animals transported within a state. Some western states have brand inspection laws that require certificates of ownership and inspection of the livestock by an inspector. In some states animals transported short distances must have certificates. Transporters should be knowledgeable of regulatory requirements. International regulations for transporting animals have recently been summarized.

LAIRAGE RECOMMENDATIONS BEFORE SLAUGHTER

After the animals are unloaded from the transport vehicle, lairage pens should be provided. There must be sufficient space for all of the animals to lie down at the same time without being on top of each other. Table lists some examples of recommended space requirements.

Table. Space Requirements for Lairage

Species	Weight, kg (lb)	Space, m^2 (ft^2)
Cattle	545 (1,200)	1.87 (20)
Pigs (market weight)	113 (250)	0.55 (6)

EMERGENCY PROCEDURES FOR THE RESEARCH FACILITY AND TRANSPORTERS

Both research facilities and people transporting animals should have a list of emergency contact phone numbers.

The following numbers should be on the list. For the contacts other than the police, fire, and ambulance, phone numbers for work, home, and mobile should be listed:

- Police
- Fire
- Ambulance
- Emergency contact 1 and emergency contact 2

Transporters should have numbers they can call if they have an accident. Some of the contacts that should be included are persons who can bring portable panels, loading ramps, or other equipment for reloading escaped animals after an accident.

6

Beef Cattle

Beef cattle includes all animals of the genus *Bos* and their close relatives that are raised primarily for meat production. As ruminants, beef cattle are capable of utilizing a wide range of feedstuffs and consequently are maintained in an array of situations ranging from extensive grazing to confined feedlot pens and intensive laboratory environments. Regardless of the housing system, basic needs for food, water, shelter, and comfort should be met.

FACILITIES AND ENVIRONMENT

IDEAL THERMAL CONDITIONS

Under most environmental conditions, temperature represents a major portion of the driving force for heat exchange between the environment and an animal. However, moisture and heat content of the air, thermal radiation, and airflow also affect total heat exchange. Thus, a combination of environmental variables contributes to the conditions to which an animal responds. Under conditions in which relative measures and comparisons of the effect of different environmental variables could be determined, the apparent ambient temperature at which animals can cope has been defined with a reasonable degree of accuracy; however, variation does exist among animals.

Environmental conditions that provide maximum comfort and require little or no energy expenditure for maintenance depend on cattle age, metabolic size, and/or body mass and surface area. The TCZ generally ranges between 15 to 25°C for most cattle less than 1 mo old; between 5 and 20°C for a mature beef cow consuming a maintenance diet; and between–10 and 20°C for yearlings with ad libitum access to energy-dense feedlot diets.

Based on physiological responses and heat load thresholds, *Bos indicus* and some heat-tolerant *Bos taurus* cattle breeds have a TCZ at least 5°C greater than typical *Bos taurus* cattle. Encompassing the TCZ is the thermoneutral zone (TNZ). Within the TNZ, an animal can maintain homeostasis through normal physiological and metabolic processes, which may require minimal expenditure of energy when the animal is exposed to conditions outside the TCZ.

The TNZ generally ranges between 10 and 30°C for most cattle less than 1 mo old; between–15 and 28°C for a mature beef cow consuming a maintenance diet; and between–35 and 25°C for yearlings with ad libitum access to energy-dense feedlot diets. Even though the upper end of the TNZ for most *Bos taurus* cattle is between 25 and 30°C, for high-producing cattle with high intakes of metabolizable energy the upper limit may be closer to 20°C on sunny days when little or no wind is present.

When given sufficient time, cattle acclimate and adapt to colder or hotter conditions. It should be noted that cattle that are adapted to–35°C may be uncomfortable at 10°C. Thus, the TCZ and TNZ serve only as guidelines to describe the limits within which cattle are comfortable and can adapt to, respectively.

Independent of these guidelines, performance standards that indicate a problem with the thermal environment include, in cold weather, shivering, huddling, and loss of body condition/weight; and in hot weather, panting, sweating, and a reduction in feed intake. Primary factors that affect thermal comfort include feed/energy intake and body condition/fat cover.

THERMAL INDICES

At the present time, the temperature-humidity index {THI; THI = 0.8 × ambient temperature + [(per cent relative humidity/100) × (ambient temperature–14.4)] + 46.4} has become the de facto standard for classifying thermal environments in many animal studies and selection of management practices during seasons other than winter. The THI, first proposed by Thom has been extensively applied for moderate to hot conditions, even with recognized limitations related to airspeed and radiation heat loads.

A THI between 70 and 74 is an indication to producers that the potential for heat stress in livestock exists. In particular, when THI values are above 70 by 0800h, it is recommended that managers of confined cattle that have high metabolic heat loads initiate or prepare to initiate heat-stress management strategies before cattle become exposed to the excessive heat load. A THI of 84 or above can cause death, especially in feedlot cattle that are within 45 d of slaughter and consuming high-energy finishing diets.

Modifications to the THI have been developed to overcome the shortcomings related to the lack of airflow and radiation heat load in the index. Eigenberg also developed similar adjustments based on predictions of respiration rates using ambient and dew point temperature, windspeed, and solar radiation. These models have merit in that the combined effects of multiple environmental factors can be taken into account when determining animal comfort. Gaughan developed a more extensive index as a guide to the management of feedlot cattle during hot weather. The heat load index (HLI) incorporates black globe temperature, relative humidity, and windspeed. A threshold above which cattle are less efficient at dissipating heat was developed for a reference animal.

The threshold for a full-blood Brahman steer is 96. Also, adjustments to the threshold are possible for use of shade, clean dry pens, cattle coat colour, and days on feed. The thresholds are lowered if cattle are sick or not acclimated to summer conditions. Very limited data exist for assessing environmental effects on reproduction.

However, Amundson found THI and daily minimum temperature to be equally good predictors of pregnancy rate at 42 d into the breeding season. However, the combination of wind speed and THI had the greatest correlation to pregnancy rate. Indices for cold stress are not as well defined as for heat stress. The wind chill index (WCI) has traditionally been used to derive an apparent temperature for humans. In 2001, the National Weather Service released a new WCI that may have merit for assessing effects of wind on domestic livestock.

RANGE AND PASTURE SYSTEMS

Acceptable systems for grazing beef cattle on pasture and rangeland vary widely. Cow body condition is an excellent performance standard for monitoring the well-being and nutritional status of range cattle. Special consideration needs to be given to environmental factors that affect grazing beef cattle. In areas where heat stress is common, provision of shade to decrease the solar heat load is the most practical intervention in pasture and range systems.

The need for artificial shade should be assessed after careful consideration of the adequacy of naturally occurring sources. Heat stress is evidenced when respiration rates begin to increase. Prolonged increases in body temperatures will result in decreased feed intake, body condition, and weight. In areas where exposure to extreme cold is likely, provision of shelter for grazing beef cattle may be desirable.

Grazing beef cows decrease grazing time and forage intake as ambient temperature decreases below 0°C, although such changes are small in adapted beef cows. Cattle use windbreaks to decrease wind chill and prevent exposure to blowing snow, although it has not been clearly established that windbreaks improve animal performance.

Supplementary feed should be provided during periods of heavy snow cover that preclude grazing. An adequate supply of forage should be available to grazing cattle. Intake and performance may be decreased when the amount of standing forage is lacking but the appropriate quantity of forage dry matter per hectare varies with the pasture or range type and the stocking rate. Guidelines for acceptable amounts of standing forage per unit of body weight at given stocking rates are available but additional research is needed with a variety of pasture and range types. Grazing beef cattle should be provided with supplements for nutrients that are known to be deficient in pasture and range forage in particular localities. In almost all grazing environments, range cattle require free-choice access to supplemental salt as a source of supplemental sodium.

Typically, these salt-based, free-choice mineral supplements will also be fortified with trace minerals. Observation and monitoring of range cattle often occur less regularly than for other livestock. When supplemental feed is provided, cattle are usually observed at least 2 or 3 times weekly. Unsupplemented cattle on open range may be observed less frequently.

However, it is recommended that range cattle be observed at least once per week. In certain areas, grazing beef cattle may be affected by predators and poisonous plants. Careful attention should be given to such problems, and efforts should be made to decrease or eliminate these adverse conditions. Availability of fresh, unfrozen water is critical for grazing beef cattle, and distance to water should be given consideration in pasture and range systems.

If cattle are required to travel long distances to water in hot, dry climates, animal performance and utilization of pasture forage can be affected. Holechek recommended that distance to water be no greater than 1.6 km in rolling, hilly country and in undulating, sandy terrain. This recommendation was decreased to 0.8 km in rough country, increased to 2.4 km in smooth, sandy terrain, and increased to 3.2 km in areas with flat terrain. Thus, the distance to water for grazing cattle should not exceed 3.2 km, and every animal should have the opportunity to drink ad libitum at least once per day.

FEEDLOT AND HOUSING SYSTEMS

Beef cattle used in research or teaching may be housed in intensive management systems, either indoors or in open lots, with or without shelter. Facilities for beef cattle should provide cattle with opportunities for behavioural thermoregulation. Management of dairy beef is similar to other cattle, although, some feeding, housing, and marketing regimens are unique to Holsteins. Proper airflow and ventilation are essential in intensive facilities.

In feedlots, cable or wire fencing has minimal effect on natural airflow in summer. However, high airflow rates are undesirable during periods of low temperature, and tree shelterbelts and other types of windbreak can decrease the rate of airflow past the cattle. An 80 per cent solid windbreak 3 m high decreases wind speed by half for about 45 m downwind and controls snow for about 8 m; a similar windbreak 4 m high decreases wind speed by half for about 65 m downwind and controls snow for about 10 m.

A windbreak is recommended in mounded, south-sloping feedlots in the northern United States to provide dry resting areas with low air velocities. Caution should be exercised when placing cattle in sheltered areas in the summer because of the adverse effects of restricted airflow on cattle reared in hot environments. During potentially stressful heat episodes, panting scores (1 = elevated respiration rate, 2 = drool or saliva present on side of mouth, 3 = open mouth breathing observed, and 4 = tongue and neck extended with open mouth breathing) can be utilized as an excellent indicator of stress levels experienced.

When cattle are beginning to experience panting scores of 2 or greater some means of cooling may be needed. Cattle learn to take evasive action to alleviate heat stress and such competition for cooler areas in a pen or around the water trough increases even during cooler days in which heat alleviation methods are not utilized. When this occurs evidence of crowding is observed, which exacerbates the heat stress problems.

Wetting the ground or floor of holding facilities can be an effective method of cooling cattle managed in unshaded, outdoor units where surface vegetation is sparse or nonexistent. Direct wetting of cattle during extreme heat is also an effective practice and is often used as an emergency measure. Benefits of sprinkling are enhanced if sprinkling is started in the morning, before cattle experience high heat loads. Generally, a daily application of 0.5 to 1.0 cm of water is sufficient to cool pen surfaces. However, applying 1.25 to 1.50 cm every other day is acceptable and will not sufficiently contribute to mud build-up in normally dry pens.

In areas with high evaporation rates additional water may be needed, which can serve to cool pen surfaces as well as eliminate potential dust problems. The size of the area needed to be sprinkled would be similar to the shade area recommendations. As a routine protective practice, wetting can be efficiently accomplished by utilizing a timer to provide 5 to 10 min of spray during each 20-to 30-min period. Fogger nozzles are often mistakenly recommended for wetting animals.

Fogger nozzles are less effective than sprinkler nozzles because of the barrier formed by the fine droplets. These droplets adhere to the outer hair coat of the animal, causing the heat for evaporation to come from the air rather than from the body. Mitlöhner *et al.* reported that misting cattle was not as effective as shade in decreasing heat stress, and in some cases, caused respiration rate to increase compared with nonmisted cattle.

Shade for cattle can provide the margin of survival for animals that are unconditioned to a sudden heat wave with high solar radiant loads in central and southern regions of the United States. Mader found limited performance benefits of utilizing shade in the north-central region of the United States, in contrast to the findings of Mitlöhner where shade was effective in southern regions

Also, use of shade in northern climates may be costly and logistically prohibitive because of snow load requirements, potential mud problems under shade and the low percentage of time that cattle may actually benefit from using the shade. However, benefits of using shade for maintaining animal comfort will almost always be found in any area or location in which abnormally hot or hot and humid conditions arise or persist, including northern climates, and when cattle have not had the opportunity to acclimate.

Mitlöhner *et al.* found excellent results when shades were provided for feedlot cattle reared in the south-central region of the United States, an area where more consistent benefits of shade would be expected to be realised. For optimum benefits shades should be 3.6 to 4.2 m high in areas with clear, sunny afternoons to permit maximum exposure to the relatively cool northern sky, which acts as a radiation sink.

In areas with cloudy afternoons, shades 2.1 to 2.7 m in height are more effective, as they limit the diffuse sky radiation received by animals beneath the shades. The amount of shade required for young cattle is 0.7 to 1.2 m^2 per animal, whereas larger cattle need 1.8 to 2.5 m^2 per animal. Shades are strongly recommended for sick cattle or for animals in hospital pens.

Cold housing can be provided for beef cattle. Open sides of any cattle building need to face away from prevailing winds. Such structures are ventilated by natural airflow, and the resultant winter temperatures are typically 2 to 5°C above outdoor conditions as a result of body heat. Totally enclosed housing requires ventilation to maintain the air temperature at acceptable levels and to minimize the accumulation in the air of water vapour, noxious gases, other odorous compounds, and dust. Ventilation systems may be either natural or mechanical.

Type of pen surface affects dustiness during hot dry weather and mud or manure build-up during wet periods. Good drainage of outside pens is imperative. Dirt pens should be regularly cleaned of animal waste residues and maintained to minimize accumulation of water. A hard surface apron in front of the feed bunks and around water troughs and shelters should be considered in dirt pens.

Mounds should be provided in dirt pens for cattle to lie on during inclement weather. Accumulation of mud in a pen or on the cattle can influence maintenance requirements and thermal balance. Properly designed pens with adequate slope are extremely important for minimizing mud and related health and behaviour problems. In areas where slope or drying conditions are limited, adding mounds is very useful for keeping cattle clean and dry. Under hot-humid conditions, mounds aid in preventing animal crowding and improve exposure to airflow for the animals that utilize them.

Additional information on feedlot/drylot pen design and layout has been published by Pohl and Henry. For hard-surfaced pens, materials should be durable, slip-resistant, and impervious to water and urine; easily cleaned; and resistant to chemicals and corrosion from animal feed and waste. Concrete floors should be scored or grooved during construction to improve animal footing.

Properly designed slotted floors are self-cleaning. Fences, pen dividers, walls, gates, and other surfaces must be strong enough to withstand the impact of direct animal contact. Configuration and treatment of contact surfaces must minimize or eliminate protrusions, changes in elevation, and sharp corners to minimize bruising and injuries and to improve the efficiency of cattle handling. Proper lighting permits inspection of animals in feedlots and other cattle housing systems and provides safer working conditions for animal care personnel. Maintenance of facilities should be timely and ongoing.

FEED AND WATER

Diets for beef cattle should be formulated according to the recommendations of the NRC. Formulation of diets should consider factors such as environmental conditions, breed or biological type, sex, and production demands for growth, gestation, or lactation. Feed and water should be offered to cattle in ways that minimize contamination by urine, feces, and other materials. Feed bunks should be monitored daily and contaminants or spoiled feed should be removed. In most situations, feed should be available at all times.

However, restricted feeding of high-energy diets may be practiced to meet maintenance requirements or targeted levels of production. When restricted feeding is practiced, feed must be uniformly distributed in the bunk to allow all cattle to have simultaneous access to the diet. When high-energy diets are fed, increased attentiveness should be given to possible occurrence of diet-related health problems such as grain overload, lactic acidosis, and bloat.

Abrupt changes in diets should be avoided. Feed deprivation for more than 24 h should be avoided, and feed deprivation for any length of time must be justified in the animal use protocol. Cattle can vary considerably in body weight and condition during the course of grazing and reproductive cycles. Feeding programmes should allow animals to regain the body weight that is lost during the normal periods of negative energy balance.

Confined cattle should have continuous free access to a source of water, except before surgery or weighing if the research or animal care protocol requires such restriction. When continuous access to water is not possible, water should be available ad libitum at least once daily and more often if hot weather conditions exist or cattle have high levels of metabolizable energy intake for purposes of achieving high output.

Under winter range conditions, Degen and Young found that snow can be used as a water source for beef cows and growing calves. However, there was evidence that the snow resulted in reduced water intakes as evidenced by compensatory water intake when water was reintroduced following 84 d of consuming water in the form of snow. When snow was the only source of water, total water intake reductions averaged approximately 10 per cent among the cattle groups.

The quantity and, possibly, quality of water available will influence animal comfort, especially under hot conditions. Evaporation of moisture from the skin surface or respiratory tract is the primary mechanism used by the animals to lose excess body heat in a hot environment. Estimates of daily water requirements for beef cattle are reported in NRC.

During summer months, in particular, waterer space available and water intake per animal becomes extremely important. Under these conditions, Mader found that as much as 3 times the normal waterer space may be needed to allow for sufficient room for all animals to access and benefit from available water. Additional waterer space recommendations are provided by MWPS.

HUSBANDRY

Adequate care of cattle and calves is especially important for establishing and maintaining optimal immune system function. Good husbandry can minimize health problems and infectious diseases. The risk of disease and mortality in young calves is related to immune status. It is critical that newborn calves nurse or ingest colostrum soon after birth. The health of young growing cattle should be assessed regularly pre-and postweaning. Animal care personnel should be taught to recognize signs of illness and external parasites.

Alert caretakers should have the ability to perceive appropriate behaviour and posture. A system of monitoring calves through critical stress periods such as weaning should be established. Any sick or injured calves should be treated promptly. Daily records should be kept. For cattle reared in close confinement assessments should be done at least once daily and more often if cattle have been stressed or potentially exposed to conditions in which their health could be compromised.

In general, confined feedlot cattle, especially new incoming cattle, require more frequent observations than nonconfined cattle because of the greater probability of animal health being compromised due to comingling, dehydration, digestive problems, respiratory problems, and interaction of any of these factors with environmental stress. Signs of healthy calves are alert ears and clear eyes, no signs of diarrhea, and, upon arising, resumption of a normal standing posture after stretching.

For feedlot cattle provided energy-dense diets, caretaker knowledge of acidosis and management regimens necessary to minimize digestive problems are essential. Appropriate medication and vaccination programmes should be used to reduce the incidence of disease and mortality, improve cattle health and performance, and ensure that no illegal residues occur in the carcass. Treatment and vaccination schemes should be based on veterinary advice and experience.

WEANING

In typical beef cow/calf production systems, calves are artificially weaned from their dams by physical separation. This process, albeit important to the efficiency of the cowherd, can be stressful to both the cow and calf. The most common weaning procedure involves an abrupt separation of cows and calves resulting in increased walking and vocalization and decreased eating and resting. An alternative to abrupt weaning and permanent separation is a period of fenceline contact between cows and calves in adjacent but separate pastures.

This weaning management alternative has been shown to decrease vocalization and walking and increase the time spent resting and grazing. This fenceline weaning procedure may also decrease the incidence of calf illness. Within the weaning pasture or pen, a mature cow can be included in the group of freshly weaned calves. This "trainer" cow can assist in introducing the weaned calves to the location and facilitating consumption of feed and water.

Despite the weaning process selected, it is important that weaned calves be provided access to clean water and a source of feed and/or forage. To encourage intake, highly palatable forage and feed sources are recommended until calves become accustomed to the separation from their dams. Additionally, feed and water sources should be placed close to the perimeter of the fenceline, because calves will typically spend a majority of their time in these areas as they seek to reunite with their dams.

SOCIAL ENVIRONMENT

Cattle are social animals. Each individual in the group should have sufficient access to the resources necessary for comfort, adequate well-being, and optimal performance. Mixing, crowding, group composition, and competition for limited resources are part of the social environment and in some circumstances, may be social stressors for certain cattle.

Generally, cows from similar environments but from different social groups can be mixed with little or no long-term adverse effect on performance; however, because introduced cows may be the recipients of aggression, the number of mixing episodes should be minimized. Mixing of older cattle, especially bulls, results in more fighting than occurs when younger cattle are mixed.

Fighting and mounting can be a problem associated with keeping bulls in social groups and can present a significant welfare problem if not managed carefully. Attempts should be made to keep bulls in stable social groups and to minimize mixing. When feed, water, or other resources critical for comfort or survival are limited, or when large differences exist among cattle in size or other traits related to position in the social order, some animals may be able to prevent others from gaining access to resources.

In properly designed facilities, all individuals should have sufficient access to feed, water, and resting sites to minimize the correlation between position in the social order and productive performance. Proper animal care includes observation of groups and of individuals within groups to ensure that each individual has adequate access to the resources necessary for optimal comfort, welfare, and performance.

FLOOR OR GROUND AREA

Area recommendations for open lots and barns are listed in Table. Every animal should have sufficient space to move about at will, adequate access to feed and water, a comfortable resting site, and the opportunity to remain reasonably dry and clean. These suggested recommendations alone do not ensure that an ideal environment exists; however, in some cases these conditions can be met with less than the recommended area.

The area required is affected by type and slope of floor or soil surface, amount of rainfall, amount of sunshine, season, group size, and method of feeding. Open feedlot pens need to be sloped to promote drainage away from feed bunks, waterers, pen dividers, and resting areas. Space allocations are related directly to slope. In temperate Midwestern climates, the following relationships have been found to be workable: 2 per cent slope or less: 37 to 74 m^2 per animal; 2 to 4 per cent slope: 23 to 37 m^2; and 4 per cent or greater slope: 14 to 23 m^2.

Space allocations can be less in drier regions of the country. In the Southwest, at 0 per cent slope, typical allocations are 14 to 23 m^2 per animal. In other regions, space allocations may need to be increased above Midwestern norms in consideration of such factors as soil type and rainfall distribution. The area requirements for cattle are greatly influenced by group size. One animal housed separately in a pen requires the greatest amount of floor area on a per-animal basis. As group size increases, the amount of area required per individual decreases.

When an animal is housed individually, the minimum pen width and length should be at least equal to the length of the animal from nose tip to tail head when the animal is standing in a normal erect posture. Acceptable indoor pen floor surfaces for beef cattle include unfinished concrete, grooved concrete, concrete slats, expanded metal, plastic-covered metal flooring, and rubberized mat. The floor surface in stanchions and metabolism stalls may be concrete, expanded metal, wood, rubberized mat, or a combination of materials that provides support for the animals' bodies; does not damage hooves, feet, legs, and tails; and can be cleaned.

STANDARD AGRICULTURAL PRACTICES

For beef cattle, management procedures may be performed by properly trained, nonprofessional personnel. These include, but are not limited to, vaccinating, dehorning and castrating young cattle, horn-tipping, ear-tagging, branding, weighing, implanting, use of hydraulic and manual chutes for restraint, roping, hooftrimming, routine calving assistance, ultrasound pregnancy checking, feeding, and watering.

Other husbandry and health practices used in beef cattle research and teaching that similarly may be performed by properly trained, nonprofessional personnel, but that require special technical training and advanced skill levels, include artificial insemination, electroejaculation, pregnancy palpation, embryo flushing and transfer, nonroutine calving assistance and dystocia treatment, emergency cesarean section, retained placenta treatment, and dehorning and castration of older cattle.

One of the main animal husbandry concerns is that of pain and distress, especially pain inflicted from standard husbandry procedures. Dehorning, castration, and branding are husbandry procedures that can cause pain and discomfort; nevertheless, these procedures are justified as a management tool to minimize injuries or other problems associated with confining horned cattle and commingling bulls.

DYSTOCIA MANAGEMENT

Matings should be planned to lessen the genetic probability of dystocia. When dystocia does occur, proper care and assistance at calving can decrease injury or death of both calves and heifers/cows. Parturition without complication is common in beef cows. Therefore, before administering assistance to a cow experiencing difficulty with calving, personnel should be familiar with the stages associated with approaching parturition and the signs of normal delivery.

As a general rule, females should be examined within 30 to 60 min following presentation of feet, nose, or fetal membranes if delivery of the calf does not appear imminent. However, heifers or cows exhibiting signs of a malpresentation, oversized fetus, fetal anomaly, or other obvious complication must be assisted immediately. Facilities should be provided that are designed for restraint of cows and heifers experiencing dystocia.

Because many animals, especially heifers, lie down during the obstetrical procedure, sufficient space should be provided to permit adequate freedom of movement. It is important that the obstetrical restraint facility be fitted with side gates, both of which are hinged at the head end, so that the animal can become fully recumbent and the obstetrical procedure can be performed with safety and efficiency. In dystocia cases where fetal presentation appears to be compromised or there appears to be a disparity between the size of the fetus and the diameter of the birth canal, assistance of the delivery by personnel appropriately trained in the judicious use of a fetal extractor may be attempted. In general, if more than slight traction is required on the fetal extractor, the procedure should be stopped and a veterinarian called immediately to perform a caesarean section or fetotomy. Use of excessive force can damage the calf and/or dam and lead to suffering and/or death. Strict sanitation should be used with all obstetrical procedures.

VACCINATIONS AND DRUG ADMINISTRATION

Vaccinations are a key component to any herd health programme. Care should be taken to ensure the proper use, handling, and storage of vaccines and approved or investigational drugs. The preferred site of injection is the neck for either intramuscular or subcutaneous injections; however, for investigational drugs used in research, alternate sites of administration may be required or preferred as dictated by the research protocol. Investigators and animal care staff should utilize best management practices associated with the use of syringes and handling needles. Use and regular replacement of disposable syringes and needles is highly recommended to avoid excessive trauma and disease transmission.

CASTRATION

Castration of male beef cattle is performed to reduce aggressiveness, prevent physical danger to other animals in the herd and to handlers, enhance reproductive control, manage genetic selection, and satisfy consumer preferences regarding taste and tenderness of meat. Castration of young bulls is a necessary management practice in beef production.

Several methods for castrating cattle are acceptable, including surgical removal of the testicles using a knife or scalpel to open the scrotum and cutting or crushing the spermatic cords with an emasculatome or emasculator. Bloodless procedures utilizing specialized rubber rings or surgical tubing bands are available to create devitalization and eventual sloughing of the tissues below the ring or band.

High-tension banding systems may be used with appropriate veterinary supervision and/or training in those situations where surgical castration may predispose to postsurgical complications or when surgical castration is not appropriate because of its effect on research protocol. The castration method used should take into account the animal's age and weight, the skill level of the technician, environmental conditions, and facilities available as well as human and animal safety. Whatever the method of castration, the procedures should be conducted by, or under the supervision of, a qualified, experienced person and carried out according to castration equipment manufacturer recommendations and accepted husbandry practices.

Surgical castration is normally a short-term event with short-term duration of pain-associated responses. Bloodless castration has been associated with lower short-term pain indicators but longer chronic pain indicators. Bloodless castration should be used when surgical castration may predispose to postsurgical complications or when surgical castration is not appropriate because of its effect on the research protocol.

Castration is least stressful when performed at or shortly after birth, but lower stress is reported if performed before 2 or 3 months of age or before animals reach a body weight of 230 kg. It is strongly recommended that calves be castrated at the earliest age possible. It may be desirable to inject local anesthetic in the scrotum of calves heavier than 230 kg when surgical methods of castration are used or when the spermatic cords are crushed.

Topical local anesthetics may also be used on open wounds. Improved animal performance, as one potential indicator of improved animal welfare, has not been observed in animals locally anesthetized at the time of castration. It should be recognized that the effect of anesthetic agents is short-lived. Nevertheless, procedures should be implemented to minimize pain and discomfort, especially in older cattle.

Castration of older, heavier bulls should be performed only by skilled individuals. When it is necessary to castrate these heavier bulls, techniques and procedures to control bleeding must also be used. No advantage to use of anesthesia is apparent when bloodless castration is practiced. The possibility of infection should be given additional consideration after castration. Equipment should be sterilized, and facilities should be clean and sanitized.

Infection following castration can be minimized by keeping the animals in a clean area and away from excessive mud or contaminants following the procedure until the wound is healed. If tetanus is a common disease associated with the premises, or if a bloodless castration method is utilized, the herd health veterinarian should schedule a prophylactic tetanus immunization programme.

DEHORNING

Horns on cattle can cause bruises and other injury to other animals, especially during transport and handling. Horns on adult cattle also can be a hazard to humans. Hornless cattle require less space in the feedlot and at the feed bunk. Polled breeds should be used whenever possible. Disbudding and dehorning of cattle in the United States is not currently regulated.

The Canadian Veterinary Medical Association recommends that disbudding be performed within the first week of life. In the United Kingdom, disbudding with a hot iron is preferred to dehorning and it is advised that this should be performed before cattle reach the age of 2 mo. In Australia, dehorning without local anesthesia or analgesia is restricted to animals less than 6 mo old.

Calves suffer less pain and stress, have less risk of infection, and have better growth rates when dehorning is performed at a very young age. Stafford and Mellor found that the use of local anesthetics virtually eliminated the escape behaviour of calves associated with the dehorning process and that a 2-h delay was observed in the cortisol response to horn amputation. Whenever possible, the use of a local anesthetic is encouraged when dehorning.

When horned breeds of cattle are selected, dehorning should be performed under the supervision of experienced persons using proper techniques. The horn buds should be removed at birth or within the first month after birth by several means, including hot cauterizing irons, cauterizing chemicals, a sharp knife, or commercially available mechanical devices. It is strongly recommended that calves be dehorned at the earliest age possible. When it is necessary to remove horns from older cattle, methods that minimize pain and bleeding and prevent infection should be employed.

Dehorning should be performed by a person knowledgeable and experienced in the appropriate procedures. Appropriate restraint and local anesthesia to control pain should be used when cattle older than 1 mo of age are dehorned. Cattle should be monitored for hemorrhage and infection following dehorning.

Adult cattle should be dehorned if aggressive behaviour is displayed towards herd mates or humans. Dehorning may temporarily depress the growth of cattle. In the event that bunk and pen space are ample, then tipping the horn may be considered as an alternative to minimize potential bruising or injury of pen mates. However, Ramsay reported that, after transport, carcass bruises were as common among tipped cattle as among horned ones.

IDENTIFICATION METHODS

Proper animal identification is essential to research, facilitates record keeping, and aids in the routine observation and repeat identification of cattle. Methods of identification include skin colour markings, ear tagging, tattooing, hot branding, freeze branding, and electronic identification. Ear tags are best used in conjunction with a more permanent form of identification such as a tattoo or brand, as ear tags are sometimes lost.

Hot branding the hide is utilized as a means of identification; however, loss in hide value and studies indicating that freeze branding is less painful than hot branding have begun to minimize the use of hot branding. Alternatives to hot branding should be considered. However, skin and hair colour in addition to a limited access to liquid nitrogen or dry ice in extensive range operations may affect the ability to achieve a quality freeze brand.

At some locations, branding is required by law. Both hot branding and freeze branding should be performed by trained personnel to minimize skin contact with the branding device to only that required to achieve a useful brand. Advent of a national animal identification system (NAIS) in the form of visual or *radio frequency identification* (RFID) ear tags serve as an additional means of identification. As this system will become standard for all cattle as part of a national programme, managers of beef cattle as part of resident herds used in research should comply with the established guidelines.

IMPLANTING

Implanting of cattle is a management practice for the administration of growth promotants and potentially as a means of delivery of investigational compounds used in research. For proper absorption and maximum response, implants should be placed correctly and in the correct location. Traditionally, implants are placed beneath the skin on the back side of the middle third of the ear; however, alternate implantation sites may be required as designated by the research protocol.

Proper disinfection of the implant site is required to prevent infection. Care should be taken not to injure major blood vessels or the cartilage of the ear when implanting in the ear location. Utilization of best management practices associated with the use of the implant device and correct needle-handling procedures are required by suitably trained personnel.

SPECIAL CONSIDERATIONS

INTENSIVE LABORATORY FACILITIES

Some research and teaching situations require that beef cattle be housed under intensive laboratory conditions. Cattle may be kept in metabolism stalls, stanchions, respiration chambers, or environmental chambers. Housing cattle in such facilities should be avoided unless required by the experimental protocol and then should be for the minimum amount of time necessary to accomplish the teaching or research objective.

Cattle that are held or penned temporarily in crowded areas, frequently disturbed, or come into close contact with humans, or exposed to unfamiliar conditions or laboratory/teaching settings should have calm dispositions and be adapted to frequent contact with animal care personnel and to those conditions that could result in the animal having an adverse reaction.

In some cases, it may be advantageous to train such animals to a halter. Time spent preparing cattle for use in a laboratory improves the quality of research and the safety of both the animals and the humans. Cattle should not be housed in isolation unless approved by the Animal Care and Use Committee for specific experimental requirements. Whenever possible, cattle should be able to maintain visual contact with others.

Unless the experimental protocol has special requirements for lighting, all animal rooms should be designed to minimize variation in light intensity.

During light periods, the minimum light intensity for intensively housed cattle is 70 lx. If possible, a diurnal light-dark cycle should be used and a standard daily schedule established. Excreta should be removed from enclosed laboratories at least once daily. Pens or stalls should be washed thoroughly at the beginning of every trial.

If excreta or other foreign materials such as wasted feed cannot be adequately removed through daily cleaning, additional washing may be needed during a trial. The method of collection of feces and urine from cattle in metabolism stalls, stanchions, and chambers depends on the design and construction of the unit. Additional management may be needed to keep animals clean when they are housed in stalls or stanchions.

Cattle may need to be washed and curried regularly to maintain cleanliness and to avoid fly infestations. Pens, stalls, and stanchions should be large enough to allow cattle to stand up or lie down without difficulty and should be long enough to allow cattle to maintain a normal standing position. Because of the operating costs associated with singlepass ventilation systems in controlled environmental facilities, partial recirculation of exhaust air from animal rooms is common and acceptable in many studies.

In facilities designed to recirculate even a small part of the exhausted air, treatment is necessary to remove odorous compounds, gases, and particulate matter. Cattle maintained in some laboratory environments have their activity restricted more than cattle in production settings. The length of time that cattle may remain in stanchions, metabolism stalls, or environmental chambers before removal to a pen or outside lot for additional exercise should be no longer than that necessary for conducting the study.

Opportunities for regular exercise should be considered if they do not disrupt the experimental protocol; care must be taken in moving animals from the laboratory to the outside environment for exercise when a large temperature differential exists. If cattle are to be housed in such laboratory environments for more than 3 wk then particular attention should be given to alertness of the animal; appetite; fecal and urinary outputs; and condition of the feet, legs, and hock joints. Rubber mats or suitable alternatives should be used to increase the comfort of cattle maintained for lengthy periods on hard surfaces.

CARE OF GENETICALLY ENGINEERED AND CLONED BEEF CATTLE AND USE OF BEEF CATTLE IN BIOMEDICAL RESEARCH

Relative size, cost of maintaining beef cattle, and the use of alternate animal models in biomedical research have largely minimized the use of beef cattle in this regard. Nevertheless, beef cattle have played a role in understanding such maladies as lysosomal storage diseases and hemochromatosis, among others, which have similarities to diseases, often genetically based, found in humans; therefore beef cattle may serve as highly valuable biomedical models in some cases.

In addition, the potential use of cattle as bioreactors for the production of human gene products or pharmaceuticals in milk, blood, urine, or tissues may further extend the use of beef cattle for biomedical applications. Standards for the care and welfare of beef cattle used in biomedical research should be the same as that applied to all beef cattle.

However, institutional or biomedical funding agencies may require more specific disease entry testing requirements for cattle used in biomedical research, in addition to having more stringent procedures with respect to adherence to alternate oversight committee guidelines for reporting, housing, observation and care procedures than might be utilized or generally accepted under typical agricultural research and production systems.

In some cases, in which in vitro reproductive technologies are used for the production of beef cattle in research, maturation, fertilization, manipulation, and/or culture, differences can exist in fetal morphology, physiology, and in the expression of developmentally important genes that may require alteration in management strategy. For example, cattle produced in this manner may exhibit "large calf syndrome" and therefore may require extra assistance at calving.

The animal biotechnology sector continues to grow, with significant advancements being made that may directly and indirectly affect beef cattle research, and it is important to recognize that alterations through the genetic engineering of beef cattle may similarly require alterations in beef cattle care practices. With respect to genetic engineering, unanticipated results from genetic modifications have been observed in several genetically engineered species that require diligence on the part of the researcher and animal care staff in assessing animal welfare.

However, the general standards of care associated with genetically engineered and cloned beef cattle should be the same as that applied to all beef cattle unless the specific genetic modification requires an alteration in management within the research environment to specifically facilitate animal welfare.

EUTHANASIA

The USDA and Food Safety and Inspection Service (FSIS) *Humane Slaughter of Livestock* regulations, floors of livestock pens, ramps, and driveways of harvest facilities shall be constructed and maintained so as to provide good footing for livestock. Animals shall have access to water in all holding pens and, if held longer than 24 h, access to feed. Also, for animals held overnight there shall be sufficient room in the holding pens for the animals to lie down.

The AVMA *Guidelines on Euthanasia* lists several methods of euthanasia that are appropriate for ruminants. Intravenous administration of barbiturates, potassium chloride used in conjunction with general anesthesia, and penetrating captive bolt are acceptable means of euthanasia in all cases. Other conditionally acceptable methods include intravenous administration of chloral hydrate, gunshot to the head, and electrocution.

In all cases, euthanasia should only be performed by trained individuals. Agents that result in tissue residues cannot be used for the euthanasia of ruminants intended for human or animal food, unless those agents are approved by the Food and Drug Administration. Carbon dioxide is the only chemical currently used in euthanasia of food animals that does not lead to tissue residues.

Use of carbon dioxide is generally not recommended for euthanasia of larger animals. The carcasses of animals euthanized by barbiturates may contain potentially harmful residues, and such carcasses should be disposed of in a manner that prevents them from being consumed by humans or animals.

Dying, diseased, and disabled livestock shall be provided with a covered pen sufficient to protect them from adverse climatic conditions. Incurably ill or injured animals in chronic pain or distress should be humanely euthanized as soon as they are diagnosed as such and according to AVMA recommended procedures. Their disposal should be accomplished promptly by a commercial rendering service or other means according to applicable ordinances and regulations.

7

Dairy Cattle

Dairy cattle include replacement heifer calves and yearlings, dry cows, lactating cows, and breeding bulls used for research and teaching purposes related to milk production. The basic requirements for safeguarding the welfare of dairy cattle are an appropriate husbandry system that meets all essential needs of the animals, and high standards of handling.

FACILITIES AND ENVIRONMENT

Physical accommodations for dairy cattle should provide a relatively dry area for the animals to lie down in and be comfortable and should be conducive to cows lying for as many hours of the day as they desire. Recent work indicates that blood flow to the udder, which is related to the level of milk production, is substantially higher when a cow is lying than when a cow is standing. Criteria for a satisfactory environment for dairy cattle include thermal comfort, physical comfort, disease control, and freedom from fear.

Cattle can thrive in almost any region of the world if they are given ample shelter from excessive wind, solar radiation, and precipitation. Milk production declines as air temperature exceeds 24°C or falls below–12°C for Holstein and Brown Swiss cows or below–1°C for Jerseys. Heat stress affects the comfort of cattle more than does cold stress. Milk production can be increased during hot weather by the use of sunshades, sprinklers, misters, and other methods of cooling as well as by dietary alterations.

Temperatures that are consistently higher than body temperature can cause heat prostration of lactating cows, but additional energy intake and greater heat production by the cow can compensate for lower temperatures, even extremely low ones. Consideration also needs to be given to humidity levels and wind chill factors in determining effective environmental temperatures.

Adaptation to cold results in a thicker haircoat and more subcutaneous fat, which also reduces cold stress. Because dairy animals adapt well to cold climates, maintaining indoor air temperature equal to or slightly above outdoor air temperature is quite tolerable to housed animals. Coincidentally, providing the ventilation rate necessary to maintain this minimum temperature difference leads to good air quality. Protecting the animal from extreme drafts, providing dry lying places that contribute to a dry, fluffy, erect haircoat, meeting the nutritional needs of the animal, and allowing the animal sufficient freedom of movement are essential. The newborn dairy calf has a lower critical temperature of 8 to 10°C. The intake of high-energy colostrum permits rapid adaptation to environmental temperatures as low as–23°C and as high as 35°C in dry, individual shelters with pens or in hutches.

Calves may be housed individually in outdoor hutches or inside buildings in bedded pens or elevated stalls. If calves are exposed to low temperatures, they should be provided with dry bedding and protected from drafts. Proper ventilation is critical in closed buildings with multiple animals. Hutches should be sanitized by cleaning, followed by moving the hutch to a different location or leaving the hutch vacant between calves.

In hot climates or during hot summer weather, calf hutches need to be environmentally modified or shaded to ensure that the calf does not experience severe heat stress. Housing and handling systems vary widely, depending on the particular use of the cattle in research and teaching. Recommended facilities for dairy cattle range from fenced pastures, corrals, and exercise yards with shelters to insulated and ventilated barns with special equipment to restrain, isolate, and treat the cattle.

Generally, headlocks, corrals, and sunshades are used in warm semi-arid regions. Pastures and shelters are common in warm humid areas. Naturally ventilated barns with free stalls are used widely in both warm and cold regions. To a lesser extent, insulated and ventilated barns with tie stalls are used in colder climates. Early research showed an economic advantage in providing housing for dairy cows during the winter instead of leaving them outside.

During good weather, to enrich the environment and to improve overall health and well-being, cows should be moved if possible from indoor stalls into the barnyard, where they can groom themselves and one another stretch, sun themselves, exhibit estrous behaviour, and exercise. Exercise decreases the incidence of leg problems, mastitis, bloat, and calving-related disorders.

Keeping cows out of mud and manure increases their productivity and reduces endoparasitic and foot infections. Current trends and recommendations favour keeping dairy cows on unpaved dirt lots in the southwestern United States and on concrete in the northern United States throughout their productive lifetimes.

Concrete floors should have a surface texture that provides good footing but does not cause injury. The concrete surface should be rough but not abrasive, and the microsurface should be smooth enough to avoid abrading the feet of cattle. Scraping a new concrete surface tends to remove microprojections formed during finishing Data are limited on the long-term effects of intensive production systems; however, concern has been expressed about the comfort, well-being, behaviour, reproduction, and udder, foot, and leg health of cows kept continuously on concrete.

As a safeguard, cows should be moved from concrete to dirt lots or pasture, at least during the dry period. An additional advantage is that the rate of detection and duration of estrus are higher for cows on recommended dirt lots or pastures than for cows on concrete. Exercise during the dry period does not adversely affect milk production, but does result in cows that are fit. Forced exercise after parturition reduces energy intake and milk production; therefore, forced exercise is not recommended.

AREA

Between and within breeds, ages, and body conditions, critical dimensions of dairy cattle vary less with weight than with age. Body length and hip width are relatively uniform across breeds at weights between 180 and 450 kg. More than 94 per cent of the dairy cattle in the United States are Holsteins, and area recommendations for female calves and heifers are usually related to age groupings for Holsteins. Average normal growth curves relate heart girth and live weight to age.

The length of individual stalls should be a little longer than the length of the animal, defined as the distance between the pin bones and the front of the shoulders or between the pin bones and the brisket. For stanchions and tie stalls, stall width to length ratio should be at least 0.7. The width of free stalls should be twice the hip width. Dairy cows prefer larger, more comfortable stalls and use free stalls 9 to 14 h daily. Free-stall systems may be adapted for feeding trials utilizing electronic gates. Free stalls are recommended for dairy cattle used in teaching, extension, and research programmes throughout much of the United States.

BEDDING

Resting dairy cattle should have a dry bed. Stalls ordinarily should have bedding to allow for cow comfort and to minimize exposure to dampness or fecal contamination. When handled properly, many fibrous and granular bedding materials may be used, including long or chopped straw, poor-quality hay, sand, sawdust, shavings, and rice hulls. Inorganic bedding materials provide an environment that is less conducive to the growth of mastitis pathogens. Sand bedding may also keep cows cooler than straw or sawdust.

Regional climate differences and diversity of bedding options should be considered when bedding materials are being selected. Bedding should be absorbent, free of toxic chemicals or residues that could injure animals or humans, and of a type not readily eaten by the animals. Bedding rate should be sufficient to keep the animals dry between additions or changes. Any permanent stall surfaces, including rubber mats, should be cushioned with dry bedding.

Bedding material added on top of the base absorbs moisture and collects manure tracked into the stall, adds resiliency, makes the stall more comfortable, and reduces the potential for injuries. Bedding mattresses over hard stall bases such as concrete or well-compacted earth can provide a satisfactory cushion. A bedding mattress consists of bedding material compacted to 8 to 10 cm and enclosed in a fabric. Shredded rubber may be used and is recommended as mattress filler. Small amounts of bedding on top of the mattress keep the surface dry and the cows clean.

VENTILATION

Ventilation permeates all aspects of the animal environment. Most often, ventilation is associated with respiratory health of animals: the quality of the air that animals breathe directly influences animal health and disease. Nevertheless, ventilation —directly and indirectly—affects many other aspects of animal health as well. Good ventilation in the lying area of lactating animals helps to keep bedding dry, a factor in favour of good mammary health.

Good ventilation along alleys helps to keep walking surfaces dry, a condition that contributes to healthy feet and a reduction in falling accidents. Good ventilation may lead to greater productivity; for example, maintaining air movement in the area of the eating area makes animals more comfortable, which is especially important during hot weather as an aid to maintaining dry matter intake. A comfortable, well-ventilated lying area encourages animals to lie down, an important contribution to many aspects of animal health.

During ventilation, outside air is brought into a barn where it collects moisture, heat, and other contaminants, all produced by the animals. Air is then exhausted to the outside. Ventilation is an air exchange process—contaminated air inside the barn is exchanged for fresh outside air. To determine ventilation rates, we focus on the moisture content of the air, as measured by relative humidity. But moisture is only one aspect; ventilation removes other undesirable contaminants as well. Ventilation is truly a process of dilution.

Air moved through a barn actually serves to dilute the inside air and, very importantly, to dilute all of its components. Dilution reduces concentrations of moisture and heat. Dilution also reduces concentrations of airborne disease organisms, harmful gases and dust, and undesirable odours. The dilution rate of ventilation is often expressed in air changes per unit time. For example, a ventilation rate of 4 air changes per hour implies that the entire volume of the ventilated space is replaced every hour.

In fact, some of the air may bypass the occupied zone in the barn, depending upon geometry of the space, the design of diffusers controlling inlet air, and so on. Thus, the effectiveness of ventilation is not often 1.0, but something less, perhaps 0.65. When ventilation is reduced below recommended levels—usually in a misguided effort to warm the barn using animal heat—less moisture is removed.

Sometimes the consequences of the resulting moisture buildup and lack of proper ventilation—usually condensation—are masked by:

1) Insulating the barn,
2) Using a greenhouse effect,
3) Providing supplemental heat, or
4) Dehumidifying the inside air.

For example, adding heat to the air reduces relative humidity, without the need for air exchange. It is quite possible to have substantial quantities of moisture added to the air and, if accompanied by heating of the air, have the relative humidity remain in an acceptable range. Thus, if relative humidity is the only measure of air quality, air quality may be deemed satisfactory.

However, even though excess moisture may not be apparent, the reduced dilution does indeed result in increased concentrations of airborne disease organisms, harmful gases and dust, and undesirable odours. If these increases are ignored, animal health problems are inevitable. Underventilation in winter is one of the most serious threats to the environment of animals.

Improper design and improper management of the ventilation may be reasons that wintertime ventilation is lacking, compromising animal health. Problems are most likely during winter, spring, and fall, especially during rainy weather and warmer days coupled with cold nights. Specific recommendations for ventilation system design are available. In general, minimum ventilation is provided by a continuous rate in winter, amounting to at least 4 to 6 air changes per hour.

Summer ventilation rates may range up to and above 90 air changes per hour. Maintaining good air quality is a fundamental aspect of that healthy environment with ventilation providing the key. Through ventilation, the air inside the barn is continually diluted, ensuring that the air the animal breathes has low concentrations of all contaminants that threaten the animal's health.

HOUSING TYPES

In colder climates, stanchion and tie-stall barns have served well for herds ranging up to 50 or 60 milk cows. However, stall barns are labour intensive, both for milking and feeding. Comfort or tie stalls are preferred over stanchions. To avoid contamination of the teat and reproductive tract orifices, manure removal must be more regular and thorough when cows are housed in tie stalls. Cow trainers and gutter grates are recommended to ensure cleaner stalls and cows.

Free-stall barns are a type of loose housing with one free stall recommended for each lactating cow. Depending upon provisions for feeding, different groups of cows can be fed differently according to their particular nutritional requirements. This has led to barn arrangements that permit division of milking herds into groups, usually by production.

One free stall is recommended for each lactating cow. The stall base and bedding provide a resilient bed for cow comfort and a clean, dry surface to reduce the incidence of mastitis. Because cows prefer to stand uphill, the stall base should be sloped forward 3 to 4 per cent from rear to front. Commonly used materials for the base include concrete, clay, sand, and stone dust; hardwood planks tend to rot. Rubber tires, if not firmly imbedded, tend to become loose.

In an ideal free stall, the stall bed and partition should define the lying position of the cow and accommodate natural lying and rising behaviour. Proper free-stall care includes daily inspection and removal of wet bedding and manure, in addition to adding dry bedding periodically. Neglected free stalls with excessive moisture or accumulations of manure can lead to an increased incidence of mastitis.

For stalls with bases that must be replenished such as sand, an upward slope of the base towards the front should be maintained. This upward slope helps position cows more squarely in the stall when lying down, which contributes to cleaner stalls and cleaner cows. Free-stall hardware and other components should be kept in good repair.

Corrals should be scraped as needed and concrete alleys should be scraped or flushed regularly to clean them effectively. Feedbunk areas should be scraped regularly and any leftover feed removed. Shades and corrals should be designed to minimize areas of moisture and mud. Pastures must be managed to avoid disease transmission. Stocking rates should maximize production per head unless forage supplementation is provided or unless production per unit of pasture area is to be studied.

This strategy minimizes the stress that may result from overgrazing and minimizes ingestion of plants from areas immediately surrounding those areas contaminated with excreta, thereby reducing the challenge of potential pathogens and helminth parasites. Some pathogenic microbes may survive more than 6 mo in fecal deposits. Shade should be provided during hot weather.

SPECIAL NEEDS AREAS

Cows with special needs are associated with greater risk and thus require special consideration with respect to facilities:

- *Preparturition*: Cows that are near the time of calving benefit from a clean, dry environment and access to an appropriate dirt lot for exercise. Feeding facili-ties should be provided to prepare cows for the high-energy ration they will receive upon entering the milking herd. Free-stall housing situated for frequent observation and proximity to the maternity area is a desirable option.
- *Maternity*: In preparation for calving, cows should be moved to individual pens that are separate from other animals, especially

younger calves. The environment should be well ventilated, and the pens should be maintained to be clean, dry, and well bedded. Recommended pen size is 3.7 m × 3.7 m or 3 m × 4.3 m. The maternity pen should have a stanchion on one side for cow restraint. A concrete curb between each stall aids sanitation. Deep bedding should be used on concrete floors to prevent cows from slipping. Grooved concrete is also recommended. Provisions should exist for lifting downer cows. Devices to aid and promote standing include hip lifters, slings, inflatable bags, and warm water flotation systems. Pen location should permit access by a tractor or loader to allow removal of downed cows. All downed cows should be promptly examined by a veterinarian and handled in a humane and appropriate manner. Each pen should be provided with adequate feeding space and fresh, clean water. Depending on local conditions, a calving pen may not be necessary. Cows can calve in a pasture area with lighting situated for observation. A calving pasture should be well sodded and drained, should be large enough to allow cows to move away from others in the group before calving, and should contain an adequate sheltered area. Use of a pasture pen can eliminate footing and bedding problems associated with calving pens.

- *Removing Calf*: Dairy calves are normally removed from their dams as soon as possible following birth. The cow and calf are more difficult to separate after 3 d. Therefore, early removal is recommended. To prevent transmission of Johne's disease, follow the National Johne's Education Initiative control programme.
- *Postcalving*: A cow that has recently calved should be placed in a special area for frequent observation before rejoining the milking herd. Individual feed intake and milk production should be monitored to determine whether the cow is progressing normally. Milk must be withheld from shipment as required by regulations. Free stalls or large, well-bedded pens may be used in this special area. For a larger herd, a special hospital and maternity barn, possibly equipped with a pipeline or portable milker, could house cows in this management category as well as cows that are calving or that have other special needs.
- *Treatment*: A treatment area in the barn is recommended for confining cows for artificial insemination, pregnancy diagnosis, postpartum examination, sick cow examination, surgery, and for holding sick or injured animals until recovery.
- *Dry-off*: Cows recently dried off should be separated from the milking herd for feeding purposes. Recommended medical treatments should be performed, and cows should be observed frequently to ensure normal progress.

LIGHTING

Lighting recommendations for dairy cattle housed in indoor environments are the same as those for beef cattle in intensive environments.

FEED AND WATER

Except as necessary for a particular research or teaching protocol, dairy cattle should be fed diets that have been formulated to meet their needs for maintenance, growth, production, and reproduction. Feed ingredients and finished feeds should be wholesome, carefully mixed, and stored and delivered to the cattle to minimize contamination or spoilage of feeds. To ensure freshness, feeds that are not consumed should be removed daily from feeders and mangers, especially highmoisture feeds such as silage.

Feed should be far enough from waterers to minimize wetting of feed. Space should be adequate for feed and water. Feeders or mangers should be designed with smooth surfaces for easy cleaning and increased feed consumption. The recommended linear space per cow at the feed bunk is 61 to 90 cm, which should allow every animal uninterrupted feeding. Feeder design should permit a natural head-down grazing posture to promote intake, improve digestive function, facilitate normal tooth wear, and decrease feed-wasting behaviour.

At least one water space or 61 cm of tank perimeter should be provided for every 15 to 20 cows in a group. At least 2 watering locations should be provided for each group of cows. Each cow in tie stalls and stanchions should have its own water bowl or drinking cup. All calves should consume colostrum in amounts of 8 to 10 per cent of body weight within 4 to 5 h after birth always before milk is fed, and another 2 to 3 L within 24 h of birth for a 36-to 45-kg calf. Colostrum should be monitored with a colostrometer for quality.

Mixed highquality colostrum pooled from several cows can be better than low-quality colostrum from a particular dam. However, it is currently suggested that individual cows be tested for colostrum quality for the use of their colostrum alone with avoidance of colostrum from known disease-carrying cows. Proper handling and storage of the colostrum is essential.

Until calves can consume dry feed at an adequate rate, they should be fed liquid feed in amounts sufficient to provide needed nutrients at a rate up to 20 per cent of body weight at birth per day until weaned. Water should be given at times other than when milk or milk replacer is fed to avoid possible interference with curd formation. However, this is not a problem with most milk replacers currently fed. Fresh water should be provided at all times.

Replenishment of water should follow milk or milk feeding by at least 15 minutes. Calves being raised as replacement heifers or for beef should be fed enough dry feed with sufficient fibre preweaning to stimulate normal rumen development. Calf research guidelines have been reported that permit uniformity in measuring and reporting experimental data.

Water intake affects consumption of dry matter and is itself influenced by individual behaviour, breed, production rate, type and amount of feed consumed, water temperature, environmental temperature, atmospheric vapour pressure, water quality, and physical facility arrangement. Nonlactating cows consume 3 to 15 kg of water/kg of dry matter consumed, depending on environmental temperature.

Lactating cows consume 2 to 3 kg of water/kg of milk produced plus that required for maintenance. Water should be available at all times; it should be checked daily for cleanliness and monitored regularly to ensure that it is free of contaminants that could potentially put zoonotic agents into the human food chain. Water sources should be readily accessible to all stock. Underfoot surroundings in watering areas should be dry and firm. Cattle should not be able to wade in drinking water.

HUSBANDRY

SOCIAL ENVIRONMENT

Dairy cattle are social animals that exist within a herd structure and follow a leader. Cows exhibit wide differences in temperament, and their behaviour is determined by inheritance, physiology, prior experience, and training. Cattle under duress may bellow, butt, or kick; however, cows are normally quiet and thrive on gentle treatment by handlers. Cows learn to discriminate among people and react positively to pleasant handling.

Aversive handling leads to more incidents during handling and transport for calves than positive handling. Similarly, heifers and cows exposed to aversive handling took longer to traverse and more force to move than those handled more gently. Although the presence of an aversive handler reduced kicking during udder preparation, residual milk was 70 per cent greater than for the control milkings.

Cows have higher milk yields if handlers touch, talk to, and interact with them frequently. Cows should have visual contact with one another and with animal care personnel. Handling procedures are more stressful for isolated cattle; therefore, attempts should be made to have several cows together during medical treatment, artificial insemination, or when cows are being moved from one group to another.

This was verified by increased heart rate, hypothalamic-pituitary-adrenocortical axis activity, and vocalizations. Pain sensitivity is reduced during isolation, suggesting a stress-induced analgesia. Care should be taken to minimize the negative impact of moving cows to new groups by avoiding frequent regrouping and by always moving more than one animal at a time to a new group. The use of a trainer cow can have a positive impact on adjustment to feedlot environments where many heifers are raised.

However, dairy calves had few indicators that repeated regrouping and relocations stressed calves. Aggression was rare and the calves seemed to habituate to the repeated mixing. Calves from larger groups after weaning had fewer incidences of displacement of other calves from the feed barrier, were more active, and had more positive interactions with familiar calves. Calves, like cows, prefer familiar calves to unfamiliar calves during stressful situations, and a familiar companion calf improved cows' reaction to separation.

Social status can affect health issues such as lameness. Low-ranking cows spent more time standing and standing half in cubicles than did middleand high-ranking cows. Standing half in cubicles correlated positively with the number of soft tissue lesions related to lameness. Dairy cattle have traditionally been kept in groups of 40 to 100 cows, although specific research protocols may require smaller or larger group sizes.

Variation in group size—small, medium and large—does not cause a problem *per se*. Expansion to a larger herd size, however, can affect management decisions because overcrowding with an insufficient number of headlocks or inadequate manger space per cow, irregular or infrequent feeding, and excessive walking distance to and from the milking parlor have a greater impact on behaviour and well-being than does group size. Cattle of all ages are gregarious.

Socially isolated cattle show clear signs of stress: increased heart rate, vocalization, defecation/urination, and cortisol levels. In addition, there are benefits of housing cattle together. For example, pairs of calves are more likely to play than isolated calves, a behaviour thought to be associated with positive welfare. Young calves should be kept in groups from 2 to 7 animals in order for animals to benefit from social contact, but larger groupings are associated with health problems and morbidity.

Management of resources is an important part of reducing aggression and other problems, such as cross sucking, in groups of animals. Adult dairy cattle should have 1 freestall/cow to reduce competition. Similarly, dairy cattle with more space at the feedbunk engage in fewer aggressive interactions and the reduction of competitive behaviour associated with more feeder space is particularly marked in post-and-rail feeder design.

Cross sucking in calves is an undesirable behaviour performed in groups. Calves are typically fed 10 per cent body weight during the milk-fed period and there is clear evidence that this feeding level is insufficient. A combination of slower milk flow, hay feeding, and access to a nonnutritive artificial teat are also recommended to reduce cross sucking. Providing additional objects for oral manipulation, such as tires, has also been shown to reduce other problems such as stereotypic tongue rolling in calves.

RESTRAINT AND HANDLING

Vaccination schedules that are appropriate for the location and dynamics of the individual herd should be established with the advice of the attending veterinarian. Certain dairy cattle behaviours put at risk the health and well-being of herdmates as well as the humans handling the cattle. These behaviours can be reduced or modified by implementing principles of low-stress handling and restraint that include appropriate movement of people, well-designed facilities, optimal lighting, nonslip flooring, and smooth, quiet restraint devices.

Stanchions, head gates, and squeeze chutes can be modified to function optimally, but acclimation and positive reinforcement by individuals trained in low-stress handling can minimize the need for additional restraint by halters, rope, tail hold, and nose tongs. Hobbles and casting ropes should be used selectively and only when necessary. Chemical sedation is always preferable to excessive use of force or application of electrical prods. Information about calving management is given by Albright and Grandin.

First-calf heifers should be bred to calving-ease bulls and be of appropriate stature and body condition to minimize the chances of dystocia or the need for calving assistance. Optimal calving conditions in a clean, quiet environment with employees appropriately trained to follow calving protocols will result in more live calves and fewer calving injuries and illness.

Calving injuries should be assessed immediately so that appropriate footing is provided and proper treatment is implemented. Cows that are unable to stand should be moved to a soft-bedded pack and examined by a veterinarian within 2 to 4 h of calving. Calves require special handling and care from the time they are born. Colostrum should be fed or ingested within the first 5 h after birth always before milk is fed. Between 1.89 L and 3.79 L of colostrum are necessary to impart adequate immunity to the calf.

In the absence of colostrum, a colostrum replacement product that delivers at least 125 g of immunoglobulin should be given by bottle, bucket, or tube feeder. Colostrum is rich in nutrients and provides the calf with vital immunoglobulins and other important immune factors. Clean navels can be dipped in a dilute chlorhexidine solution as soon as possible after birth. Good nutrition as supplied by a combination of milk starter grain, and fresh water along with proper handling and close monitoring starts a calf on its way towards a healthy life.

STANDARD AGRICULTURAL PRACTICES

All animals should be individually identified. Heifer calves should have supernumerary teats removed at an early age. Removal may be performed in the first 3 mo of life with a scalpel or sharp scissors. Older calves and heifers close to calving that have supernumerary teats should be examined by a qualified person. The removal of extra teats at this advanced age is necessary if they will later disrupt the milking process or be at risk of becoming infected.

If so, they can be removed with proper restraint and use of appropriate anesthesia by a qualified and trained person. Milking procedures should follow National Mastitis Council guidelines. Routine breeding programmes should include housing and handling facilities that allow for effective implementation of artificial insemination programmes. Castration may be performed on male calves.

DISBUDDING AND DEHORNING

A review of horn anatomy and growth and dehorning and disbudding of cattle was provided by the AVMA. The AVMA also provides guidance on use of sedation, anesthesia, and analgesia and alternatives to horn removal. The AVMA policy on dehorning/disbudding should be followed. Calves should be observed closely for 1 to 2 h following dehorning. No food or water should be offered until the sedation is completely worn off or reversed. Persistence of a depressed attitude, head-pressing, or an abnormal head tilt for more than 2 h should result in a complete examination.

TAIL DOCKING

The bovine tail has several physiological and behavioural functions including dissipation of heat, and facilitation of visual communication among cattle and with human caretakers; the tail often serves as a primary mechanism of fly control. Removal of the lower portion of a cow's tail is commonly referred to as "tail docking" and the use of tail docking as a routine dairy farm management tool apparently originated in New Zealand.

New Zealand farmers responding to a 1999 survey believed removal of tails resulted in faster milking, reduced risks to the operator, and reduced rates of mastitis. Similar unsubstantiated claims have been made for the US dairy industry. Several European countries, some Australian states, and California have prohibited tail docking. Both the Canadian and American veterinary medical associations have policy statements that oppose the practice of tail docking for routine management of dairy cattle.

The policy statement of the *American Association of Bovine Practitioners* (AABP) indicates that scientific evidence to support tail docking is lacking and recommends that "if it is deemed necessary for proper care and management of production animals in certain conditions, veterinarians should counsel clients on proper procedures, benefits, and risks. Scientific studies have been performed to evaluate both the potentially negative and positive aspects of tail docking. Important welfare issues that have been evaluated have included pain caused by tail docking, changes in fly avoidance behaviour, immune responses, and changes in levels of circulating plasma cortisol.

Experiments that have been performed on both calves and preparturient heifers have consistently concluded that the process of tail docking does not induce significant acute or chronic changes in plasma cortisol or other selected physiological measures. Modest changes in general behaviour of calves that have been docked using rubber rings or cautery irons have been reported but these changes have not been associated with significant differences in normal feeding, ruminating, or grooming behaviours. Likewise, few significant differences in general behaviour of docked preparturient heifers have been noted.

However, greater changes have been observed in tail surface temperatures of docked heifers compared with heifers with intact tails, indicating that heifers may experience chronic pain similar to the phantom pain reported by human amputees. Research has demonstrated that tail-docked heifers flick their tails more often and are forced to use alternative behaviours such as rear leg stomps, feed tossing, and head turning to try to rid themselves of flies.

More flies settle on tail-docked cows than on intact cows, and the proportion of flies settling on the rear of the cow increases as tail length decreases. In another study, there were no significant differences in the numbers of stable flies found on the front legs of cows but docked cows had nearly twice as many flies on their rear legs compared with those with intact tails.

Fly avoidance behaviours were increased in the docked animals, whereas tail swinging was increased in the control animals. Foot stamping was identified only in docked animals and, overall, fly numbers and fly avoidance behaviours were increased in docked animals. Researchers have been unable to identify improvements in udder health or udder cleanliness for animals in commercial herds that have docked tails. In one study, the effect of tail docking on cow cleanliness and *somatic cell counts* (SCC) was evaluated over an 8-wk period for lactating cows that were housed in a free-stall facility.

Standardized cleanliness scores obtained from the rump, midline of the back, or rear udder were not significantly different between docked and intact animals nor was there any significant difference in SCC or the number of teats containing obvious debris. In another study, SCC, occurrence of *intramammary infections* (IMI), and udder and leg hygiene scores were evaluated over an 8-mo period for lactating dairy cows that had been blocked by farm and randomly allocated to tail-docked or control groups.

No significant differences were found in SCC or udder and leg hygiene scores. The prevalence of contagious, environmental, and minor pathogens was not significantly different between cows with docked or intact tails. Although current studies do not indicate that the process of tail docking modifies physiological indicators of stress, several studies have documented changes in fly avoidance behaviour and recent research has suggested that docked tails have enhanced sensitivity to heat.

No benefits to cattle welfare have been associated with tail docking. The routine use of tail docking in research or teaching herds should be discouraged, and alternatives to tail docking are recommended when appropriate. Any use of tail docking, other than for medical reasons, should be reviewed and approved by the IACUC.

FOOT CARE

Lameness in dairy cattle is a major source of economic loss to the farmer and a serious cause of pain and discomfort to the cow. It is perhaps the most important condition affecting the welfare of cows on dairy farms. Lame cows suffer lowered milk production and reduced fertility, and are culled at 2 to 4 times the rate of healthy control cows.

The pain associated with lameness results in changes in the animal's gait that include:

- Arching of the back;
- Shortening of the stride length on the affected limb;
- Sinking of the dew claws on the unaffected contralateral limb;
- Head bob in a vertical plane;
- Reduction in walking speed, and frequent stops; and
- Swinging the affected limb in or out depending on the location of the painful lesion.

These alterations can be used to provide a locomotion score for each animal, and the most commonly used system in North America utilizes a 5-point system of scoring where 1 is nonlame and 5 is severely lame. Herd workers should be taught how to score locomotion so that they can identify cows with scores >2 for treatment by an attending veterinarian or hoof-trimmer.

Around 85 per cent of lameness in dairy cattle is associated with lesions in the rear feet, particularly the outer claw, because of the overgrowth of horn resulting from the redistribution of weight as the cow walks on hard concrete surfaces, with a large udder occupying the space between her rear legs. This overgrowth of the outer claw may be removed and the weight transferred equally between the inner and outer claw by regular hoof-trimming.

Trimming to restore a normal toe length along the dorsal hoof wall of around 75 mm for mature Holstein cattle, combined with balancing weight between the inner and outer claw, lasts around 4 mo on average. Therefore, it is recommended that cattle be trimmed at 6-mo intervals, typically at the time of dry off and in mid-lactation around 90 to 150 d in milk. Some cows with pre-existing hoof disease may require attention more frequently.

Hoof lesions causing lameness may be broadly classified into 2 groups:

1. Infectious and
2. Claw horn.

Infectious lesions include digital dermatitis, interdigital phlegmon, and heel horn erosion. These lesions are associated with poor feet and leg hygiene and are a particular problem in free-stall environments, where the cow is exposed to alleyways contaminated with wet manure when she is not occupying a stall. Putative agents such as several species of *Treponema* and *Fusobacterium necrophorum* are involved in the pathogenesis of these conditions, but hydropic maceration of the skin of the interdigital space appears to be a prerequisite for the development of disease. Infectious causes of lameness are controlled by improving leg hygiene by removing manure from the walkways and by the use of a topical antibacterial administered either directly to the lesion by a hand-held spray or via a footbath. The frequency of foot bathing is dependent on the degree of manure contamination of the cows, and a variety of chemicals are available for use, such as copper sulfate, zinc sulfate, and formalin.

Use of any of these chemicals should be done under veterinary direction. Claw horn lesions include sole hemorrhage, sole ulcer, toe and heel ulcer, and white line disease. These are clinical signs on the surface of the claw that represent the result of several possible causative pathways. Sinking of the third phalanx within the claw horn capsule, due to a breakdown in the connective tissue of the suspensory apparatus, may be caused by hormonal changes at calving time and nutritional events such as subacute ruminal acidosis.

Sinking of the third phalanx compresses the corium below, interrupting the flow of blood and nutrients to the cells responsible for horn growth. As a result, a defect develops that becomes apparent several months later as the sole horn continues to grow. Excessive removal of sole horn, either through poor hoof trimming or due to excessive wear from walking long distances on rough concrete will also contribute to lesion development.

Flooring surfaces should be nonslip, avoid excessive trauma to the claw surface and be dry. Concrete should be grooved to improve traction; a pattern that utilizes parallel grooves 3/4 inch wide and deep, spaced 3 inches on center appears to provide a good compromise between sufficient traction to reduce injury while limiting the amount of wear.

For transfer lanes between milking centers and the living accommodation, a 1-m wide strip of rubber flooring has been used successfully to reduce trauma and wear, and rubber flooring has been used in parlor holding areas to provide cushion for cows that have to stand for long periods of time. The severity of the claw horn lesions that develop is influenced by the time spent standing each day, which results in increased loading of the claw and increased compression of the tissues below the third phalanx.

Time spent standing may be increased by:

- Poor stall designs that fail to provide surface cushion, room to lunge, and sufficient resting area;
- *Overstocking*: Providing fewer usable stalls than there are cows in a pen;
- Excessively prolonged milking times;
- Time spent locked up away from the stalls for management tasks; and
- *Heat Stress:* Cows may stand more in an attempt to cool off.

In addition, lame cows struggle to use stalls with hard surfaces because the act of rising and lying down becomes more challenging due to foot pain. These cows stand more in the stall and fail to gain adequate rest for lesion healing. For this reason, deep sand-bedded stalls provide the gold standard in cow comfort. If sand stalls are unavailable, lame cows should be treated and returned to a bedded pack area for rest and recuperation until normal ambulation returns.

Failure to identify a claw horn lesion early in its course may result in deep digital sepsis. This is a complication caused by infection of the deeper structures of the claw, including the distal interphalangeal joint and tendon sheaths. Such animals are usually severely lame and require euthanasia or extensive surgery. Seeking veterinary assistance is recommended for individual cows that show signs of lameness or if a significant lameness issue exists for the herd.

SPECIAL CONSIDERATIONS

MILKING MACHINE AND UDDER SANITATION

The milking facility should have a programme for regular maintenance of milking machines and follow the recommended mastitis control programme of the National Mastitis Council. Appropriate equipment and competent personnel should be available for milking. Personnel responsible for milking should receive ongoing training about proper milking procedures as the frequency of training has been associated with adequacy of milking performance.

Animal care facilities should be designed and operated to standards meeting or exceeding those of grade A dairies as defined in the Pasteurized Milk Ordinance. Areas where milking takes place must be designed and constructed in accordance with the 3-A Sanitary Standards Inc. Accepted Practices. Cows should be maintained in housing areas that provide for adequate hygiene to ensure that udders are visibly clean. Cows should be milked on a regular schedule that is appropriate for the goals of the herd or specific research project.

Written operating procedures should be established to control potential contamination of milk with antibiotics or other pharmaceutical agents. Antimicrobial treatments should be administered based on approved defined protocols. All extra-label treatments must be administered under the supervision of a veterinarian that has an appropriate veterinary-client-parent relationship.

Milking machine and udder sanitation are vital to an effective preventive programme against mastitis and follow guidelines as established by the NMC. Care should be used to minimize the excessive use of water before and during udder preparation. Emphasis should be placed on ensuring that cows enter the milking parlor with clean, dry teats. Udders, especially teat ends, should be clean and dry when teat cups are applied for milking. The removal of foremilk before teat disinfection is encouraged as a means to detect mild cases of clinical mastitis. Teat sanitation, predipping, and wiping immediately before machine attachment reduce udder infection caused by environmental pathogens. Postmilking disinfection of teats is an essential management practice that greatly reduces the incidence of mastitis. Milkers handling cows should pay meticulous attention to their own personal hygiene and wash their hands thoroughly before milking and frequently during milking.

The use of clean nitrile or latex gloves during milking is highly encouraged to prevent contamination of the udder. Cows with subclinical cases of contagious mastitis should be milked last to reduce the spread of mastitis throughout the herd. Udder hair removal is recommended as a means to improve milking hygiene and udder health. Cleaning of milk handling equipment is accomplished by a combination of chemical, thermal and physical processes and cleaning regimens should be designed to meet appropriate regulatory standards.

Recommended cleaning and sanitizing practices are a balance between the cleaning temperatures, cleaning chemical concentration, contact time and mechanical action. Effective cleaning programmes for milking machines include use of hot water; use of disinfectant solutions and other chemical agents effective for removing mineral, milk fat, and protein deposits from equipment between milkings; disinfection of teat cups between cows; and flushing of teat cups with warm water, cold water, boiling water, or chemical disinfectant solution.

The most common routine in the United States is a combination of prerinse, alkaline detergent, acid rinse and premilking sanitize. Very small herds may utilize manual cleaning and disinfecting that involves hand-cleaning of some or all of the milk harvesting and storage equipment. Small to medium herds commonly use automatic washing equipment.

This equipment will automatically mix the chemicals with the appropriate water volume and temperature and circulate these solutions through the milking machine. On large farms, an attendant may be present to mix chemical solutions and operate valves for circulation. The effectiveness of milking system cleaning can be evaluated by examination of standard plate counts and laboratory pasteurized counts performed on bulk tank milk samples.

STRAY VOLTAGE

The term stray voltage describes a special case of voltage that develops on grounded metal objects on farms. If this voltage reaches sufficient levels, animals coming into contact with grounded devices may receive a mild electrical shock that can cause a behavioural response. At voltage levels that are just perceptible to the animal, behaviours indicative of perception such as flinches may result, with little change in normal routines. Studies by numerous independent research groups in several countries are in agreement that the most sensitive cows begin to react to 50 or 60 Hz electrical current of 2 mA applied from muzzle to hooves or from hoof to hoof. This corresponds to a contact voltage level of about 1 V. As the voltage and current is increased, a greater percentage of cows will react with behavioural responses becoming more pronounced. Numerous studies have documented avoidance behaviours at levels above the first reaction threshold.

The median avoidance threshold for 50 or 60 Hz current flowing through a cow is about 8 mA. Even when the threshold is exceeded not all cows would be expected to show a behavioural response but as the voltage increases, signs in a herd would be expected to be more widespread and uniform. The scientific evidence strongly suggests there is no relationship between behavioural responses to stray voltage and physiological or hormonal responses.

There is no apparent relationship among behavioural modifications, milk production, and animal health. The only studies that have documented adverse effects of voltage and current on cows had both sufficient current applied to cause aversion and forced exposures. It is typical for voltage levels to vary considerably at different locations on a farm. Decreased water and feed intake or undesired behaviours will result only if current levels are sufficient to produce aversion at locations that are critical to daily animal activity.

These locations include feeders, waterers, and milking areas. Controlled research has shown that if an aversive voltage was administered to a water bowl once per second, water intake was reduced. However, when the same voltage was applied once every 10 min and once per day, no reduction in water intake was observed. If an aversive current occurs only a few times per day, it is not likely to have an adverse effect on cow behaviour.

The more often an aversive voltage occurs in areas critical to cows' normal feeding, drinking, or resting, the more likely it is to affect cows. No one sign is pathognomonic; a variety of signs has been reported in cows exposed to different levels of voltage. Documented signs are behavioural changes and decreased drinks of water per day and length of time per drink. The amount of water consumed may not be affected even when behavioural modification occurs.

Intermittent periods of poor performance, poor milk letdown, and incomplete or uneven milk-out, abnormal behaviour during milking, increased milking time, refusal of feed or water, increased SCC in milk, and increased mastitis are signs often attributed by farmers to stray voltage; however, none of these signs were evident in numerous controlled studies. These signs are often caused by other factors such as abusive cow handling, faulty milking machine, poor milking techniques and hygiene, and nutritional deficiencies. Therefore, animal behaviour or other symptoms cannot be used to diagnose stray voltage problems. The only way to determine if stray voltage is a potential cause of abnormal behaviours or poor performance is to perform electrical testing. A thorough investigation of the entire production unit should be conducted to determine other sources of problems. Electrical systems should comply with wiring codes and standards at all times to protect both animals and people.

Whenever suggestive signs cannot be attributed to other causes, measurements should be taken to determine if a voltage potential exists, and the results recorded for future comparisons. A diagnostic confirmation of stray voltage must include a competent electrical measurement indicating at least 2 to 4 V between 2 points that a cow might contact, with some cows should exhibiting avoidance behaviours at this location. Voltage levels may need to be monitored at different times of the day and on different days because the threshold level may be exceeded intermittently.

All voltage readings should be made with a 500 to 1,000 Ω resistor across the 2 measuring leads to the cow contact points in addition to open circuit measurements. Readings without the use of a shunt resistor are meaningless. Although the resistance of cow and human tissues is similar, the contact resistance is generally lower for cows than for humans, particularly if cows are in a wet environment. The resistance of a cow's body plus the contact resistance with the floor is commonly estimated as 500 Ω. This is a reasonable value for a cow standing on a wet floor.

Cows standing on a dry surface will typically produce 1,000 Ω resistance or higher. Cows standing or lying on dry bedding will have a resistance many times higher than this. The resistance of a human can be as low as 1,000 Ω for wet hand-foot contact to >10,000 Ω for dry handfoot contact. The contact voltage to produce sensation can therefore be higher for humans than for cows, depending on the conditions of the contact points. If more than 1 V is detected at the cow contact points, it is advisable to have a qualified electrician or the local power supplier evaluate the situation.

BULLS

The feeding and watering of growing and mature bulls should meet requirements of the National Research Council. Bulls should be housed in clean, well-lit, and ventilated buildings or outside in facilities that protect them from inclement conditions and allow them to remain clean and dry. Young bulls kept in small and uniform groups should be observed carefully as they mature to make certain that one or more individuals are not injured.

A panel can be installed in the center of group-housing pens to allow subordinate bulls to escape aggressive behaviour of dominant pen mates. Aggressive behaviour increases with age, and group housing should be discontinued by around 3 yr of age. Smaller or subordinate bulls should be removed from the group, and a bull removed from a group for over a few hours should never be returned to the group. Visual and vocal social interactions with other bulls may be stressful. The safety of humans and animals is the chief concern underlying bull management practices. By virtue of their size and disposition, bulls may be considered as one of the most dangerous domestic animals. Management procedures should be designed to protect human safety and to provide for bull welfare. Electroejaculation of bulls is sometimes necessary and should be performed by a qualified person using equipment that functions properly and is in good repair.

A programme of annual self-regulation should be followed for:

- Semen identification and sire health auditing service and
- Minimum requirements for health of bulls producing semen for artificial insemination.

8

Poultry

FACILITIES AND ENVIRONMENT

The physical environment afforded by a poultry research or teaching facility should not put birds at undue risk of injury or expose them to conditions that would be likely to cause unnecessary distress or disease. The facility should be maintained in such a way as to allow the birds to keep themselves clean and free from predators and parasites, prevent bird escape and entrapment, and avoid unnecessary accumu-lation of bird waste.

Environmental conditions are known to have major implications on the health, performance, and welfare of poultry. Air quality and the thermal environment should be maintained by ventilation, cooling, and heating to provide birds with the right environmental conditions for their age and time of the year. Welfare of the caretaker, in addition to bird wellbeing, deserves consideration in evaluation of housing systems and should receive attention during remodeling and development of future designs and concepts.

Bird exposure to high levels of ammonia causes irritation of the mucous membranes of the respiratory tract and eyes, increasing susceptibility to respiratory diseases. Birds detect and avoid atmospheric ammonia at or below 25 ppm. The *National Institute for Occupational Safety and Health* (NIOSH), the recommended exposure limits for humans should be no greater than 25 ppm for an 8-h day; for short-term exposure of 15 min, the threshold is 35 ppm. Ideally, ammonia exposure for birds should be less than 25 ppm and should not exceed 50 ppm. Design of all housing systems should facilitate cleaning of the house and equipment as well as the inspection of birds.

Cages with multiple decks should allow for cleaning of equipment and inspection of birds without handling them, yet the birds should be easily accessible. Adequate lighting should be available for examination of all birds, and a movable platform or other system should be provided for examination of higher level decks, if those cannot be readily seen by attendants standing on the floor. Feeding and watering equipment also should be accessible for easy maintenance.

ADVANTAGES AND DISADVANTAGES OF CONVENTIONAL AND ALTERNATIVE HOUSING SYSTEMS

Although there are a variety of systems that can be used for housing poultry, including conventional and furnished cages, aviaries, littered floor systems, and free range, no housing system is perfect, with each system having its own health and welfare advantages and disadvantages. Research into alternative housing systems has been extensive in recent years including furnished cages, aviaries, and free-range systems as alternatives to conventional cages for egg-laying strains of chickens.

Conventional cages lack nests, perches, and dust baths to meet the behavioural needs of hens, but conventionally caged hens have less cannibalism and pecking because of smaller group sizes leading to a reduced trend in mortality compared with hens in non-cage systems. Because conventional cages lack perches and do not have access to litter, poor foot health and keel bone deviations and deformities are not as problematic in cages as they are in non-cage systems or furnished cages; however, because of lack of exercise, conventionally caged hens are susceptible to osteoporosis.

Moreover, freerange birds are able to express behaviours such as freedom of movement, running, short-distance flying, and the scratching of soil, and have the opportunity to be exposed to a variety of environmental stimuli. They are also leaner with more muscle mass and plumage than caged birds.

However, ranged birds are more susceptible to problems caused by inclement weather and have increased risks of bacterial disease, parasites, cannibalism due to larger group sizes, predators, environmental contaminants such as dioxin, and increased frequency of old bone fractures. No housing or management system is likely to be ideal in all respects. Therefore, ethically acceptable levels of welfare can exist in a variety of housing systems.

ALTERNATIVE HOUSING

Furnished Cages for Egg-Laying Strains of Chickens

Furnished cages are available to house large, medium, and small group sizes. The European Commission offers standards for furnished cages that include perching space for all hens and a nest and dust bath area, with minimum available space per hen of 750 cm^2 per bird.

Appleby suggests that group sizes of 8 hens or more in furnished cages should have 800 cm^2/hen and that smaller groups of 3 or less should have 900 cm^2/hen, plus an area with litter. In these systems, claw-shortening devices are helpful to maintain short claws, and perches can help to increase leg strength. Problems observed in this type of housing include increased keel bone deformities associated with high perch use and should be monitored.

Aviaries or Multi-tier Systems for Egg-laying Strains of Chickens

Aviaries, designed to use vertical space, consist of a ground floor plus one or more tiers consisting of perforated or slatted floors or platforms with manure belts underneath. Providing a littered area allows for dust bathing and reduces the incidence of cannibalism and feather pecking. The scratch area also allows the hens to keep their claws trimmed. The litter should cover enough area to allow for proper mixing of manure and avoid excessive manure and moisture accumulation.

The depth of the litter should be sufficient to prevent hens from coming in contact with the floor. Likewise, the depth of the litter should not be so deep that it encourages the laying of eggs on the floor. Opening and closing the littered areas for specified periods can be used as a management tool to prevent the laying of floor eggs. The European Commission recommends that the littered areas cover at least 30 per cent of the useable floor area of the house.

The recommended floor space per hen for aviaries excludes nest space. Only the floor area and the tiers can be counted as usable space when calculating stocking density for hens in aviaries. Hens housed in aviaries have a high incidence of bone fractures during the laying cycle because of crash landings or failing to jump gaps effectively. Each tier should allow hens to safely access other vertical tiers, including the littered floor. For example, a ramp can be used to allow birds to move from the littered floor area to the first raised tier.

If ramps are used, they should be designed to prevent droppings from falling on the birds below. Hens should have access to the entire littered floor area, including the area under the raised tiers. Raised tiers need a system for frequent removal of manure. To reduce the incidence of hen injury, including broken bones, the highest tier should not exceed 2 m.

Vertical distance between tiers, which also includes the floor to the first tier, is recommended to be between 0.5 and 1.0 m. Measurements may be taken from the top of the littered floor or slat area to the underside of the manure belt. When adjacent tiers are staggered to allow for diagonal access to tiers of different heights, the hen's angle of descent should not exceed 45°.

The horizontal distance between tiers should not be more than 0.8 m. Where design discourages horizontal movement between different tiers, there should be a minimum distance between tiers of 2 m. For flock sizes that exceed 3,000 hens in a room, no more than 2 raised tiers above the floor are recommended. Smaller flock sizes of 3,000 or less can have up to 3 raised tiers in a room.

Birds that are to be housed in aviaries as adults should be reared as pullets in similar aviaries to facilitate adaptation to perches and nests. Typically, day-old chicks are housed in a central tier the first 10 d of age and then about half of the pullets can be distributed to the lower tier to provide more space as they age. In this manner, the pullets quickly find the feed and water and are provided proper brooding temperatures during the early stages of growth. By 15 to 21 d of age, pullets are given full access to the aviary. Ramps are provided to allow pullets easy access to all levels of the aviary. Perch space per pullet is recommended to be 8 cm/pullet during the first 10 wk of age and 11 cm/pullet after 10 wk of age. Welfare standards for pullet aviaries are still in the investigational stage.

OUTDOOR ACCESS OR FREE RANGE

Poultry may also be raised with access to the outdoors. Poultry raised under an organic protocol require outdoor access, which can be a range or a semi-enclosed yard often referred to as a veranda or winter garden. During inclement weather or for health-related reasons, birds should remain indoors or in shelters until such conditions are improved. A range is an outside fenced area. Fence height and fencing material should be of appropriate mesh size to retain domesticated poultry and prevent predator entry.

A permanent fence can be extended underground to a minimum depth of 0.25 m to prevent ground predator entry. The fence can be surrounded by an electric wire 25 to 45 cm above the ground and 0.6 to 1.0 m away from the primary fence. Overhead fine netting, as used for game birds, can be used to protect domestic poultry from wild avian predators and minimize disease transmission from wild species to domesticated poultry.

Ranges should be free of debris such as large rocks and fallen trees, environmental contaminants, and be designed to prevent muddy areas, to avoid injuries and foot problems, and to promote overall bird health. Vegetation should be used for ranges or sections of the range where soil erosion is problematic. Range rotation is one tool for minimizing the threat of a disease outbreak and to provide opportunity for land to recover from bird activity.

A covered veranda provides shade and is connected to the house and is made available to the hens during the daylight hours. The floor of the veranda can be solid and may be covered with litter. To minimize the probability of cannibalism, natural light or high-intensity artificial light can be used during early stages of rearing to facilitate the transition of birds from indoor to outdoor lighting conditions. Free-ranged birds without access to a permanent building should have covered shelters that provide shade, protection from inclement weather, litter, food, and water.

The sheltered area should provide space to allow all ranged birds to rest together without risk of heat stress. Mobile shelters should be moved on a regular basis or managed to minimize the probability of a disease outbreak or muddy conditions. Elevated perches designed for poultry can be provided on the range or inside the indoor shelter. All range, veranda, or any other type of outdoor access should be managed so that birds are protected from potential predators. Weather permitting, birds should be given access to the outside as soon as they have full feather coverage to encourage ranging behaviour. Vegetation such as small bushes, crops such as corn, or cover panels that provide a sense of protection in the outdoor area can be used to encourage the use of the range. When indoor birds are allowed free access to the outdoors, they should have appropriately sized openings of sufficient number to facilitate bird exit from and entrance into the building; alternatively, the doors of the house can be opened to allow birds freedom of movement.

The size of each pophole should allow for easy passage of a bird to and from the outside. The number of popholes provided should allow birds to comfortably access the outside or inside without significant congregation of birds on either side of the pophole. A roof can be placed over a pophole to provide protection and baffles installed to reduce entry of wind into the house.

Slats can also be used to prevent the formation of muddy areas around the popholes. For whole house configuration without individual pens, popholes should be evenly distributed down the entire length of the building to prevent birds from blocking the access in and out of the building. On windy days, it may be wise to open popholes only on the leeward side, so providing more than the minimum number of popholes is advisable.

Egg-laying Strains of Chickens

The approximate age that egg-laying strains of chickens are allowed access to the range is about 12 wk of age. Before 12 wk of age, they are brooded in confinement. To allow for range rotation, provide each hen with 4 m^2 of outdoor access. Shade should be evenly distributed in the outdoor area and provided at a minimum of 8 m^2 per 1,000 hens.

Meat-type Chickens

Fast-growing strains of broilers should have access to a minimum of 1 m^2 of outdoor access, whereas slower growing strains require 2 m^2 of outdoor access.

Turkeys

The age that turkeys are given access to outdoors may vary from 5 to 12 wk depending on weather conditions and predator risk, with 8 wk being the most common age. A flock can gradually be transitioned to range by moving one-third of the flock the first morning and then moving the remainder of the flock a day or two later. The following formula can be used to calculate the minimum amount of shelter recommended: area, m^2 = [W]/D, where n is the number of birds in the flock, W is the expected average weight at depopulation, and D is the maximum stocking density in kg/m^2. Growing turkeys are allowed a minimum space allocation of 6 m^2/bird of free range.

Ducks

Information for porches or winter gardens for ducks is not available. When growing ducks are first introduced to the range, they need to be shown the location of the feeders, drinkers, and shelters. The outdoor feeders and drinkers should be surrounded by slatted or solid flooring to prevent the ground in the immediate area from becoming muddy. Free-ranged growing ducks are allowed a minimum of 2.5 m^2/bird when reared on well-maintained ranges with ground cover.

If the vegetation is poor, then a minimum of 4 m^2/growing duck should be provided. If ponds are available, they should be well maintained so as to avoid stagnant water containing decaying vegetation. Botulism in ducks can be a problem when pond water is not well aerated or not filtered to remove plant debris. Developing breeders may be raised outdoors on well-drained soil with open shelter. A minimum of 1,290 cm^2 of shelter area/bird is recommended for developing breeders.

FEED AND WATER

FEED

Circular or linear troughs can be used to supply feed. Feed troughs can be located either inside or outside the area where the birds are housed. If feed troughs are located outside the area where the birds are housed, then only one side of the trough is available to the birds. Unless the feeder is mounted on a wall, feeders located in the area where the birds are housed generally provide bird access to both sides of the trough.

Depending on species, specifications are for birds housed in multiple-bird pens and cages, individual cages, or aviaries. Feeder space allocation is presented as linear trough space per bird when both sides of the trough are available. If only one side of the trough is available, then the amount of feeder space per bird must be doubled. Because meat-type chickens, ducks, and turkeys have been bred for rapid growth to market age, excessive *body weight* (BW) gain of broiler breeders, duck breeders, and male turkey breeder stocks is a problem unless energy intake is controlled beginning early in life.

Because breeders are allocated limited feed to allow for a gradual increase in BW each week, birds are hungry as indicated by motivational test, stereotypic pecking on nonnutritive objects, and excessive drinking of water. Stress is also apparent in feedrestricted broiler breeders between 8 and 16 wk of age. Feed restriction of breeders allows for controlled BW gain, reduces skeletal problems, increases activity, and improves livability, fertility, immune function, egg production, and disease resistance. Evidence to date indicates that the welfare of breeders is better if they are feed restricted. Feed should be allocated and BW routinely monitored to maintain the recommended BW for the particular stock and age. Rations may be either a fixed amount of feed allotted daily or under various alternate-day feeding schemes. Alternate-day feed restriction as opposed to limited feed each day allows more-timid birds access to feed, resulting in better flock uniformity. Inhibition of feeding by subordinate birds is likely if feeder space is limited.

Therefore, procedures that require restricted feeding should have enough feeder space so that all birds can eat concurrently. It may also be helpful to use low-density diets and to provide birds with environmental enrichment such as devices that they can manipulate to obtain small amounts of food to fulfill their feeding behaviour. Although adult broiler breeders are housed together for mating, they are fed separately to control BW gains.

If both sexes have access to the same feeder, the more aggressive males will consume more than their share of feed. The female feeder is fitted with a 4.3-cm grill sufficiently wide to allow feeding, whereas the male trough is fitted with a 5.1-cm grill. In this manner, the installation of narrow grills over the female feeder may prevent males with larger heads from consuming the hen's feed.

However, some genetic lines of male breeders have smaller heads allowing them access to the female feeder, which not only deprives the hens of proper nutrient intake, but may lead to excessive BW gains for those males eating the hen's feed. University research uses a multitude of genetic lines in their studies; therefore, a one-size restriction grill does not exist to meet the head size of all breeds of meat-type chickens. To rectify this situation, small plastic pegs that are 6.3 cm in length are inserted through the nares of genetic lines of male broiler breeders known to have small heads at 20 to 21 wk of age to minimize male access to female feeders.

The behaviour of males with Noz-Bonz inserted did not appear to be affected, with resumption of foraging activities immediately post-insertion. Use of breeds or genetic lines that do not require Noz-Bonz is highly encouraged. Ducks experience difficulty consuming mash because the mash, as it becomes moist, may cake on their mouth parts. Therefore, it is recommended that all feeds for ducks be provided in pelleted form. Pellets no larger than 0.40 cm in diameter and approximately 0.80 cm in length should be fed to ducklings less than 2 wk of age. Pellets 0.48 cm in diameter are suitable for ducks over 2 wk of age.

WATER

Recommendations for watering space vary widely, depending on species, type of bird, bird density, and whether water intake is restricted. Depending on type of poultry, specifications are for multiple-bird pens and cages, individual cages, or aviaries. These recommendations assume moderate ambient temperatures. Newly hatched birds may have difficulty initially obtaining water unless they can find the waterers easily. Similar difficulties may occur when older birds are moved to a new environment, especially if the type of watering device differs from that used previously by the birds.

Watering cups that require birds to press a lever or other releasing mechanism involve operant conditioning. Because individuals may fail to operate the releasing mechanism by spontaneous trial and error, shaping of the behaviour may be required. Thus, it may be necessary to press the individual bird's beak or bill to the trigger to facilitate finding the water source.

Watering cups may need to be filled manually for several days until the birds have learned the process. Water pressure must be regulated carefully with some automatic devices and watering cups. In such cases, pressure regulators and pressure meters should be located close to the levels at which water is being delivered. Manufacturer recommendations should be used initially and adjusted if necessary to obtain optimal results. Automatic watering devices require frequent inspection to avoid malfunctions that can result in flooding or stoppage. Waterers should be examined at least once per day to ensure they are in good working condition. The height of drinkers should be adjusted to meet bird size. Birds accessing nipple drinkers should raise their heads up while standing to activate the trigger pins.

As a general guide, the bottom of the water trough should be approximately even with the back of the bird. Poultry ordinarily should have continuous access to clean drinking water. However, with some restricted feeding programmes, overconsumption of water may occur, leading to overly wet droppings that can hamper health and performance of poultry due to poor litter quality.

This situation can be controlled by restricting excessive water intake, usually by limiting water availability to certain times of the day, in accordance with accepted management programmes that consider the amount of time that feed is available and also environmental temperature conditions. There is little effect on welfare indicators of breeders with limited access to water compared with breeders consuming water ad libitum.

Water should be provided each day and also made available during the time that feed is being consumed. Adequate drinker space is needed to prevent undue competition at the drinkers when the water is turned back on. Water may also be shut off temporarily in preparation for the administration of vaccines or medications in the water. Most conventional poultry drinkers may be used for ducks, except for cup drinkers that are smaller in diameter than the width of the duck's bill.

Nipple drinkers support slightly poorer duck performance during hot weather than do trough waterers. Ducks can grow, feather, and reproduce normally without access to water for swimming or wading, but weight gain may be improved slightly during summer months if such water is provided. If ducks are provided water for swimming or some other wet environment, they should also have access to a clean and dry place; otherwise, they are unable to preen their feathers and down properly, and the protection normally provided by this waterproof, insulated layer may be lost.

HUSBANDRY

SOCIAL ENVIRONMENT

All poultry species are highly social and should be maintained in groups when possible. However, certain social environments can be stressful to poultry and should be avoided. For example, repeated movement of individuals from one socially organized flock to another may induce stress in those individuals that are moved. Human interactions with chickens can also contribute, either favourably or unfavourably, to the social environment of the animal.

A calm, friendly interaction between known animal caretakers and the birds will result in reduced stress and better performance compared with abrupt, careless interactions. Chickens, turkeys, and ducks are likely to panic when sudden changes occur in their environment. When birds are kept in group housing, this panic reaction may result in birds trampling each other and piling up against barriers or in corners with resulting injury and mortality.

Husbandry methods should be used to prevent death loss caused by smothering. Such sudden changes should be prevented to the extent possible. Alternatively, young birds, which are less reactive to such stimuli, can be habituated to conditions that are likely to be encountered and could cause panic responses later in life.

Chickens

Excessive fighting and mounting may occur in groups of mature males residing in floor pens. If such abuse is likely to be encountered, as when aggressive stocks are used, late adolescent or mature males should be placed in environments where those behaviours are not possible or are less injurious; for example, in individual cages, in multiple-bird cages with moderate density or in mixed-sex flocks with appropriate sex ratios.

The proportion of mature males in sexually mature flocks should be low enough to prevent injury to females from excessive mounting. Male to female ratios for breeding purposes can be variable in regard to different breeds and strains of chickens. The optimal ratio in most breeder flocks is 1 male to 12 to 15 females for egg-type strains and 1 male to 9 to 11 females for meat-type chickens.

Some environmental enrichment techniques can be used to control aggression and over-mating in poultry. Recent research has shown that social dynamics in layers and chickens raised for meat are complex and increments in group size or density do not necessarily result in a linear increase in aggression or reduced welfare and performance. Intermediate group sizes of around 30 birds were found to be more problematic than smaller or larger groups of layers in floor pens. Chickens kept for meat production can be safely maintained in large groups of several hundreds or thousands of birds with no increased aggression or behavioural problems, as long as sufficient feeding and drinking space is provided to prevent competition for resources. The welfare of broiler chickens tends to be affected more by environmental conditions than by group size or density effects, as long as density is maintained within a reasonable range.

Turkeys

Tom turkeys are prone to excessive aggression as they become older. Early beak trimming reduces the likelihood of injuries from fighting among toms. Breeder toms are housed separately from breeder hens using artificial insemination to produce fertile hatching eggs.

Ducks

Ducks, being very sociable animals, do not perform well in isolation. Therefore, it is imperative that individually caged ducks have some means of social interaction such as a wire partition between adjacent cages so that they can see and touch each other. For sexually mature breeder ducks, injury to females resulting from excessive mounting by drakes may be exacerbated in the presence of other stressful conditions such as lameness associated with foot pad trauma caused by improper flooring. For Pekin breeders, the ratio of males to females should not exceed 1:5 and may require periodic adjustment throughout the breeding cycle because of higher mortality rates for females than for males.

FLOOR AREA AND SPACE UTILIZATION

Chickens, turkeys, broilers, and ducks should have sufficient freedom of movement to be able to turn around, get up, lie down, and groom themselves. Use of floor area by birds within groups follows a diurnal pattern and is influenced by the dimensions and design of the facilities. Birds may huddle together for shared warmth or spread out for heat dissipation. They generally use less area during resting and grooming than during more active periods and will often seek the protection offered by the walls of the enclosure.

Floor space allowances for layer-type chickens in conventional cages are based on extensive research. In a survey of experiments involving density effects, Adams and Craig made multiple comparisons within specific categories for several production traits and for livability. Their survey indicated that livability and hen-housed egg production were reduced significantly when areas of 387 cm^2 and 310 cm^2 were compared with 516 cm^2, amounting to reductions of 2.8 and 5.3 per cent in livability and 7.8 and 15.8 eggs per hen housed, respectively. Decreases in livability and other measures of wellbeing were also associated with high density. Craig *et al.* found that livability and egg mass were significantly lower with 310 cm2 than with 464 cm^2; Okpokho *et al.* and Craig and Milliken found livability was lower at 348 cm^2 than at 464 cm^2 and 580 cm^2; and Craig and Milliken found lower hen-day rate of lay and egg mass per hen at the highest density. In the same studies, however, no differences in survival and egg production measures were detected between the 2 lower densities.

From data on plasma corticosterone concentrations, Mashaly *et al.* concluded that more than 387 cm^2 of space per hen should be provided; Craig *et al.* found that plasma corticosterone concentrations were greater at 310 cm^2 than at 464 cm^2. Similarly, feather condition was worse and fearfulness was greater when estimated at 40 wk of age or older. Using data on egg production, mortality, and serum corticosterone concen-trations, Roush *et al.* concluded that 3 hens, rather than 4, should be kept in cages of 1,549 cm^2 area; that is, within the goals and constraints employed, hens should have 516 cm^2 rather than 387 cm^2 area.

Using operant determination for laying hens' preference for cage size, Faure indicated that a stocking density of 400 cm^2 was sufficient most of the time, although hens would work to obtain more space up to 25 per cent of the day. Modification of commercial cages from those currently in wide usage for chickens may improve the health and welfare of birds. Thus, cage height should allow birds to stand comfortably without hitting their heads on the top of the cages.

Studies have indicated at least 40 cm over 65 per cent of the cage area and not less than 35 cm at any point is desirable. Taller cages may be necessary for larger breeds. Cage floors with a slope of no more than 9° in shallow, reversed cages may result in better foot health. However, such low slopes may not be desirable in deeper cages, because difficulties are encountered in getting eggs to roll out efficiently. Horizontal bars across the front of the cage appear to allow egg-laying strains of chickens to feed easily and with reduced probability of entrapment.

White Leghorn hens housed in cages with horizontal cage fronts had better feather scores than hens in cages with vertical bars fronts. The cage door should be wide enough to allow easy removal of the bird. Caged hens may cease egg production temporarily or birds may undergo a molt if removed from the cages to which they have become accustomed; for example, for cage cleaning.

Therefore, hens and roosters may be kept in their cages for 18 mo or longer, as long as air cleanliness is maintained and excreta are disposed of regularly from under the cages. However, the incidence of osteoporosis and weak bones may be higher in hens caged for prolonged periods compared with hens housed in systems where greater freedom of movement is possible.

The welfare of meat chickens is not compromised at densities of 15 to 17 birds/m^2 as long as adequate environmental conditions are maintained. However, welfare status for a given density will depend in part on the final

BW at which the birds are grown and managed. For example, heavy male broilers raised to 49 d of age at a stocking density of 30 kg of BW/m^2 had the lowest incidence of foot-pad lesions, the lowest incidence of scratches on the back and thigh, and had the best market BW compared with higher stocking densities of 35, 40, and 45 kg of BW/m^2.

With 35 d-old male broilers grown to a lower BW of 1.8 kg, feed consumption, feed conversion, BW gain, and foot pad lesions were adversely affected with increasing stocking densities. These results on lighter weight broilers suggested that the best bird performance and welfare was achieved at 25 kg of BW/m^2. In terms of space use, there is no scientific evidence to suggest that social restriction on use of space occurs in large groups of broilers, even in mature broiler breeders.

Although less active than layer strains, meat chickens will use more space when available to them. Studies have also shown that provision of partitions such as cover panels help to maintain a more-even bird distribution in the facility and can help to control behavioural problems. Use of space can be improved by providing rectangular rather than square pens for the same available area.

Although broiler chickens can be maintained in cages, it is best for their health and welfare to use floor pens provided with some type of litter such as wood shavings. Because of a relative absence of research on well-being indicators for turkeys and ducks, recommendations are based on professional judgment and experience. Generally, area allowances are assumed to be adequate when productivity of the individual birds is optimal and conditions that are likely to produce injury and disease are minimal.

Singly caged birds are frequently used in agricultural research and teaching to establish or demonstrate fundamental principles and techniques. Because withincage competition for feed and water is absent, feeding and watering spaces are not critical; however, individually caged birds must have ready access to sources of feed and water except during feed-restriction periods for meat-type breeder birds.

FLOORING

Poultry may be kept on either solid floors with litter or in cages or pens with raised wire floors of appropriate gauge and mesh dimension. When poultry reside on solid floors, which are more adequate for heavy strains of poultry, litter provides a cushion during motor activity and resting and absorbs water from droppings. The ideal litter can absorb large quantities of water and also release it quickly to promote rapid drying. A dry, dusty litter or a litter that is too wet will have a negative effect on the health, welfare, and performance of poultry. Litter, when sampled away from the drinkers, needs to be moist but not so moist that it forms into a ball when handled. Litter should not emit excessive dust when disturbed. The poultry house should be ventilated to maintain litter in a slightly moist condition. Avoiding excess moisture in the litter improves bird health by reducing dirty foot pads, hock lesions, leg defects, and fecal corticosterone.

Some examples of acceptable materials used for litter, depending on local availability, include rice hulls, straw, wood sawdust or shavings, and cane bagasse. Because litter materials differ in their ability to absorb and release water, husbandry practices should be varied to maintain proper litter conditions. Litter being stored for future use should be kept dry to retard mold growth. When poultry are kept in cages or on raised floors, accumulated droppings should not be permitted to reach the birds. Droppings should be removed at intervals frequent enough to keep ammonia and odours to a minimum.

Ducks

Particular attention should be paid to the type of floor provided in pens or cages for the common duck because the epidermis of the relatively smooth skin on the feet and legs of this species is less cornified than that of domesticated land fowl and, therefore, is more susceptible to injury. Properly designed, nonirritating floor surfaces minimize or prevent injury to the foot pad and hock and minimize subsequent joint infection.

Dry litter floors are least irritating to the feet and hock joints of ducks and should be used whenever possible, particularly if ducks are going to be kept for extended periods. Litter floors that are not kept dry present a serious threat to the health of the flock. Wire floors and cage bottoms of proper design may be used without serious adverse effects if the ducks are not kept on wire for more than 3 mo.

Younger ducks and smaller egg-type breeds are less susceptible to irritation from wire than are older and larger meat-type breeds. Properly constructed wire floors and cage bottoms should provide a smooth, rigid surface that is free of sags and abrasive spots. The 2. 5-cm mesh, 12-gauge welded wire is usually satisfactory for ducks of all ages over 3 wk.

Mesh size should be reduced to 1.9 cm for ducklings less than 3 wk of age. Vinyl-coated wire is preferable, but stainless steel or smooth, galvanized wire floors are satisfactory. Slats are not recommended for ducks because leg abnormalities have developed in ducks kept in research pens with slatted floors. Raised plastic flooring is commonly used in commercial duck production and is superior to wire in terms of reducing foot and hock damage.

Irritation to the feet and legs of ducks is reduced greatly if hard flooring such as wire occupies only a portion of the total floor area of a pen. In large floor pens, one-third wire and two-thirds litter is a satisfactory combination, provided that drinking devices are located on the wire-covered section of the pen, which greatly reduces the transport of water from the drinking area to the litter.

Maintenance of litter in a satisfactorily dry condition is considerably more difficult in housing for ducks than for chickens and turkeys. Ducklings drink approximately 20 per cent more water than they need for normal growth and, as a result, the moisture content of their droppings is relatively high—approximately 90 per cent. To offset this extra water input in duck houses, extra litter and removal of excess water vapour by the ventilation system are essential. Supplemental heat may be necessary to aid in moisture control.

PERCHES

Egg-laying strains of chickens housed in cage-free systems are highly motivated to use perches at night. An entire flock will utilize perches at night if sufficient roosting space is provided. Perches allow hens to roost comfortably with a minimum of disturbance and provide the opportunity for hens to seek refuge from aggressive birds so as to avoid cannibalistic pecking. Perches also minimize bird flightiness. Early exposure to perches during rearing encourages adult perching behaviour leading to a lower incidence of floor eggs.

Adult Spanish breeds of chickens housed on a slatted/litter combination floor with perches compared with no perches were less stressed. However, if perches are not designed properly, they can lead to keel bone deformities. Perches should be designed to allow hens to wrap their toes around the perch and to balance themselves evenly on the perch in a relaxed posture for an extended period of time.

The perch should be elevated high enough from the surface floor to allow hens to grasp the perch without trapping their claws between the perch and the floor and to discourage the harboring of mites. The center of the upper surface of the perch should be flat to allow for weight distribution so as to minimize keel deformities and foot problems.

Perch edges should be smooth and round. The perch should be made of non-slip material. Ideally, perches should be positioned over slats or wire to prevent manure accumulation under the perches. Perch placement should minimize fecal contamination of birds, drinkers, and feeders below.

Egg-laying Strains

All hens should be able to roost at the same time; therefore, provide a minimum of 15 cm of usable linear perch space per egg-laying strain of chicken. Perforated floors that have perches incorporated into the floor structure and the rail in front of nest boxes can be counted as perch space. A minimum of 20 per cent of the perch space should be elevated above the adjacent floor.

Perches also need to be away from the wall at a sufficient distance to allow birds to use the perch. The height of the perch should not exceed 1 m above the floor so as to minimize skeletal fractures during bird flight from a perch. Provide enough space to allow a bird to jump down from its perch at an angle no steeper than 45°. Perches should be at least 30 cm apart to minimize cannibalistic pecking between birds on parallel roosts.

Meat-type Chickens

Only about 20 per cent of broilers in a flock will use perches at a single time. Depending on bird size, each broiler requires a perch space of 15 to 20 cm. If colony size is 100 birds and bird size indicates 20 cm of perch space/bird, then provide 400 cm of perch space/100 birds for 20 per cent usage. The width of the perch can range from 4 to 6 cm with perch heights of 10 to 30 cm depending on bird size. Broiler breeder hens prefer a roost with a width of 5 cm over narrower roosts of 3.8 cm and 2.5 cm. For adult broiler breeders, provide 28 cm of elevated roost per bird.

Turkeys

If perches are to be used for turkeys, provide a minimum of 30 cm to 40 cm of elevated roost per bird. Perch height is dependent on bird size relative to breed, sex, and age of marketing with ranges from 20 to 150 cm. Turkeys appear to do well on wooden perches with rounded edges with dimensions of 5 cm in height and 7.5 cm in width.

NESTS

Hens place a high value on accessing nests, and their motivation for use increases greatly as the time of oviposition approaches. Hens without prior exposure to nests also show strong motivation to use nests for egg laying. Nests facilitate egg collection and minimize the risk of cloacal cannibalism. Because eggs laid in nests are cleaner and more sanitary, every effort should be made to avoid floor eggs.

Use of electrical hot wire near walls outside of the nests may discourage the laying of floor eggs, as may a bright light that eliminates shadows when directed towards the corner. Pullets intended for systems with nests should be reared with access to raised areas and perches from an early age to become adept at moving up and down in space. Pullets allowed to access perches during rearing are less likely to lay eggs on the floor during the laying period.

Birds should be transferred to the layer house before sexual maturity to allow for sufficient time for exploration of the house and to find the nests before onset of lay. Nests should be dark inside. Lights in nest boxes should be avoided because of increased risk of cannibalism. Nests should be constructed and maintained to protect hens from external parasites and disease organisms. Nests should be closed to bird access at night and re-opened before lay early in the morning. Nests should be regularly inspected and cleaned as necessary to ensure that there is no manure accumulation.

Nests should be provided with a suitable floor substrate that encourages nesting behaviour. Nests with wire floors or plastic-coated wire floors alone should be avoided. The provision of loose litter material in nests can be useful for training hens to use nests. For individual nest boxes with a single opening, provide a minimum of 1 nest box per 5 birds. Nest size for hens of egg-laying strains, which includes egg producers and layer breeders, can be 30 cm wide by 30 cm deep by 36 cm high.

Nests for broiler breeders are slightly larger than those for egg-laying strains of chickens with recommendations of 36 cm wide by 30 cm deep by 36 cm high. Turkey breeders require a nest size of 51 cm wide by 61 cm deep by 61 cm high, whereas duck breeders are provided a nest size of 36 cm wide by 45 cm deep and 30 cm high. For colony nests, provide a minimum of 0.8 m^2 of nest space per 100 chickens. Use of colony nests with duck breeders is not recommended because of increased incidence of floor eggs, egg breakage, and egg eating compared with individual nests. Hotter climates may require more nest space.

BROODING TEMPERATURES AND VENTILATION

Because thermoregulatory mechanisms are poorly developed in young chicks, poults, and ducklings, higher environmental temperatures are required during the brooding period. Requirements of young birds may be met by a variety of brooding environments. Ventilation is ordinarily gradually increased over the first few weeks of the brooding period. Whether ventilation is by a mechanical system or involves natural airflow, drafts should be avoided, and streams of air that impinge upon portions of pens or groups of cages should be minimized.

In relatively open brooding facilities, as in houses having windows for ventilation and with chicks kept in floor pens, draft shields may prove beneficial up to 10 d after hatching. Young birds may huddle together or cluster when sleeping but are likely to disperse when awake. Within limits, birds can maintain appropriate body temperatures by moving away from or towards sources of heat when that is possible and by seeking or avoiding contact with other individuals.

Extreme huddling of young birds directly under the source of heat, especially during waking hours, usually indicates a need for more supplemental heat; dispersal associated with panting indicates that the environment is too warm. With brooding systems that allow birds to move towards or away from heat sources, the temperature surrounding the brooding area should be at least 20 to 25°C during the first few weeks but not be so high as to cause the young birds to pant or show other signs of hyperthermy.

When the entire room is heated and chicks are not free to move to cooler areas, the minimum temperatures that are recommended below may be too high. Thus, during the first week after hatching, a lower temperature may reduce the lethargy and nonresponsiveness that is otherwise likely to be seen. Areas with minimum temperatures that are adequate for comfort and prevent chilling should be available to young birds.

The following minimum temperatures and weekly decreases are suggested until supplementary heat is no longer needed:

- For chicks, a 32 to 35°C ambient temperature initially, decreasing by 2.5°C weekly to 20°C; however, for some well-feathered strains, supplemental heat may be discontinued at 3 wk if room temperature is 22 to 24°C;
- For poults, 35 to 38°C, decreasing by 3°C weekly to 24°C;
- For ducklings, 26.5 to 29.5°C, decreasing by 3.3°C weekly to 13°C. After the brooding period, ducklings are comfortable at environmental temperatures of 18 to 20°C.

Ducks

The recommended ventilation rates for chickens and turkeys have also given good results with ducks. Generally, however, lower relative humidity is desirable in duck houses to help offset the higher water content of duck droppings. Proper screening underneath watering equipment in houses with litter floors and the addition of generous amounts of litter are necessary features of the moisture control programme. When outside temperature allows, supplemental heat may be used to help to control moisture build-up in duck houses.

SEMEN COLLECTION AND ARTIFICIAL INSEMINATION

Semen collection and artificial insemination may be used in poultry depending on the species and type of research being conducted. Methods for semen collection and artificial insemination in poultry were developed in the 1930s and put into practice by the turkey industry such that artificial insemination is commonly used in commercial turkey breeding. Under conditions of artificial insemination, the breeder males and females are usually housed separately.

Careful and calm handling of the birds is needed to prevent injury and facilitates the success of the collections. Collection of semen from poultry involves restraining the male by the legs during the process. After stimulating the male by manual massage of the back area towards the tail, the semen is removed by squeezing the upper part of the cloaca and collected into a clean container. The number of cloacal strokes used should be limited to 4 strokes to avoid damage to the cloacal tissues.

The semen may be inseminated without dilution or diluted with an extender. Males may be used for semen collection several times a week on alternate days although more than 3 collections per week may result in reduced semen volume and sperm concentration. The males must be acclimated to the handling and the semen collection process. Males may need to go through the procedure 3 to 4 times before they have a good response, but this can vary largely from male to male.

During the insemination process, the hen is gently restrained by the legs or held between the legs of the inseminator. Manual pressure is applied to evert the cloaca and expose the opening to the vagina. Semen is placed into the vaginal opening with an insemination straw, a small syringe or a pipette tip. Depth of insemination will vary with species.

As insemination occurs, the pressure on the cloaca is gradually released. After insemination, the hen should be gently released. If done correctly, the process takes only a few seconds to complete and should cause no pain or discomfort to the hen. Hens should also be acclimated to handling and the insemination process. If females are stressed or nervous, they may expel all or a portion of the semen immediately after the insemination.

A typical insemination schedule that will give the highest level of fertility involves 3 inseminations within the first 10 d at the onset of reproduction, followed by insemination on a weekly basis. In turkey hens, morefrequent inseminations may be necessary to maintain fertility as they become older. Actual insemination schedules will vary depending on the research objectives.

STANDARD AGRICULTURAL PRACTICES

For handling birds and for all practices under this heading, experienced and skilled persons should carry out or train and supervise those who carry out these procedures.

BEAK TRIMMING

Trimming of the tip of the beak is done to minimize injury and death due to aggressive and cannibalistic behaviour. Outbreaks of cannibalism among egg-laying strains of chickens, turkeys, and ducks can occur with any housing system, resulting in a serious welfare problem. If the trimmed beak grows back, a second trim may be needed. An alternative to beak trimming is use of low light intensity in housing systems where light control is feasible. Genetic stock that shows little tendency towards cannibalistic behaviour and feather pecking should be used when possible.

Egg-strain Chickens

Production, behaviour, and physiological measurements of stress and pain as indicated by neural transmission in the trimmed beak are used as criteria to determine well-being in beaktrimmed birds. In addition, the welfare of those hens that are pecked by beak-intact hens has been evaluated. Disadvantages of beak trimming include shortterm stress as well as short-term, and perhaps long-term, pain following the trimming of the beak. Because feeding behaviour must adapt to a new beak shape, a bird's efficiency in eating is impaired following a trim.

Welfare advantages include decreased mortality; reduced feather pulling, pecking, and cannibalism; better feather condition; less chronic stress; and less fearfulness and nervousness. Welfare advantages are more applicable to the interactive flock, whereas welfare disadvantages are applicable to individual birds whose beaks are trimmed. Genetic lines differ in their aggressiveness and beak-trimming requirements.

Genetic selection is effective in reducing or eliminating most feather-pecking and beak-inflicted injuries and heritability estimates for survival suggest that the prospects for improving livability through genetic selection are good. Therefore, when feasible, stocks should be used that require either minimal or no beak trimming. Nevertheless, beak trimming is justified in stocks that otherwise are likely to suffer extensive feather-pecking and cannibalistic losses.

Management guides, available from most breeders, indicate methods for beak trimming to reduce these vices. Beak trimming should be carried out when birds are 10 d of age or younger. The amount of beak removed should be 50 per cent or less to avoid neuroma formation and to allow the keratinized tissue to regenerate. The length of the upper beak distal from the nostrils that remains following trimming should be 2 to 3 mm. The lower beak should be slightly longer than the upper beak. If a second trim is needed due to regrowth of the beak, it is recommended that it be done before the pullets are 8 wk of age to avoid a decrease in egg production.

Broiler-type Chickens

Beak trimming is generally not required in young broilers raised for meat production. For broiler breeders, early beak trim before 10 d of age is generally sufficient to control feather-pecking and cannibalism in breeder stocks.

Turkeys

Beak trimming of turkeys is a standard management practice. Strains of turkeys and sexes differ in their requirement for and their response to beak trimming. In strains of turkeys that exhibit a high incidence of beak-inflicted injuries, arc-type beak trimming at hatching is effective in reducing such injuries. Severe arc-type beak trimming increased mortality relative to hot-blade trimming of the upper beak at 11 d of age.

There was no evidence that arc-type beak trimming 1.5 mm from the nostrils at hatching or hot-blade trimming of the upper beak at 11 d of age increased mortality relative to leaving beaks intact. Beak trimming completed shortly after hatch did not modify performance or behaviour in commercial market toms compared with nontrimmed controls and also reduced pecking damage when beak regrowth did not occur. Arc-type beak trimming 1.5 mm anterior to the nostrils or hot-blade trimming of the upper beak at 11 d of age is recommended to prevent cannibalism in strains of turkeys that exhibit a high incidence of beak-inflicted injuries.

Ducks

Feather pecking is a behaviour that sometimes occurs in ducks and may be controlled either by partial removal of the nail of the upper bill or inhibition of the growth of the nail by heat treatment. If not controlled, feather pecking injures the feather follicles of the tail, wings, and back, and the protective feather and down covering breaks down. Tip searing using cautery only may be a preferred method of bill trimming in Pekin ducks because of better weight gains following a trim and fewer changes in the morphology of the bill. For all species of poultry it is critical that the equipment used to trim beaks is maintained in good working condition. Personnel involved in beak trimming should receive species-specific training on proper procedures to use during beak trimming.

TOE TRIMMING

Because of the size and weight of the birds involved and the sharpness of their toenails, broiler breeder males and market turkeys generally have certain toes trimmed to prevent them from inflicting serious injuries to the hens during natural matings or to their penmates. Toe trimming should be done at 1 d of age using an electrical device that removes and cauterizes the third phalanx of the toes involved.

Microwave energy application to the tip of the toe is also used to restrict toenail growth and is conducted using specialized equipment at the hatchery. In chickens, the microwave method did not result in increased stress or fearfulness. Provision of abrasive strips or hard surfaces in the facility may help to control excessive claw growth and reduce the need for declawing. Trimming toes for the purpose of identification is unjustified and should not be performed.

Egg-laying Strains of Chickens

Leghorn hatchlings whose claws were trimmed through use of microwave energy experienced increased mortality and reduced feed consumption and BW during the pullet grow-out period. Removal of the claws resulted in a reduced foot spread allowing the toe of some pullets to slip into the wired mesh of the cage floor. The pressure on the web between the toes led to a splitting of the foot epidermis in 24 of the 1,200 pullets whose claws were trimmed. Compton *et al.* reported similar results when using a hot blade to reduce claw length and suggested that chick movement about the wired cage was difficult until the toe grew long enough to allow the foot to spread across the wired cage floor. These results suggest that trimming the claws of egg-laying strains of chickens is not recommended.

Broiler Breeder Males

When meat-type males of certain genetic lines are to be used in natural matings, the practice of trimming certain toes at 1 d of age can be considered; toe trimming of breeding males may prevent injury to the female during natural mating. However, there is also evidence that toe trimming may impair the mating ability of males. The removal of one nail does not appear to cause chronic pain. For those genetic lines with long spurs, the spur bud on the back of the cockerel's leg may be removed at 1 d of age using a heated wire. Use of genetic lines with short, blunt spurs is preferable over spur removal. Most commercially available broiler breeder lines do not need to have their spurs removed.

Turkeys

Toe trimming is a widespread management practice in turkey production. The number of toes trimmed per foot varies from 1 to 3 plus the dewclaw. Carcass grade of turkeys may or may not be improved by toe trimming, although rate of early mortality may be increased. Toe trimming may be justified when excessive injuries are likely to occur, but alternative methods should be considered to prevent bird injury.

SNOOD REMOVAL

Turkeys have a frontal process called a snood, which is an ornamental appendage for the adult male. The snood can be grasped by other turkeys during fighting and can be torn or damaged. Breaks in the snood skin can be a health concern among older turkeys or those housed on pasture or on ranges. Data collected from industry showed that snood removal in tom poults reduced the odds of mortality.

To avoid injury and possible infection, the snood can be removed from the newly hatched male poult by clipping or pinching the snood from its base on the head. If removed, the process should occur as soon as possible after hatching and no later than 3 wk of age. Snood removal after 3 wk of age is possible by clipping but not recommended without veterinary advice as the snood will continue to increase in size and vascularization especially in the males.

4PARTIAL COMB AND WATTLE REMOVAL

Removal of part of the comb and wattles of chickens may be needed if birds are kept in cages. Combs and wattles can get caught in wire openings or feeders after significant comb and wattle growth has occurred. Comb and wattle removal is more commonly performed on cockerels because these structures are larger in males. Dubbing or removal of part of the wattles should only be used as a last resort when equipment or housing conditions cannot be modified to prevent torn or damaged combs or wattles. To perform successful comb and wattle removal with minimal bleeding and excellent long-term results, surgical scissors, scalpel blade, or electrocautery/radiosurgery electrode should be used to remove part of the comb and wattle during the first few days after hatching. To reduce risk of infection between birds, the scissor blades can be disinfected.

PINIONING

Surgical pinioning, which involves amputation of the wing tip from which primary feathers grow, or tendonotomy is used mainly in exhibit birds to render them permanently incapable of flight. Pinioning is not recommended as a means of reducing bird flightiness in chickens broilers, and ducks used for research and teaching. If flightiness is problematic, the primary feathers of one wing may be clipped.

INDUCED MOLTING

In birds, plumage is normally replaced before sexual maturity through a natural molt. Molting also occurs naturally after sexual maturity and is associated with a pause in egg production, which can be lengthy and take place out of synchrony with others in the flock. Inducing synchronized molting is used to rejuvenate laying flocks to extend the productive life of hens for 2 or 3 cycles of production. Molting has become a common procedure for commercial table-egg layers and sometimes for broiler breeders and turkey breeders.

In recycled egg-laying strains of chickens, molting decreases the demand for chicks by 47 per cent and thereby reduces the need to process, render, or bury the same percentage of spent hens. Rejuvenation of flocks also prevents the annual euthanasia of one hundred million additional male chicks. Additional advantages of molting include feather rejuvenation, thus improving thermoregulation. After a molt, livability and egg quality are improved during the second cycle of egg production compared with a nonmolt control group.

Egg-strain Chickens

Several procedures used to induce a molt have included short-term and long-term feed withdrawal; manipulation of dietary energy, protein levels, and dietary ingredients such as calcium, iodine, sodium, or zinc; and addition of feed additives that influence the neuroendocrine system such as iodinated casein. These procedures have been used coupled with a reduction in the daily photoperiod. These methods cause a cessation of egg production along with decreased BW and feather loss.

To allow for a return to egg laying, feather regrowth and BW gain are accomp-lished by feeding a diet designed to meet the nutritional requirements for a nonovulating, feather-growing hen. Until 2000, the most common procedure used to induce a molt was to withdraw feed for 4 to 14 d without water restriction. Feed withdrawal for inducement of ovarian arrest is stressful leading to increased mortality during the first 2 wk of the molt. Hens are more fearful during a fasted molt compared with before and after a molt.

Temporary frustration as indicated by a moderate increase in aggression on the first day of feed removal has been noted in molted hens compared with nonmolted full-fed controls. Aggression dissipated by the end of the first day, and molting hens showed elevated activity on the second day of fasting as indicated by increased nonnutritive pecking, standing, and head movement.

Resting behaviour increased by d 3 of fasting, and although non nutritive pecking decreased from d 2, this pecking, interpreted as a redirection of foraging activity, remained higher than in control hens. Resting behaviour persisted for the remaining part of the fast. Similar changes in behaviour of hens subjected to a fasting molting regimen have been reported by Simonsen and Aggrey *et al.* with the notation of an additional behavioural repertoire of increased preening on d 8 to 10 post-feed removal, most likely coinciding with the dropping of feathers.

Hens subjected to a fasting molt compared with nonmolted controls demonstrated decreased skeletal integrity, immunity, helper T cells and heterophil phagocytic activity. In addition, hens subjected to a fasting molt showed an increase in *Salmonella enteriditis* (SE) fecal shedding, the prevalence of SE in organs, inflammation of the intestines, the recurrence of a previous SE infection, and susceptibility to SE infection compared with nonmolting controls. *Salmonella enteriditis* was readily transmitted horizontally among molting birds under simulated field conditions, whereas in actual field settings, increased environmental *Salmonella* was observed in molted versus nonmolted hens.

As an alternative to fasting, hens subjected to nonfeed-removal molting regimens show post-molt performance not unlike the hens of the fasting molting regimen. Examples of successful non-feed-removal molting methods include the ad libitum feeding of diets high in corn gluten, wheat middlings, corn, or a combination of 71 per cent wheat middlings and 23 per cent corn. *Salmonella* shedding, intestinal inflammation, and internal organ contamination of SE-challenged hens were reduced and bone mineral density improved through the use of non-feed-withdrawal molting programmes compared with hens of a fasted molt.

Environmental presence of *Salmonella* increases during the molt in rooms containing fasting hens, but not in rooms of hens molted through wheat middlings. *Salmonella* fecal populations did not increase during a non-feed-removal molting programme compared with the pre-molt and post-molt periods, with *Salmonella* prevalence being the lowest during the molting period.

Biggs *et al.* reported no differences in social behaviour between fasted hens and hens subjected to a non-feed-removal molting programme. These results on increased resistance to *Salmonella* and improved skeletal integrity suggest that non-feed-withdrawal methods of molting should be used rather than the more conventional feed-withdrawal molting regimens. During the non-fast molt, hens should be monitored for health, mortality, and body weight. Water withdrawal or restriction, which can lead to increase mortality especially during hot weather, is not recommended.

Broiler Breeders, Turkey Breeders, and Duck Breeders

Induced molt is occasionally done on parent breeding stock using feed withdrawal methods. Molting methods for breeder ducks are similar to those used for broiler breeders. Nonfasting methods of inducing a molt have not been reported in breeder stock.

SPECIAL CONSIDERATIONS

GENETICALLY MODIFIED BIRDS

To date, there are no special animal care requirements for transgenic or cloned poultry. Transgenic birds are cared for in the same manner as conventionally domesticated birds unless the genetic manipulation affects basic bird needs. Future transgenic animals may have special requirements and they should be cared for based on their genotype and phenotype rather than based on the technology that was used to create them.

SURGERIES

All intrathoracic and intraabdominal invasive surgeries require anesthesia. Caponization, or removal of the testes, is an invasive surgical procedure that requires anesthesia.

OTHER BIRD SPECIES

Gaunt and Oring and the Canadian Council on Animal Care offer recommen-dations on the care and use of wild birds, pigeons, doves, nondomesticated waterfowl, budgerigars, and quail. Parkhurst and Mountney provide animal care recommendations for geese, Coturnix quail, Bobwhite quail, chukar partridge, pheasants, guinea fowl, peafowl, pigeons, and swan. The Standing Committee of the European Convention for the Protection of Animals Kept for Farming Purposes provides recommendations and minimum standards for the welfare of ostrich and emu. Recommendations from New Zealand provide animal care guidelines for ratites. These references are given not as an endorsement but as referral material only.

EUTHANASIA

Agricultural Animal Health Care and by the American Veterinary Medical

Association (AVMA) *Guidelines on Euthanasia.* For the purpose of euthanasia, the AVMA accepts administration of barbiturates, inhalant anesthetics, carbon dioxide, carbon monoxide, gunshot and stunning followed by exsanguination, and conditionally accepts nitrogen and argon gases, cervical dislocation, decapitation, and maceration. Methods of euthanasia should ensure death and be selected to take into account any special requirements of experimental protocols so that useful data are not lost.

Anesthetic agents are generally acceptable, and most avian species can be quickly and humanely killed with an overdose of a barbiturate administered intravenously. When relatively large numbers are involved, exposure to gas euthanasia agents such as carbon dioxide in enclosed containers may be used.

Atmospheres containing a significant amount of carbon dioxide, with or without the presence of oxygen, cause birds to head shake and breathe deeply, but scientific evidence indicates that these behaviours are not associated with distress. These behavioural changes are not caused by irritation of mucosal epithelia in the nares or throat because they occur at carbon dioxide levels considerably below the threshold of trigeminal nerve nociception; that is, 40 to 50 per cent carbon dioxide based on lab study of nerve fibre activity in chickens.

Furthermore, although poultry can detect atmospheres containing significant concentrations of carbon dioxide and may show responses indicative of some degree of aversion, several studies have demonstrated that most chickens and turkeys will voluntarily enter carbon dioxide concentrations as high as 60 to 80 per cent. Because poultry can be rendered unconscious with 30 per cent carbon dioxide in air, or less if enough time is allowed, and concentrations of carbon dioxide above 50 per cent quickly kill adult birds, it is not necessary to measure the carbon dioxide concentration closely when performing euthanasia.

However, it is important that the process be observed and carbon dioxide added, if necessary, to ensure that death is attained without undue delay. Although euthanasia of poultry in high concentrations of carbon dioxide is relatively rapid, it also tends to promote vigourous convulsive wing flapping after loss of posture. Although the birds are not conscious when this occurs, the sight can be disagreeable to human observers.

Slower induction of unconsciousness using lower concentrations of carbon dioxide appears to sedate birds and greatly reduces convulsions after loss of posture. Newly hatched chicks and poults have a greater tolerance to carbon dioxide so concentrations of 60 to 70 per cent should be used to kill these birds. Anoxia using argon or nitrogen, or mixtures of these gases with carbon dioxide, has been found to be effective and to produce minimal distress, but residual oxygen should be kept below 2 per cent. Anoxia causes strong convulsive wing flapping after loss of posture. When employing anoxia, the final gas concentration should be achieved quickly to avoid development of ataxia in conscious birds. It is acceptable for an individual who has been properly trained to use cervical dislocation without stunning or anesthesia when small numbers of birds that are small in size require euthanasia.

When enough experienced personnel are available for a given period of time, large numbers of birds can be euthanized via cervical dislocation, as long as operator fatigue is avoided. Cervical dislocation is not recommended with larger poultry such as turkeys and adult ducks or when one individual is required to kill a large number of birds. Following cervical dislocation, the necks of small birds should be checked for dislocation of vertebrae to ensure that the procedure was done correctly.

Use of a captive bolt device for euthanizing large birds such as adult ducks and turkeys can be used by a skilled operator provided bolt diameter, mass and velocity, and angle of bolt impact are appropriate. Restraint of the head without compromising the handler is a major concern with use of captive bolt, so safety and restraint issues need to be considered. Both cervical dislocation and captive bolt killing are followed by severe convulsive wing flapping.

A Burdizzo, a flatedged clamp used for crushing tissue, may be used by trained individuals for the euthanasia of large poultry, particularly turkeys older than 10 wk of age. Birds must be rendered insensible before crushing the cervical vertebral column with a Burdizzo. Embryonated eggs may be destroyed by chilling or freezing at a temperature of 4°C for 4 h. Decapitation or anesthetic overdose are suitable methods for embryos that have been exposed for experimental purposes.

Maceration in a purposedesigned macerator, a mechanical apparatus with rotating blades, is also considered a humane method for killing embryos and surplus neonatal chicks. Chicks are rapidly fragmented by maceration, which results in immediate death.

SLAUGHTER

Slaughter of animals entering the human food chain must comply with regulations as outlined in the *Federal Humane Slaughter Act*. The processing area for poultry slaughter should be designed and managed to minimize bird discomfort and distress. The manager or person in charge of the processing area should be competently trained in animal slaughter and is responsible for training all staff to carry out their duties responsibly and humanely. The holding area for birds to be processed should be adequately ventilated and protected from temperature extremes and adverse weather such as wind, rain, sleet, snow, and hail.

Upon arrival, birds should be inspected to ensure that none are injured or suffering from heat or cold stress. Injured birds with signs of severe stress should be humanely killed or slaughtered immediately. If numbers are in excess, the farm manager should be contacted immediately. Birds should be processed as soon as possible once they arrive at the slaughter facility. All birds should be slaughtered within 12 h of feed and water withdrawal. Feed withdrawal minimizes microbial contamination of the carcass by preventing breakage of the gastrointestinal tract during processing. All transport crates and trucks should be inspected to make sure that all of the birds have been removed for processing. Birds should be handled carefully when removed from crates or, in the case of large turkeys, from livestock trailers.

In plants with automated lines, birds should be shackled with a line running at a speed that permits the proper positioning of the birds to prevent injuries such as broken bones or bruising and to minimize discomfort and stress. Shackles should be of proper size to prevent bird escape and discomfort. Both legs should be hung on the shackles. To keep birds in the proper position for stunning, the height of the line should be adequate.

Measures should be taken to minimize wing flapping such as use of funnels, breast bars, curtains, low light intensity or blue lights, reduction in noise, running a hand down birds after shackling, and avoiding bends in the line between the shackling area and the stunner. In nonautomated systems, cones should be of appropriate size. Birds should not be suspended upside down in cones or shackles for more than 90 s before they are stunned. Poultry killed using exsanguination should first be stunned using electrical or gas methods.

Stunned birds may recover consciousness quickly; therefore, exsanguinations should be accomplished immediately after stunning to avoid recovery from consciousness. Exsanguination itself results in a rapid loss of consciousness if both carotid arteries are completely severed. Considerations involved in electrical stunning are discussed by Gregory and Wilkins, Bilgili, and Raj and Tserveni-Gousi. Electrocution is acceptable if the current travels through the brain and through the heart.

Occasionally some birds may not develop ventricular fibrillation after electrocution, so any birds showing signs of recovery should be immediately killed by other means such as by cervical dislocation, decapitation, or gas. Electrical stunners adjusted for sufficient current should render birds immediately insensible before neck cutting, and they should remain insensible during exsanguination. Acceptable stunners include a hand-operated stunner, stunning knife, a dry stunner incorporated into a metal bar or grid that is electrically live, or an electrical water bath.

Hand-held electrical stunners may be used for shackled birds or for those birds that are restrained in a cone. The electrodes are applied to either side of the head between the ear and eye. The stunner should be applied to shackled birds until wing flapping stops or until the legs become rigid and extended when using the cone. With respect to use of a water bath for stunning, the water level in the bath should be set so that the heads of all birds make effective contact with the water.

Use of an ammeter is recommended to monitor current flow through the water bath while it is loaded with birds. The water bath should be deep enough to prevent water overflow and the electrodes should extend the length of the water bath. Birds exiting the water bath should be regularly checked to ensure that stunning is effective. Characteristics of adequate stunning include rigidly extended legs, rapid and constant body tremors, wings held close to the body, open eyes, and an arched neck with the head directed vertically.

If cardiac arrest is induced during stunning, birds become limp with no breathing or reflex of the nictitating membrane. Pupils are dilated and the birds do not respond to a comb pinch. Stunning equipment should be maintained properly to ensure an adequate stun. Gassing birds before exsanguination may be a humane method of rendering birds insensible, but further research is needed to determine if it is a superior method.

If birds are gassed before or immediately after removal from transport crates or vehicles, they avoid the stress of shackling and the potential of pre-stun electrical shock. Post-stun exsanguination should be initiated by making a ventral cut in the neck, wherein at least both carotid arteries or the carotid artery and the jugular vein on one side are severed. Properly stunned birds will not show voluntary behaviour such as eye blinking, coordinated head or limb movements, or attempt to escape the shackle or cone during exsanguination.

Some involuntary convulsive movement, such as a wing flap, is not unusual as the blood supply to the brain becomes depleted. In some cases there may be a need for kosher or halal slaughter of birds, which does not allow stunning. For this purpose a very sharp knife with a straight surface that is at least twice the length of the head should be used to cut the arteries, veins, trachea, and esophagus. A poultry scalpel can also be used effectively.

An aggressive single stroke cut is most effective. Birds must be permitted to bleed out before further work is conducted. This process should only be performed on birds that are adequately restrained such as by the use of a cone. Birds must be rendered insensitive in less than 30 s. Following exsanguination, birds must not be breathing when they enter the scalder. Birds must be monitored to make sure they are dead before entering the scalding tank. If any bird shows signs of consciousness, they must be removed from the processing line and promptly stunned.

9

Sheep and Goats

Domestic sheep and goats are small ruminants, and, as such, their general care and management are often similar. However, because they are a different genus and species, their behaviours, foraging practices, diet selections, uses, and several physiological characteristics can be different. Thus, facility design and husbandry must be consistent with the behaviours, nutrient requirements, use, and physiology of each species.

For optimal results, the people who care for these animals should be well trained, have appropriate education, certifications, and relevant experience, understand the species requirements, and have good observational and communications skills. In many countries, and states and provinces within countries, various laws and regulations define and govern animal husbandry practices.

Local Institutional Animal Care and Use Committees and people using sheep and goats in research and teaching should be familiar with laws and regulations that govern animal husbandry practices, and they should be certain that animal care and use protocols are in compliance.

FACILITIES AND ENVIRONMENT

Sheep and goats used in research and teaching may be produced and managed under a variety of environmental conditions, including completely or partially enclosed buildings, drylots, pastures, and remote rangelands. Regardless of the production environment, the management system should be appropriate for the research or teaching objectives and must ensure that the animals are cared for properly.

Because of their adaptability and the insulating value of wool and hair, artificial shelter for sheep and goats may not be necessary. Site-specific needs for artificial shelter should take into account the geography, local environment and climate, and anticipated extremes of temperature. For shelter from wind, cold, or sun, sheep and goats typically seek shelter near terrain and structures, such as trees, shrubs, swales, boulders, ridges, and artificial windbreaks. Wind-chill effects can be predicted for small ruminants.

Shelter for goats to provide warmth, shade, and protection from wind and precipitation is important. When barns or sheds are provided, adequate ventilation and clean, dry surroundings are necessary to improve air quality, reduce the incidence of disease, and increase animal comfort.

Poor ventilation has reduced the performance of dairy sheep, and recommendations for adequate ventilation have been published. Guidelines for facilities layout and housing can be found in *Management and Diseases of Dairy Goats, Goat Production, Goat Farming, Goat Husbandry, Sheep Housing and Equipment Handbook, Sheep Production Handbook, Small Ruminant Production Medicine and Management: Sheep and Goats'* and *Hoop Barns for Horses, Sheep, Ratites, and Multiple Utilization;* Caroprese has discussed sheep housing and welfare. In range, pasture, or outdoor drylot conditions, harvested feed resources, desirable forage, and prevailing weather conditions are key determinants of area requirements. The space required per animal depends on the intent of the research and teaching, type and slope of floor or ground surface, weather conditions and exposure, and group size. Floor or ground area requirements vary considerably among locations, depending on conditions, husbandry, and management.

Acceptable floor surfaces include well-drained compacted soil, nonskid concrete, concrete-slatted floors, composition mats, wood, and expanded-metal or wovenmetal flooring or other materials that allow for proper footing and comfort for small ruminants. When goats have access to outside lots or pastures, an adequate sheltered area is 0.5 m^2 per goat. Stall feeding of dairy goats requires 1.5 m^2/goat. Sheep and goats are relatively intolerant of mud, so access to welldrained, dry shelter is desirable.

Crushed stone or stone dust is a suitable surface for heavily trafficked areas. Dust control in pens may reduce respiratory and other health problems and improve fleece quality. The surface of floors, pens, pastures, and other enclosures can affect hoof wear and health. Thus, an effective hoof care programme is an important component of sheep and goat management and welfare, although this is occasionally overlooked when sheep and goats are kept indoors for prolonged periods.

Provision of additional feed and protection from wind and precipitation should be provided if the animals may experience extremes in temperature. Relationships between environmental conditions and nutrition have been described. Within intensive production facilities, ventilation and structural design should prevent moisture condensation during cold weather, provide cooling during hot weather, and ensure that air quality standards are met.

Newborn lambs and kids and recently shorn sheep and goats are susceptible to hypothermia, hyperthermia, and sunburn. Frequency of neonatal observations should be increased, and appropriate shelter should be provided if natural conditions do not offer sufficient protection. The water requirements of sheep and goats increase during hot and humid weather, and it is essential that animals have access to an adequate supply of potable water. Consideration for freezing of the water supply should be addressed in cold environments. Even though an adequate supply of liquid water is preferred, sheep will consume enough soft snow, as opposed to hard crusty snow, to meet their water requirements. Established equations can be used to estimate water requirements under a variety of conditions·

Additional information is available in the Feed and Water section of this chapter. Small ruminants may need special attention when respiratory rates increase in response to increased air temperatures. During hot weather, handling or driving of sheep or goats should be restricted to the cooler times of day. Cold and cold stress should also be considered when using sheep and goats for research and teaching.

FENCING

Fences allow managers to keep their animals together and isolated from unwanted animals. Proper fences and the appropriate use of fences can improve nutrition, health, and biosecurity, ensure the integrity of experimental designs and protocols, and protect the physical security of animals used in research and teaching. Because there are numerous research and teaching objectives, and many sizes, ages, and behaviours of sheep and goats the appropriate fence design varies with experimental or teaching objectives.

However, there are a few general recommendations for fencing:

- Understand the behaviour of sheep and goats and how they respond to, or cope with, fences. The agility, natural curiosity, and inquisitive nature of goats can make some difficult to contain. Because of their behaviours, goats and the occasional sheep will defeat traditional gate or pen latching mechanisms. Thus, safeguards or redundant measures for securing entrance and exit points should be considered. Sheep and goats may become entrapped in poorly constructed or inappropriate electric fencing, and one must consider this in the design and upkeep of any fencing with an electrical component. Sheep and goats frequently attempt to harvest forage that is beyond the perimeter of the fence. Sheep and especially horned goats can get their heads and legs trapped in an inappropriate fence. During the breeding season, rams and buck goats often attempt to escape from their enclosure to reach ewes and does. Rams in adjacent enclosures will attempt to fight, which often destroys the fence between them and allows the rams to escape.
- Design, construct, and maintain fences so that they do not endanger the animals being enclosed.
- Determine the objectives for research or teaching activity and the features of the fence. Is the fence designed to keep animals enclosed? Keep animals enclosed and isolated from unwanted animals such

as domestic, feral, or wild predators or other wildlife? Keep animals quarantined? Keep animals enclosed, but allow wild ungulates to safely enter and leave the enclosure? Provide a permanent enclosure? Provide a temporary enclosure?

- Choose fencing designs and materials that offer the greatest and most affordable opportunity to accomplish the objectives for the fence.
- Fence design should be consistent with institutional, local, state, and federal requirements, some of which may be legal requirements. Those requirements often vary among states, and they are likely to evolve and may become more stringent· Livestock laws, including fencing
- Ensure that a fence is constructed according to the appropriate design, make sure the fence is maintained properly, remains effective, and does not endanger the animals being enclosed.
- Fencing is not always required and federal rules in some locations prevent the construction of fences. Under these conditions, trained herders should stay with the sheep to protect the sheep and direct their grazing patterns. Sheep herding dogs and guardian animals such as special breeds of dogs and llamas may be used for the care and protection of sheep on open rangeland or wherever there is a need for guardian animals.

LIGHTING

Sheep or goats confined in a barn should experience diurnal cycles of light and dark, unless research protocols require alternative lighting regimens. Photoperiod and light intensity should be adequate for inspection, maintenance of activity patterns, and physiological control of reproductive functions in breeding animals. Illumination of 220 lx is recommended· A window area of 0.5 m^2 per goat can provide adequate light and ventilation. Although natural daylight ordinarily is sufficient in most situations, supplemental light of 170 lx is recommended for ease of observation during lambing or kidding.

In outdoor pens, lighting may deter predators, but it may interrupt reproductive cycles or alter feeding behaviours. Either natural or artificial light may be used to control reproductive cycles of sheep and goats. Unless the experimental protocol has special light or photoperiod requirements, illumination in all animal rooms should minimize the physiological effects of variation in light intensity and duration. The diurnal cycle of light and darkness may also affect the performance of sheep and goats; therefore, maintaining a defined photoperiod is recommended.

However, specified altered diurnal lighting may at times be implemented, for example, for certain reproduction research or for accelerated management systems that include autumn lambing and kidding because sheep and goats are sensitive to, and can be manipulated with, changing cycles.

FEED AND WATER

FEED

Sheep and goats should be fed according to established nutrient requirements to provide for proper growth of young animals and long-term maintenance of body weight, body condition, which can be assessed as body condition score, and reproduction of adults. Body weight and condition of sheep and goats may vary considerably during different parts of the grazing and reproductive cycles. Feeding programmes should make it possible for animals to regain BW after the normal periods of BW loss.

However, excessive feeding beyond what is needed to achieve defined production goals can result in nutrient wasting and metabolic disorders. Nutrient requirements for sheep and goats and factors affecting nutrient availability and intake are addressed in *Nutrient Requirements of Small Ruminants: Sheep, goats, cervids, and New World camelids*. Furthermore, comprehensive descriptions and solutions for assessing and managing feed and metabolic-related diseases in sheep are discussed in the *Sheep Production Handbook*.

A variety of feedstuffs may be fed to sheep and goats, but changes in relative amounts of forage and concentrates in diets should be made gradually. Animals should be managed during transition periods or sufficient potentially fermentable fibre should be fed to avoid the development of digestive disorders such as acidosis. Male sheep and goats consuming diets with moderate to large amounts of concentrate are prone to urinary calculi.

Occurrences of this condition can be prevented or minimized by maintaining a dietary Ca:P ratio of at least 2:1, including urine-acidifying agents such as ammonium chloride in the diet, and increasing dietary salt content to promote water intake. When feeding nontraditional feedstuffs their composition should be evaluated and potential nutrient toxicities or deficiencies should be corrected.

Feeding equipment should be constructed and located to be available for ready access, provide sufficient feeder space, prevent injury to animals, and minimize contamination of feed with excreta. Providing sufficient feeder space is important for sheep and goats when feeding limited amounts of feedstuffs that are ingested quickly so that all animals have access to feed.

If feeder space is limited so that all animals cannot eat at the same time, sufficient potentially fermentable neutral detergent fibre should be included in concentrate diets to provide substrate for rumen fermentation and to prevent metabolic disturbances. Sheep and goats in some production settings undergo periods of nutrient deficiencies that result in considerable BW loss. Hence, research to address such scenarios may necessitate simulation of such conditions.

Researchers should be aware that, even though restricted nutritional planes can decrease BW and BCS, adaptive decreases in the maintenance energy requirement can minimize the negative effects of such changes. In research dealing with limited nutritional planes, individual BW and BCS of sheep and goats should be monitored frequently so that excessive decreases are avoided. Thus, if a study has a target BCS for a group of 2 on a scale of 1 to 5, some animals will have lower BCS, perhaps ≤1.5, which is undesirable particularly if the research requires maintaining such a BCS for an extended period. Furthermore, animals on limited planes of nutrition with low BCS can be more susceptible to health concerns under adverse environmental conditions and, thus, less competitive for limited feeder and shelter space, compared with animals in better condition.

Animals reaching very low BCS should be placed on a higher plane of nutrition to regain BW and increase their BCS. Sheep and goats can consume a variety of plants when grazing on pasture or range. Goats in particular will selectively browse small woody plants and brush. Thus, pasture and range forages for sheep and goats can vary from season to season and among geographic locations. Nutritional management of pastured animals is mainly controlled by movement of sheep and goats to pastures of varying forage density and by supplying appropriate minerals and water as necessary. Sheep and goats differ somewhat in susceptibility to adverse effects or tolerance of some plant secondary metabolites, and physiological conditions in animals can change over time and confer some degree of adaptation to some plant secondary metabolites.

When risks of plant secondary metabolite exposure are expected from pasture or a fed diet, animal conditions should be closely monitored. In research and teaching settings, sheep and goats are sometimes used as biological control agents for managing invasive plant species. In such cases, animals may graze plant communities with limited plant diversity, be required to remove the majority of standing biomass, or graze plants that are potentially toxic or have large amounts of antiproductive secondary metabolites. Because sheep and goats differ in their susceptibility to plant secondary metabolites, grazing animals should be monitored regularly once grazing commences to ensure adequate forage availability and to identify potential or manifested nutrient deficiencies and plant-related toxicities. Any animals showing signs of nutrient deficiencies or toxicosis should be removed and treated accordingly.

WATER

Water requirements of sheep and goats are based on, but not limited to, physiological state, dry matter intake, climatic conditions, and environment. A comprehensive discussion of water requirements is beyond the scope of this chapter, but NRC contains thorough descriptions of water use, sources, quality, and requirements for sheep and goats.

Careful consideration of water source, location, and quality will enable caretakers to effectively assess and meet the water needs of sheep and goats in research and teaching settings. Sheep and goats satisfy their water requirements from free-standing sources, food and metabolic processes. In some research and teaching settings, sheep and goats consume water from sources such as ponds, streams, and springs.

Even though it is common and preferred for liquid water to be continually available to sheep and goats, this is not practiced in some production and research settings. For example, in extensive production systems, sheep and goats may derive their water requirement from fresh forages, as preformed water, or snow. Except under extremely hot temperatures, sheep that consume sufficient fresh forage to meet nutrient requirements also obtain enough moisture from the forage to meet their water requirements.

When cold drinking water is consumed in large volumes, the temperature of the rumen may decrease, which reduces the activity of rumen microorganisms. However, when water is available in the form of snow, sheep will consume it in small amounts along with the forage. Therefore, the cooling effect on rumen temperature may be less because of the temperature buffering capacity of water already present in the reticulum-rumen.

Another example of when water is not continually available to research animals might be a head-box respiration calorimetry system in which water is offered at discrete times, perhaps twice daily, to avoid accumulation of excessive moisture in the calorimeter. Regardless of the specific setting, water availability should be appropriate for the desired level of productivity of the particular animal of interest and should be adequate to avoid dehydration, unless dehydration is a component of an approved research protocol.

Depending on source, drinking water can contain a variety of contaminants such as excessive sulfates and salts that are harmful or impair sheep and goat productivity. The NRC for dairy cattle and beef cattle are excellent sources of information on water contaminants that reduce livestock production. Historical records of water quality should be investigated or appropriate analyses should be conducted on drinking water sources. Water contaminants, not necessarily harmful to sheep, may interfere with results of experiments, such as in mineral balance studies. Manufactured watering receptacles should be inspected, cleaned, and, if needed, repaired regularly to ensure that adequate supplies of good-quality liquid water are available.

Watering receptacles should be designed and positioned to minimize feed and fecal contamination, be free of electrical and mechanical hazards that are harmful to animals and personnel, be protected from freezing, and accommodate the needs and behaviour of sheep and goats. Improperly installed or defective electrically heated livestock waterers may allow stray voltage to flow through the water and metal in the waterer and deter animals from consuming adequate amounts of water.

Several publications describe how to test for and prevent or eliminate stray voltage and the effects of stray voltage on livestock. Receptacles should be located in areas that facilitate research and teaching goals and do not compromise the surrounding environment. In some locations, watering receptacles must contain ladders to allow birds and small mammals to escape. This adds to the maintenance of the watering receptacles, but it protects birds and small mammals, reduces contamination from birds and small mammals, and complies with federal or state regulations in some regions.

HUSBANDRY

People involved in using sheep and goats for research and teaching should be trained and skilled in performing a variety of routine management procedures. Injections, ear-tagging, ear-notching, eartattooing, tail-web tattooing, deworming, shearing, and hoof care, including hoof trimming and detection, treatment, eradication, and prevention of contagious foot rot and other causes of lameness, are among the routine husbandry procedures that may be performed on sheep and goats at any age. Correction of entropion should be performed as soon as possible after birth. Immunization should be provided against pertinent diseases. Colostrum, preferably that obtained when a lamb or kid suckles its dam, should, unless it conflicts with an approved experimental protocol, be provided as a source of antibodies soon after birth to avoid disease during the neonatal period.

To eliminate a possible route of transfer of disease into research and teaching settings, the practice of using raw colostrum from outside sources to supplement or replace colostrum from a lamb's or kid's dam should be avoided. The transfer of Johne's disease or paratuberculosis in cow colostrum is an important concern. In addition, viral diseases, such as the lentivirus diseases can be transferred through raw ewe and doe colostrum and milk. Pasteurization may reduce the likelihood of transferring pathogenic bacteria and viruses, but it may denature antibodies. For goats, husbandry and management information can be found in several references, including *Management and Diseases of Dairy Goats, Goat Production, Goat Husbandry, Goat Farming, Small Ruminant Production Medicine and Management: Sheep and Goats,* and *Meat Goat Production Handbook.* In addition, a webbased training and certification programme for meat goat producers is available.

SOCIAL ENVIRONMENT

Sheep and goats are social herbivores that typically live in flocks or herds of familiar animals and engage in frequent social interactions, especially during the active period of the day. These interactions include establishment or maintenance of a social dominance hierarchy, grooming, competition for space or other resources, or play in young animals. At night, sheep and goats typically bed in close proximity to others in the flock or herd. Housing sheep and goats in groups of familiar animals is desirable whenever this practice does not conflict with research and teaching objectives.

When practical, a minimum group size of 3 is desirable. This provides for continuous social grouping even if one animal is removed. Social isolation is a source of distress for sheep and goats, and this stress may interfere with many physiological and behavioural variables. Isolation and restraint distress have been effective research tools for studying the effects of distress on physiology, behaviour, and well-being. Animals that are isolated from the flock or herd or that have recently been separated from close social companions should be monitored frequently to reduce the possibility of injury or distress after separation. New animals may be introduced into sheep and goat flocks and herds with relatively little social strife. However, unacquainted rams or buck goats may fight and severely injure each other. Occasionally, injuries can be fatal, especially when older, less agile rams are mixed with younger, stronger rams.

Care should be taken to prevent excessive fighting among males when they are newly mixed. One method to reduce injury among newly grouped males is to severely restrict the space allocation for each animal for a few days to limit the distance available when rams run towards each other to butt heads. After rams appear to have established a social hierarchy, the space allocation per animal can be increased to provide sufficient space. Goats have a strong social hierarchy, and the addition of several goats to an established group is generally less stressful and more successful than the addition of an individual. Although horned and polled animals may be penned together, care should be taken to protect the polled animals when new animals are introduced to a flock or herd. Sufficient space and multiple feeders should be provided to prevent individuals from dominating feed and water supplies.

In intensive production conditions, dividing larger flocks or herds into smaller groups, modifying facility design, increasing the frequency of observation, and using claiming pens may enhance the survival rate of neonatal lambs or kids. Ewes and does should not lamb or kid in claiming pens because the pens are typically too small to allow the animals to move about freely during labour and parturition, become wet and very difficult to keep clean, and become sources of disease. Restricting the periparturient female's movements may increase the chances that a ewe or doe will step or lie on her offspring. Ewes and does should lamb or kid in a relatively large and open area that can be observed easily and, if necessary, then moved with their offspring into claiming pens to ensure bonding.

PARASITE CONTROL

Internal and external parasite control is essential, especially when sheep and goats are on pasture. Internal parasite control programmes should be devised for each particular location with the recognition that programmes that work for sheep may not be effective for goats at the same location, and *vice-versa*. One should also recognize that most available anthelminthics are no longer adequately effective against *Hemonchus contortus*, which is the internal parasite of primary concern for sheep and goats. Because of this, new internal parasite control programmes have been devised that emphasize the strategic, rather than general, use of anthelminthics, combined with new diagnostic procedures, alternative treatments and preventatives, and managing to maximize resilience and resistance and minimize the development of infestations. Descriptions of internal parasite control programmes can found at the Southern Consortium for Small Ruminant Parasite Control Web site.

Small Ruminant Production Medicine and Management: Sheep and Goats contains descriptions and images of how to administer dewormers to sheep and goats. In intensive feedlot or laboratory environments, where pasture is not a potential route for parasite lifecycle maintenance, parasites such as *H. contortus* may not be a concern. However, in these same environments, parasites that are not primarily pasture driven may be a greater problem and require added preventative and treatment considerations.

Coccidia should be a concern when sheep and goats, especially younger animals, are managed under any confined conditions, which may include pastures of various sizes. External parasites are usually arthropods. They typically feed on the skin, wool, hair, and blood of sheep and goats and cause discomfort. External parasites may also be disease vectors and they can compromise the health and productivity of sheep and goats. Effective external parasite control programmes should be developed and implemented to guard the health of sheep and goats. Kaufman *et al.* described various external parasites and typical control strategies.

SHEARING

Because wool breeds of sheep do not shed their wool naturally and fibre is harvested from some breeds of goats, shearing may be necessary for the physical wellbeing of the animals, depending on specific environmental conditions and breed type, and to accomplish research and teaching objectives.

Cashmere-producing goats are often sheared as well. Shearing lambs and kids during hot weather may improve feed intake and growth rates. Shearing ewes before lambing can increase lamb birth weights, and it is often easier for newborn lambs to find a teat and suckle when ewes are shorn. In addition, shorn ewes usually transport less moisture into barns or claiming pens, are usually cleaner, and occupy less space. Crutching, the practice of shearing the wool from around the dock and udder, is an acceptable alternative when ewes are not completely shorn.

However, shearing ewes before lambing is a more desirable management practice. Hair-breed sheep and short-haired goats do not require shearing.

Wool-breed × hair-breed crossbred sheep may require occasional or partial shearing, or they may shed. In any case, the decision of whether to shear wool-breed × hair-breed crossbred sheep should be based on the characteristics of the sheep and on the goal of ensuring the health and well-being of the animals.

The shearing facility should be clean and dry. Information on design is in the *Sheep Production Handbook* and Barber and Freeman. To minimize the spread of infectious disease between flocks, shearing equipment should be disinfected between flocks. When infectious disease conditions are present or suspected, equipment should be disinfected between animals. A good shearer is a skilled professional. A proper shearing technique restrains and positions the sheep correctly to ensure control and comfort of the animal.

Late-pregnant ewes may be shorn if handled properly. To facilitate the comfort of the animal during shearing, animals may be held off feed and water for 6 to 12 h before they are shorn. Sheep and goats should be dry when they are shorn. After shearing, sheep and goats should have protection from severe cold, windy, or wet conditions. Raised or stubble combs, which leave some wool on the sheep, may be used if sheep are likely to be exposed to inclement winter weather conditions.

Another practice when sheep are shorn in cold climates is to increase the energy density of the diet for a period before and after shearing. In hot, sunny weather, shade may be necessary to prevent sunburn in recently shorn white-skinned sheep. Wind breaks, which may also provide shade, are beneficial under many environmental conditions.

STANDARD AGRICULTURAL PRACTICES

Other husbandry and health practices used in sheep and goat research and teaching that require special technical training and advanced skills include artificial insemination, semen collection, ultrasound examinations for pregnancy detection or predicting carcass traits, embryo flushing and transfer, and venipuncture. The *Sheep Production Handbook, Small Ruminant Production Medicine and Management: Sheep and Goats,* and several other references cited in this chapter contain descriptions of and images depicting many of these management practices. However, peer-reviewed scientific journals are often the preferred sources for descriptions of specialized technical procedures. The publication *Producing Customer Products from Sheep: The Sheep Safety and Quality Assurance Programme* contains information that may enhance training programmes for the people who manage and care for sheep and goats for research and teaching.

TAIL-DOCKING

Tail-docking of lambs is performed to reduce the possibility of soiling the long tail with urine and feces and the subsequent development of fly strike, a potentially fatal condition. With hair-breeds of sheep, tail-docking may not be necessary. Goat kids have an erect tail that is not docked. Tail-docking of wool-breed lambs is recommended unless the life span is limited to a season when fly infestations are unlikely and when the feed used does not result in a heavily contaminated fleece. There are several acceptable methods for tail-docking. These include rubber rings, hot-iron cautery, surgical removal, surgical removal after application of an emasculator, and various combinations of the basic procedures. Tails should be docked when lambs are as young as possible, preferably before 2 wk of age. Very short tail docking should not be permitted because it increases the incidence of rectal, and perhaps vaginal, prolapses. Based on recent research, tails should be docked at the distal end of the caudal folds, where the caudal folds on the underside of the tail attach to the tail; this practice reduces the incidence of rectal prolapse to negligible rates.

CASTRATION

Rams and bucks are castrated to prevent indiscriminate breeding and fighting, thus exercising genetic control, regulating the time of year of lambing, controlling the minimum age of first parturition and lactation, and reducing injuries. There are 3 commonly accepted methods for castrating rams and bucks: application of rubber rings, crushing the spermatic cord with an emasculator, and surgical removal of the testicles; various combinations of the three are also common.

For each method, the lamb's or kid's scrotum should be palpated to make sure that it contains 2 testicles and that there is no evidence of an inguinal hernia. The castration procedure should remove both testicles unless an approved experimental method precludes bilateral castration. Detailed descriptions of castration procedures are available in various publications. A common recommendation is to castrate lambs and kids when they are between 24 h and 7 d of age, although recommendations vary. Nevertheless, castrating lambs and kids as early in life as possible, considering weather, nutritional stress, environment, and the presence of complicating disease processes, seems prudent.

Lambs are typically castrated and docked at one time to reduce the number of times they are handled. Ideally, ewes and does should be vaccinated prepartum against clostridial diseases so that their lambs and kids receive passive immunization via colostrum. This will reduce the incidence of tetanus after docking or castration. If ewes and does are not vaccinated prepartum, tetanus antitoxin may be administered at castration and docking when there is risk of tetanus.

ACUTE DISCOMFORT AND PAIN AFTER TAIL DOCKING AND CASTRATION

Tail docking and castration can cause acute alterations in the behaviour of lambs, and the alterations in behaviour are consistent with evidence of acute discomfort and pain. The use of rubber rings without the use of analgesics, local anesthetics, or denervation increases the signs of acute discomfort and pain. Analgesics, local anesthetics, and denervation can reduce or eliminate the signs of discomfort and pain associated with using rubber rings for tail docking and castration. The Australian Veterinary Association recommends that tail docking and castration of sheep older than 3 mo should be treated as a major surgical procedure, and appropriate analgesia or anesthesia should be used. The people working with sheep and goats in research and teaching and the local IACUC should determine whether the methods used for tail docking and castration cause signs of acute or chronic discomfort and pain.

Observational studies can be conducted locally, and a considerable body of scientific literature is available to make an informed decision, although not all methods for tail docking and castration have been studied. If the methods used cause signs of discomfort and pain, the IACUC should then work with the people who are using sheep and goats for research and teaching to develop and implement efficacious procedures for reducing or eliminating discomfort and pain after tail docking and castration.

DISBUDDING AND DEHORNING

Disbudding of goats should be performed at less than 1 mo of age for ease of the procedure and effectiveness of removing all of the horn bud. Cautery with heat should be used when possible and be considered the method of first choice, although surgery, freezing, and an acidic paste are other options. If disbudding or dehorning of young goats causes signs of significant discomfort, stress, and pain, the local IACUC should work with the people using the goats for research and teaching to develop and implement efficacious procedures for reducing or eliminating discomfort, stress, and pain. Horns of adult goats should be removed under general anesthesia or sedation and local anesthesia due to the anatomy and tissues involved and the significant development of horny tissue in older goats, especially bucks. Dehorning is not a recommended management practice for sheep.

Even though procedures for dehorning ram lambs have been reported, horn growth was not completely eliminated, even after a second procedure approximately 1 mo after the first; dehorned sites were prone to fly strike; and dehorning did not duplicate the phenotype of genetically polled rams. However, the horns of a mature ram may curl and become long enough to grow into the ram's head. To prevent this, a ram's horns should be trimmed or tipped but the living tissue inside the horns should not be cut. A finetoothed saw blade may be used to trim and shape the horns so that they are not a danger to the ram, other sheep, and humans.

MULESING

Because of their wrinkled skin and heavy fleece, Merino sheep seem to be more susceptible to fly strike, which causes severe discomfort, pain, and often death, than are other breeds. A surgical procedure called mulesing was developed to remove wrinkled, wool-bearing skin and reduce fly strike. Mulesing has been a common practice in a few countries, but not the United States or other countries where Merino sheep are a minor breed. Even though mulesing seems to reduce the incidence of fly strike, it has been severely criticized because of the apparent discomfort and pain associated with the procedure.

Thus, Australia and New Zealand, where mulesing has been used routinely, are phasing out the practice. The Australian wool industry announced in 2004 that the practice of mulesing will end by 2010. Until then, the *Model Code of Practice for the Welfare of Animals, The Sheep* describes the mulesing procedures that must be followed. A recent study indicates that a combination of a local anesthetic and a long-acting nonsteroidal antiinflammatory drug can reduce the discomfort and pain associated with mulesing. Nevertheless, mulesing is no longer an acceptable procedure, and an IACUC should be reluctant to approve the use of mulesing in research and teaching.

SPECIAL CONSIDERATIONS

DAIRY SHEEP AND GOATS

Sheep and goats have been used as dairy animals for centuries, and dairy sheep and goats have been used for research and teaching in many countries for decades. However, dairy sheep and goat research and teaching are relatively new in North America. Publications such as *Principles of Sheep Dairying in North America, Management and Diseases of Dairy Goats* and *Sheep Production Handbook* describe the management and care of dairy sheep and goats.

Dairy Cattle of this guide are also applicable to sheep and goats, although the details of sheep, goat, and cattle dairying are species-specific and management plans should be developed with that in mind. Even though the basic requirements and management of dairy sheep and goats are similar to those for meat animals, machine or hand milking to harvest milk for further processing introduces several conditions that are unique to dairy animals.

Those include the design, sanitation, and maintenance of milking parlors and milk handling and storage equipment; frequent animal movement and handling; continuous udder care; increased risk of mastitis; artificial rearing of offspring to prevent them from competing for milk that can be harvested for processing; manipulating nutrition to increase and sustain milk yield; and nutrient intervention to exert some degree of influence on milk quality. Before research and teaching programmes with dairy sheep and goats are initiated, each element of dairy production should be evaluated so that the health and well-being of the sheep and goats are ensured.

ZOONOTIC DISEASES

Zoonotic diseases, the risk of acquiring zoonotic diseases, how to reduce the likelihood of acquiring a zoonotic disease, and the signs, symptoms, and treatment of common zoonotic diseases should be explained to people who work with sheep and goats in research and teaching.

PREDATOR CONTROL

In certain geographic locations and during certain seasons, protection from predators is an important part of providing adequate care for sheep and goats. Nonlethal means of predator control are preferable but may be inadequate. Special fencing such as electrified netting may be used to exclude some predators from livestock pastures. Lethal means of control are appropriate when necessary to reduce injury and loss of sheep and goats.

Federal, state, and local laws and ordinances must be followed. Animal and Plant Health Inspection Service, Wildlife Services, USDA, which provides expertise for resolving wildlife conflicts and protecting agricultural resources, is an important source of information and may be contacted to assist with developing effective and legal predator control programmes.

INTENSIVE LABORATORY ENVIRONMENTS

Certain laboratory settings do not allow for or utilize any range or pasture. These environments may include traditional outdoor feedlot operations, indoor/outdoor operations, or entirely indoor housing with natural or manufactured surfaces and several bedding possibilities. Some research and teaching objectives require sheep and goats to be housed under intensive laboratory conditions.

Sheep and goats that are used for intensive procedures requiring prolonged restraint, frequent sampling, complete collection of feces and urine, or other procedures may experience less stress if they are pretrained and adapted to their intensively managed environments. Sheep and goats may be kept in pens, metabolism stalls, stanchions, respiration chambers, or environmental chambers to facilitate these procedures.

Sheep and goats are social animals and prefer companionship when they are housed. In general, sheep and goats should not be housed alone in intensive environments, and they should be able to maintain visual contact with other animals. Only under scientifically justified and approved protocols that dictate isolation should this type of housing be considered for sheep and goats.

A common and beneficial practice is to shear sheep and fibre-producing goats before they are moved to intensive laboratory conditions; this improves animal and facility hygiene, often prevents reductions in feed consumption, and reduces the size of the animals, effectively providing more usable space per animal. If sheep and goats are managed under intensive laboratory conditions for extended periods, a hoof-care programme should be developed and followed. Sheep and goats housed in intensive laboratory environments should be kept clean and dry, and excreta should be removed on an appropriate schedule to achieve clean animals. Pens and stalls should be washed thoroughly at the beginning of every experimental period and as needed thereafter. Collection vessels for feces and urine depend on the design and construction of the units. Cleanliness should be maintained, and fly infestations should be avoided.

Pens, stalls, and stanchions should be large enough to allow sheep and goats to stand up and lie down without difficulty and to maintain normal standing and lying postures. The activity of sheep and goats maintained in intensive laboratory environments is restricted, and animals in these environments should be observed at least daily. The period of time that sheep and goats may be maintained in these environments before removal to a larger space for additional exercise should be based on professional judgment and experience.

The IACUC should carefully evaluate studies that require sheep and goats to be housed in intensive laboratory environments; particular attention should be given to the duration that activity is restricted. Opportunities for regular exercise should be provided if exercise does not affect the experimental protocol. For sheep and goats housed in intensive environments, one should pay particular attention to appetite, fecal and urinary output, and soundness of feet and legs.

The floor surface of pens in intensive laboratory environments is likely to be less abrasive than the ground surface of outdoor enclosures, and the reduced activity of sheep and goats in intensive laboratory environments may limit hoof wear. Thus, the frequency of hoof trimming may be greater when sheep and goats are housed in intensive laboratory environments.

Another aspect of intensive laboratory environments that should be addressed is unwanted animals and vermin, such as birds, rodents, insects, and feral cats. Whether it is in a complete indoor laboratory environment, a feedlot, or confined barn-type housing, vermin can be sources of disease for sheep and goats. Depending on the type of operation, studies, and production environment, local management or the IACUC should review the need for adequate pest-control measures.

Birds nest and roost in barns and can spread diseases to sheep and goats. Adequate bird control measures may include netting or flaps at openings into buildings and an overall elimination of perching areas where possible. For rodents, which may vector a number of specific diseases, establishing a monitoring and trapping programme should be considered. Rodent attractants should be kept to a minimum or eliminated where possible. For insects where fly strike can be a concern or mosquitoes that can transmit viral agents such as West Nile virus, an active removal and destruction programme should be considered. As always, the local management or governing IACUC is responsible for reviewing each programme and determining whether such measures are necessary or appropriate for the animals under their care.

TRANSGENICS AND CLONING

Transgenics as a technology was initially pioneered with mice, with the production of the first transgenic sheep, pigs, and goats following soon thereafter. Since then, the field has expanded considerably, and transgenic animals have become commonplace in many programmes and facilities. The applications for transgenic animals are vast with utility not only in the investigation of gene function but also for development of animal models, increased disease resistance, altered or enhanced production traits, and production of proteins in several biological fluids such as milk, blood, urine, and semen·

Transgenics and cloning bring additional and unique aspects of care, health, and welfare for sheep and goats. Specifically, a thorough understanding of normal endogenous gene function and homeostasis is required to increase the likelihood of detecting abnormal gene function, often manifested as abnormal sheep and goat physiology from exogenously introduced transgenes or constructs, which may occur in some animals. Additionally, carrying a transgene in a homozygous state may elicit abnormalities or lethal conditions not seen in the hemizygous state. Another concern relates to whether the protein being produced as a result of a transgene is already found endogenously in sheep or goats or whether the protein is novel to the transgenic animal.

Understanding the function of the protein is important for anticipating the potential for adverse effects on the animal. In some cases, the diet must be modified or fortified to provide increased concentrations of specific nutrients or classes of nutrients. With the development of cloning technology, nuclear transfer has become the preferred method for propagating transgenic sheep and goats and cloning has improved the overall efficiency of the process.

However, cloning by nuclear transfer has created additional health concerns in a small percentage of animals. For example, fetal survival may be decreased, with an increased in utero loss rate through resorption or an increased rate of abortions if fetal loss is during late pregnancy. Protocols should address the possibility of increased fetal loss and describe the appropriate care for the animals and situations.

The potential for abnormal physiology, without or with clinical signs, in transgenic and cloned animals may continue after birth and into the neonatal and early prepubertal periods. In some large-animal species, renal, cardiac, respiratory, hepatic, hematopoietic, and immune system abnormalities have been documented. However, if the small percentage of animals with these physiological abnormalities can be clinically supported over time as the animals grow, many of the abnormalities resolve, and the animals can lead normal and healthy lives. Protocols should recognize these potential abnormalities and contain clear plans for addressing them should they occur. Research results, risk assessment, and regulatory guidance for meat, milk, reproductive efficiencies, and other variables indicate that most cloned animals are normal and healthy.

Subsequent generations of animals produced from first-generation clones have been studied, and they do not seem likely to have the health-related issues observed in a small percentage of original clones. Indeed, passage through the germ line may reverse abnormal patterns that are detected at the DNA level in first-generation clones.

Nevertheless, appropriate monitoring of subsequent generations would address the possibility that abnormal patterns may not be corrected in subsequent offspring. Production of transgenic sheep and goats using microinjection or nuclear transfer are no longer scientific research endeavors and are now established production systems.

However, this field of research and development is still relatively young, and the full nature and extent of the potential effects of cloning by nuclear transfer on animal health and welfare have not yet been revealed.

Operations or institutions that house and care for transgenic sheep or goats should be prepared for and capable of handling the issues that are associated with these animals and the increased oversight required from a regulatory perspective. Thus, the local management or governing IACUC must be responsible for reviewing each programme and determining whether animal care and use standards and practices should exceed the usual standards and practices.

ALLERGENS OF SHEEP AND GOATS

Allergens related to sheep are not very common. There are reports of dermatitis due to handling sheep's wool and contact with sheep or wool. There are no known caprine allergens that affect humans.

10

Housing of Cattle

OVERVIEW OF PRODUCTION SYSTEMS

Each production system-veal calf, suckling calf, dairy bred calf, steer and heifer-implies different rearing, management and housing systems. The calves will be reared with their destination in mind. For the different systems the rearing period and the corresponding feeding system will be extended over a shorter or a longer period depending on productivity targets. Each enterprise may require a specific type of housing and, in some cases, rules are imposed for animal comfort as in the situation of organic production systems.

CATEGORIES OF PRODUCTION SYSTEMS

Veal Calves:

- *Feeding*: Based on whole milk or milk replacer.
- *Housing*: Individual pen or collective pens (with automatic milk feeder)
- Slaughtered when they reach about 110 to 250 kg

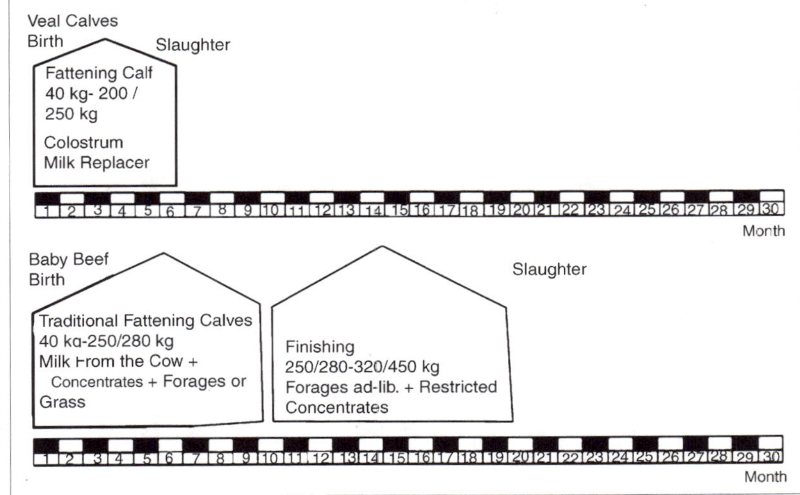

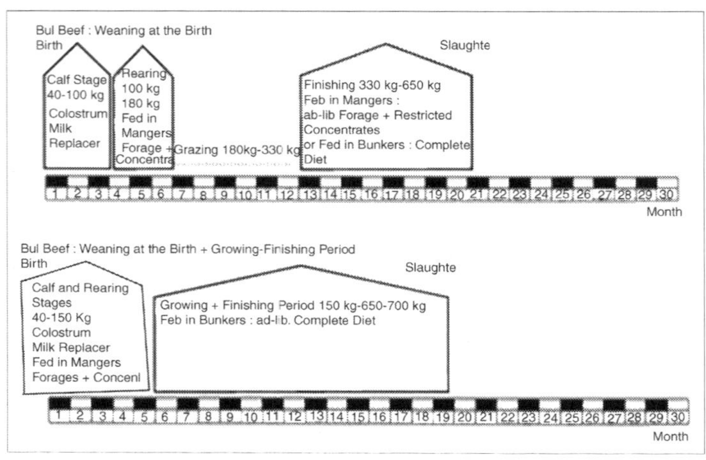
Bul Beef : Weaning at the Birth
Birth
Calf Stage 40-100 kg Colostrum Milk Replacer
Rearing 100 kg 180 kg Fed in Mangers Forage + Concentra
Grazing 180kg-330 kg
Finishing 330 kg-650 kg Feb in Mangers : ab-lib Forage + Restricted Concentrates or Fed in Bunkers : Complete Diet
Slaughte
1 2 3 4 5 6 7 8 9 10 11 12 13 14 15 16 17 18 19 20 21 22 23 24 25 26 27 28 29 30
Month
Bul Beef : Weaning at the Birth + Growing-Finishing Period
Birth
Calf and Rearing Stages 40-150 Kg Colostrum Milk Replacer Fed in Mangers Forages + Concenl
Growing + Finishing Period 150 kg-650-700 kg Feb in Bunkers : ad-lib. Complete Diet
Slaughte
1 2 3 4 5 6 7 8 9 10 11 12 13 14 15 16 17 18 19 20 21 22 23 24 25 26 27 28 29 30
Month

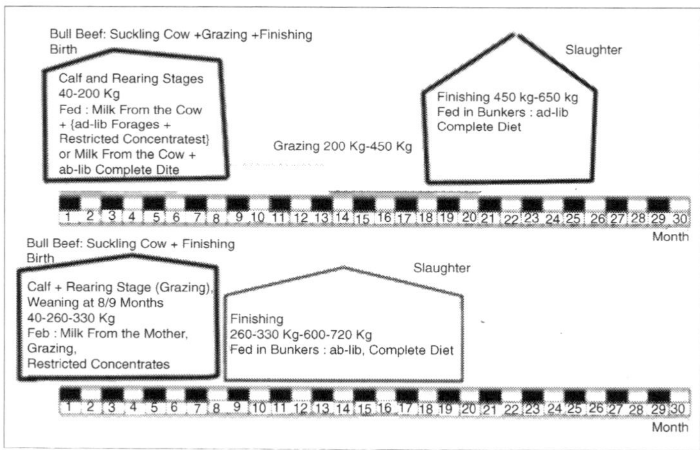
Bull Beef: Suckling Cow +Grazing +Finishing
Birth
Calf and Rearing Stages 40-200 Kg Fed : Milk From the Cow + {ad-lib Forages + Restricted Concentratest} or Milk From the Cow + ab-lib Complete Dite
Grazing 200 Kg-450 Kg
Finishing 450 kg-650 kg Fed in Bunkers : ad-lib Complete Diet
Slaughter
1 2 3 4 5 6 7 8 9 10 11 12 13 14 15 16 17 18 19 20 21 22 23 24 25 26 27 28 29 30
Month
Bull Beef: Suckling Cow + Finishing
Birth
Calf + Rearing Stage (Grazing), Weaning at 8/9 Months 40-260-330 Kg Feb : Milk From the Mother, Grazing, Restricted Concentrates
Finishing 260-330 Kg-600-720 Kg Fed in Bunkers : ab-lib, Complete Diet
Slaughter
1 2 3 4 5 6 7 8 9 10 11 12 13 14 15 16 17 18 19 20 21 22 23 24 25 26 27 28 29 30
Month

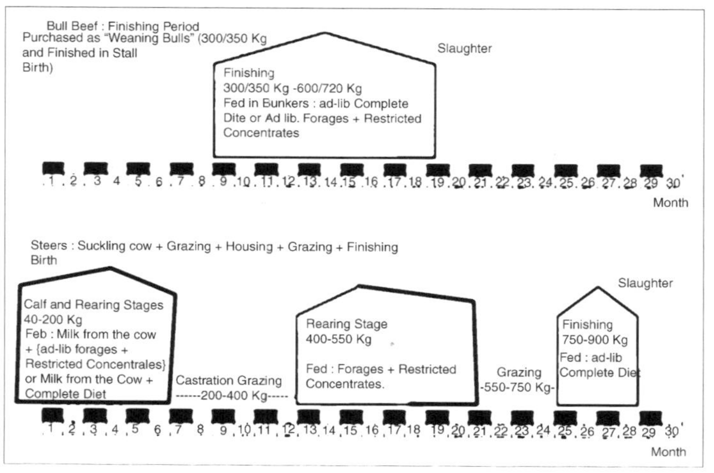
Bull Beef : Finishing Period
Purchased as "Weaning Bulls" (300/350 Kg and Finished in Stall Birth)
Finishing 300/350 Kg -600/720 Kg Fed in Bunkers : ad-lib Complete Dite or Ad lib. Forages + Restricted Concentrates
Slaughter
1 2 3 4 5 6 7 8 9 10 11 12 13 14 15 16 17 18 19 20 21 22 23 24 25 26 27 28 29 30
Month
Steers : Suckling cow + Grazing + Housing + Grazing + Finishing
Birth
Calf and Rearing Stages 40-200 Kg Feb : Milk from the cow + {ad-lib forages + Restricted Concentrales} or Milk from the Cow + Complete Diet
Castration Grazing ------200-400 Kg-----
Rearing Stage 400-550 Kg Fed : Forages + Restricted Concentrates.
Grazing -550-750 Kg-
Finishing 750-900 Kg Fed : ad-lib Complete Diet
Slaughter
1 2 3 4 5 6 7 8 9 10 11 12 13 14 15 16 17 18 19 20 21 22 23 24 25 26 27 28 29 30
Month

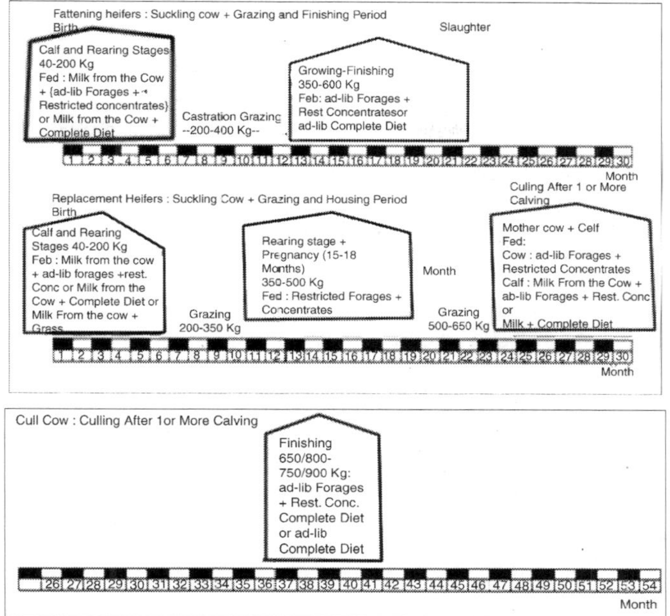

Fig. Schematic Representation of the Different Categories of Production Systems

Suckling Calves:

- *Feeding:* Natural suckling, complemented with concentrates (when grazing and indoors) if they are to grow to adult age
- *Housing*: With their mothers in cubicles or others loose housing
- Reared to become replacement animals or to be fattened.
- Slaughtered at about 200-250 kg

Bull Calves:

- Reared in groups until weaned.
- *Feeding:* Milk replacer automatically or manually distributed
- *Housing*: Group housing
- Slaughtered at about 11 to 15 months

Bull Beef:

- First period.
- *Second Period:* Fattened until they are slaughtered
- *Feeding:* Silage and concentrates from troughs
- *Housing:* Usually in small groups (no more than 20 animals per group)
- Slaughtered at about 18 months

Steers:

- Castrated animals, from suckling calves or dairy bred calves
- *First Period*: Fed on their mothers' milk or artifical milk, then gradually turned to concentrates and forages.

- *Housing*: With their mothers
- *Second Period*: After the weaning and castration, fed on grass and kept out doors
- *Third Period (Finishing)*: Fed on concentrates and usually housed in free stalls.
- Slaughtered between 24 and 30 months.

Heifers:

- Heifers are reared along the same pattern as bull calves or steers.

Cull Cows:

- Cull cows may be fattened after when milk production ceases on the same pattern as steers.

Suckler Cows:

- Although not directly reared for beef, suckler cows are an essential link along the production line and hold a very important role in the production system.
- The quality of the animals produced depends on the quality of the suckler herd.
- *Feeding:* Grass and some concentrates if necessary during the summertime; silage, hay and concentrates during the wintertime.
- *Housing:* Outdoors in the summertime; indoors, inside the barns (loose housing) in the wintertime.

HOUSING FACILITIES REQUIRED FOR GOOD MANAGEMENT

In beef production, the calf remains with its mother from birth until weaning, which may occur at the age of 2 to 6 weeks or at the age of 2 to 6 months, and sometimes more. During the time with its mother, the calf is fed by its mother and has the opportunity to eat concentrates, hay or forages.

In dairy production (and sometimes in beef production), weaning may occur at birth or just a few hours after birth (10 to 36 hours). The new-born calf receives colostrum, then milk for a few days or weeks, and then milk replacer. In beef production this occurs mainly in the double muscled breeds in order to decrease mortality at a very young age.

Period from 0 to 6 Months: Calves Weaned at Birth

At birth, the calf has no immunity against the infectious germs living in the environment. It will be immunized passively by the mother's colostrum. Afterwards, the calf will progressively build its own immunity by contact with the germs (infectious and non-infectious) of the environment. The new-born can be separated from its mother and other animals immediately after the birth in order to avoid a contamination with infectious germs, which are generally passed on from older animals to younger ones.

The calf should be housed lonely so as to avoid any possible contact with contagious animals that might contaminate it. Individual hutches placed outdoors make it possible to remove the calf from the other animals in the first minutes after birth. Besides, it is recommended to take the calf outdoors as soon as it is dry and it has received colostrum. The new-born calf may stay with its mother for 1 to 3 days to give him the opportunity to build relationship with its mother. The hygiene of the pen and the provision of colostrum immediately after the birth are of great importance to protect the health of the new-born calf. The calves must be kept in accordance with regional regulation of animal welfare.

Provision of Colostrum

As soon as possible after birth the calf should be given colostrum with the aim of acquiring immediate protection against various infectious diseases and to be assured the calf has received the recommended amount.

Provision of Milk

Milk or milk replacer can be distributed manually or by automatic milk feeder. In this case, calves are brought together within a period of 3 to 4 weeks to have 20 to 30 calves per group or pen. The amounts of distributed milk may be adjusted to the particular needs of any calf.

Housing in Individual Pens

During the period that calves are fed on milk (whole milk or milk replacer), which lasts for about 2 months, it is preferable to adopt single housing so that feed consumption may be checked (both milk and dry feeds such as cereals, concentrates...). The optimal weaning time may be fixed but delayed if necessary when it appears that the calf does not eat the amount of concentrates required to satisfy its needs when milk is no longer supplied. An obligation of the EU is to bring animals into physical contact with their equals.

In non-EU countries, the regulation of animal welfare must be taken into account. To prevent spreading of diseases, it is recommended to limit the number of calves having physical contacts to two or three. Physical contacts give the opportunity for calves to suckle ears, navels and teats, which may lead to deformations and sometimes even cause infections.

Group Housing

Housing several calves (8-10) together might only be considered if the animals are of the same size. Calves can be housed in groups from the age of one week with appropriate management to reduce the negative effect of competition.

Dehorning

To prevent accidents with the persons involved in animal care and animal handling and injuries to the other animals, it is recommended to dehorn the animals at a very young age by burning with a proprietary heating element by specially trained staff. Local anaesthesia may be required by legislation in specific countries.

Cleaning and Disinfection

Between successive uses, it is absolutely necessary to clean and disinfect the pens or the hutches. Moreover, it is highly recommended to let the pen or the hutch remain empty for about two weeks for health reasons.

Period from 0 to 6 Months: Calves Remaining with their Mothers

Calving

It is highly recommended to let the cow calve alone in a pen with enough surface and bedding material (fresh straw of good quality...) but close to her herd mates to prevent stress.

Provision of Colostrum

Normally the new-born calf nurses within a short time after birth. But the calf may not drink enough colostrum to receive a strong protection against infectious diseases. It is advisable, especially when the calf is weak or calving has been difficult, to give the calf additional colostrum as soon as possible after the birth.

Fattening Animals

Unusual Behaviour

There is a real social order among male uncastrated animals. In feed lot systems, the consequences will be controlled through providing a large area and limiting the number of animals in that area. On the other hand, aggressive behaviour is likely to occur with small groups.

Thus, it is necessary to:

- Check regularly that no animal is kept away from the group. It may become necessary to remove a weak animal.
- Dehorn all the animals.
- Provide sufficient area.

Grouping Strategies

- Groups should be formed after watching the behaviour of the animals during first stage of the rearing.

- Groups should be homogeneous in terms of weight and height at the withers of the animals and behaviour to avoid possible accidents, especially since mounting is impossible to avoid in that type of production.

Sufficient Area

Whatever the type of animal, minimum areas should be provided. When animal density exceeds recommended standards, diseases and injuries are likely to occur.

A Healthy Environment

Disease hazards remain high and environment standards should strictly be respected to reduce possible infections.

Treatment against the External Parasites

When the animals enter the barns for fattening or winter time, it is recommended to treat them against the external parasites living in their hair. To improve the effectiveness of chemicals used to destroy parasites it can be useful to shave the animals to remove long hair. If the barn is inadequately ventilated, removing the hair will help the animals regulating their body temperature.

DESIGNING FACILITIES TO MEET ANIMAL NEEDS

At present, it is generally agreed that the basic requirements for welfare of livestock are:

- The provision of readily accessible fresh water and nutritionally adequate food as required;
- Adequate freedom of movement and ability to stretch limbs;
- Sufficient light for satisfactory inspection;
- The rapid diagnosis and treatment of injury and disease;
- Emergency provision in the event of a breakdown of essential mechanical equipment;
- Flooring which neither harms nor causes undue strain;
- The avoidance on unnecessary mutilation.

Fig. Natural Lying Positions

BEHAVIOUR

Over thirty years ago discussions about animal welfare led to basic rights for animals being formulated in the Brambell Report. This report recognised certain basic physical needs in relation to housing.

These were the right of an animal to have sufficient freedom of movement to allow it to get up; lie down; groom normally; turn around; and stretch its limbs, without difficulty. Since Brambell, much research has been done to clarify behavioural needs or goals.

Work of relevance to the achievement of behavioural goals, which are fixed in the animal, deserves special mention. Animal motivation and the functional consequences of behavioural processes are the most important aspects, since they play an important role in evaluating animal welfare and predicting and controlling the underlying environmental conditions that influence behaviour.

Motivation

Cattle are highly motivated to rest, feed, drink and move around. However, the need for an animal to carry out a certain behaviour at a certain time is still not clear. This model, an animal always tries to proceed from the present situation (Existing value) to the goal (Required value). Only when the goal can be reached, the behaviour will end in an appropriate way and welfare will be assured.

Functional Consequences

When an animal is motivated, it will perform one or more behaviour patterns. The HUGHES and DUNCAN model of foraging behaviour, proper functional consequences are the main reason for an animal ceasing the behaviour. Therefore, creating opportunities for appetite behaviour alone (one part of the total foraging process) is not enough. This simply strengthens the animal's motivation but does not allow the animal to achieve satiation. Even the presence of the means to achieve a behavioural goal is not always enough; since providing a food supply for even a short duration will also strengthen motivation. Only completing the whole cycle (in foraging this means allowing satiation to be achieved) leads to a longer term decrease of motivation.

Predictability and Controllability

The predictability and controllability of environmental conditions should be included in any discussion about behavioural needs. They are of crucial importance in evaluating stress. Control of environment factors; *e.g.*, those influencing social interactions and feeding times, should be optimal. The predictability of response to certain behaviour should be high and there should be opportunities for synchronisation to avoid frustration or competition.

Stress

This has to be at the correct level. Too little stress can be just as harmful as too much. Intelligent animals need a complex and changing environment just as much as they need predictability and controllability. Besides ethological and physiological disturbances, excessive stress can also have negative effects on the animal's immune system and make animals more sensitive to infectious disease. Boredom can exactly have the same effect.

Housing submissive animals in a building with insufficient space can create a chronic stress, because they fear close contacts with dominant animals and undergoing severe aggressions from their herdmates. The climatic environment can cause stress since animals may have difficulties maintaining their body temperature. The unfriendly herdsman behaviour will enhance the animal fear and stress, especially if he comes too close to the animal.

HEALTH

In many cases, concern about welfare is largely about the physical health of the animals and the economic consequences of their health. However, even if consideration is confined to the very limited issue of keeping the animals free from costly diseases, the situation will be far from simple. Disease is generally multifactorial and housing is only one of many factors involved.

Furthermore, housing cannot be considered as a single factor, since a housing system can comprise a number of different designs and might include or exclude details that influence the incidence of a certain disease. What can be done is to find out how some detail is involved in the disease; *e.g.* how does the length of a stall or the area of the straw yard per animal affect contamination of the lying area and how does such contamination influence the incidence of mastitis within suckling cows.

Even with such information one must be careful since a different stall design might well have features that would alter the desired length, or the incidence of mastitis might rely more on other factors (*e.g.*, immune status, productivity or feeding) than on contamination of the lying area.

Consequently, predicting the consequence of all the details combined in any one housing system can only be speculative. In the unnaturally dense populations of housed farm animals, the risk of infection will be high. To some extent, this elevated risk can be counteracted by an increase in activity of the animals' immune systems. It is a question of getting the balance right. What is required is a level of infection that allows animals to develop immunity to disease, but not such a high level that it causes disease in animals with immunity.

Non infectious contaminants, such as inert dust particles and ammonia gas, can also harm animals by causing damage to the respiratory defence mechanism. Such agents can make the animal less resistant to infection allergies. In beef production, the facultative pathogens normally living in the air and causing respiratory diseases will become dangerous only, if they find favourable conditions: animal overcrowding, high air humidity, air with too many dust particles, draughts, excessively high air temperature, etc.

To prevent diseases, it is advisable to limit the number of facultative pathogens living in the air because it is not possible to destroy them completely. Good ventilation and a favourable animal occupation density are two important measures to prevent respiratory diseases. To prevent contagions within the herd it is recommended to isolate ill animals as soon as possible although it is difficult to have enough room or pens for them.

The cohabitation of animals of various age and the bringing together of animals coming from different farms represent a situation with many risks. A quarantine practice (facilities + management) for purchased animals is advisable to diminish the risk of disease outbreak. Number of animals per pen should not be higher than 12 to prevent social pressure: submissive animals are frequently disturbed by dominant animals. Control of microbe populations and comfortable housing are the two major points to preserve the beef cattle health.

HOUSING SYSTEMS

In many modern beef units animals are kept indoors all the year round. Therefore, it is important to ensure that, what ever housing system is provided, behavioural needs (*e.g.* resting, feeding and drinking) are properly met. In loose housing systems, the freedom of movement of the animals means that both individual and group behaviours must be satisfied.

Resting

In loose housing systems cattle rest for many hours per day. Resting behaviour depends on various factors including times of feeding, feeding frequency and management. Resting time is divided into lying time without sleep and lying time with total muscle relaxation sleep. For the latter, the cattle should be able to lie down with its head resting on and supported by the shoulder, so that the neck muscles can relax. To avoid disturbance and ensure suitable opportunities for resting, enough space should be available for each animal.

Cattle spend about 50 per cent of their time lying, for about 10-15 periods per day, each of about 60-80 minutes duration. The duration of each lying period is influenced by the housing environment but total lying time seems to be fixed. An animal will not stay recumbent for too long before it becomes uncomfortable. This is because the large body weight of heavy animals causes high pressures to be imposed on those parts of the body that are in contact with the ground.

Lying entirely on one side is only possible for about 10-15 minutes at a time. This is because the pressures exerted cause disturbances in pulmonary blood flow and the disposal of rumen gases. For socially gregarious animals like beef cattle, synchronisation is important to their behaviour and competition in groups. To avoid competition in communal lying areas, there should be enough space for all animals to find a resting place and to lie down together. If cubicles are used there should be a cubicle for each animal.

Increasing the floor space per animal in growing-finishing period from to 2.0 to 4.2 sq m for example resulted in appreciably greater daily weight gain. As a consequence of insufficient lying area there may be an increase in aggression and/or disturbances of behavioural rhythms (eating and resting times). In addition, animals that are unable to lie down will spend significantly longer time standing and will have an increased lying requirement when they do lie down. Animals lying on slatted floor may show abnormal standing and lying behaviour. Abnormal standing up and lying down are caused primarily by factors associated with a hard floor.

Feeding

Cattle spend many hours per day eating. If the feed is fed restrictively, there should be sufficient feeding places for all animals to feed at the same time to avoid competition, frustration and aggression. Any restriction in number of places may result in low-ranking animals receiving insufficient feed and, as a consequence, their daily weight gain will be too low or they may lose excessive weight. If the feed is fed ad libitum and if there is one eating place per two or three animals, each animal will have enough time to eat all the feed it needs. If roughage is fed ad libitum and concentrates restrictively, there should be sufficient feeding places to feed the concentrates to all animals at the same time.

Drinking

Drinkers should be located where they are easily accessible. They should not be located where it is impossible for submissive animals to leave when a dominant animal approaches, *e.g.* in corners or at the end of a passage. There should be enough room around the drinkers to avoid difficulties for animals to drink. Care must be taken to ensure that the drinker will not be fouled with faeces or urine.

When the straw is spread it is recommended to ensure it is not to throw it into the drinkers. The cleanliness of the water and of the drinkers and the functionning of the drinkers should be checked every day. Good functionning of the drinkers is especially important for animals being fed a feed with a high dry matter content. Freezing of the drinkers should be prevented during the cold days, especially if animals receive dry feed.

Locomotion

Floors should not be slippery when beef cattle walk or move on them. Any slips that occur during, or as a result of, confrontations can bring the animals into a state of chronic stress. Slippery floors can also cause beef cattle to reduce their movement, grooming activities and mounting activities. Movement difficulties can cause irregular hoof wearing and lameness.

Group Size

In buildings the groups are made on basis of sex (no males with females except for reproductive purposes), age of animals (bulls of the same age and weight, calves or heifers of the same age and weight), reproductive purposes (mother cows with their calves with or with-out a bull), diet, future of the animals (fattening, breeding..), physiology status (pregnant cows, cull cows)... To prevent disturbances with fattening bulls (excitation, bellowing) and low growing performance it is recommended to house the bulls in a building without females.

To prevent aggressiveness and negative effects of hierarchy problems it is recommended to regroup animal of the same age in group of limited size (10 to 12 bulls in the same pen, 12 to 16 cows with their calves in the same pen...). If the calves are with their mother, it is necessary to have a separated pen accessible only to calves: calves should be able to move freely or during limited periods to their mother, not the opposite. In practice, group size depends on management factors such as herd supervision and feeding. The formation by the farmer of smaller groups within a herd is usually based on factors such as age of the animals, weight, sex and diet.

Hygiene

Every effort should be made to prevent animals from becoming dirty. It is most important to keep the beef cattle lying area clean, which can be achieved by correct design and by sufficient use of bedding material. If animals are dirty, they will be uncomfortable, development of (ekto-)parasites in their coat could be increased, heat losses could be increased and their market value could be decreased. The use of bedding and the frequency of cleaning and adding new bedding are important for the hygiene of the lying area.

Walking areas should also be kept reasonably dry and clean since any dirt picked up on the hoof will be deposited on the lying area and will soil the animal. In addition, dirty hind legs may be in contact with the udder when the suckling cow is lying. A dirty udder can cause suckling problems with the calves. Wet and dirty walking areas will also reduce the durability of the hoof horn and make the beef cattle susceptible to foot diseases.

Animal Injuries

In loose housing two kinds of injuries are common: leg or claw injuries and other surface injuries. Floors have to be designed to prevent leg and claw injuries and to realise sufficient wear of the hoof to avoid overgrowth of the hoof. It is important to trim the claws as often as necessary. Other surface injuries mainly result from aggressive behaviour, often aggravated by too little space being provided for submissive animals to escape and inadequate equipment design. Emphasis on adequate dimen-sioning of all areas and on optimal equipment is therefore essential.

Aggressive behaviour furthermore strongly depends on the quality of herd management, especially on the feeding regime and the ability of the herdsman. The dehorning of animals, especially of males, decreases the aggressiveness, decreases the consequences of aggressiveness and prevents animal injuries caused by the horns. Dehorning diminishes the danger for man during animal handling.

ENVIRONMENT AND HEALTH

Air Quality and Ventilation

In well ventilated barns the air generally is of good quality and is not the cause of respiratory diseases. In livestock buildings, animals are densely stocked, floors may be covered with faeces and urine, underfloor slatted tanks may hold stored slurry and there can be large quantities of dusty feed and bedding. As a consequence the air in these buildings heavily can be contaminated with inorganic dust, spores, moulds, bacterial and viral organisms, gases, vapours and other pollutants.

Airborne particles may cause infections, al-lergies and other responses while gases and vapours may be poisons, asphixiants, or irritants. These aerial pollutants may be very small or invisible and may not smell; indeed one may not know they exist. They are easily inhaled. In cattle buildings, the most dramatic effect of air pollution is seen in young calves. These animals, with their immature immune systems, cannot resist the massive challenge of airborne infectious agents and serious respiratory problems are common.

Adult animals are more resistant and able to tolerate such aerial contaminants. However, while adult animals seldom exhibit clinical symptoms of respiratory disease, their production performance or general health status might be diminished. Little is known about such relationships, but it is clear that amongst people working for prolonged periods in intensive animal buildings there is a high incidence of chronic respiratory disease.

In housing for beef cattle, air hygiene problems are easy to solve. Because beef cattle can tolerate cold conditions, high ventilation rates can be employed to dilute and remove contaminated air from buildings.

However, very young calves can require special measures to prevent diseases caused by low environmental temperature. If the calves are not nursing, it will be recommended to keep calves apart of the cows *e.g.* outside the barn in hutches. Natural ventilation of buildings by wind effect allows air quality to be maintained at a low economic cost.

Light

Illumination is important in housing, since animals need to see so they can behave normally, *e.g.* move, feed, or lie. It is also important for the stockman so he can inspect and care for the animals. Minimum levels of illumination (lux) are often recommended for men carrying out routine tasks and such illumination may be provided by artificial or natural light. Because natural light is cheaper, it is recommended often that an area of translucent material must be provided in the roof or walls. If in the roof, a translucent area equivalent to 8 to 10 per cent of the floor area is recommended. If in the walls, a translucent area 10 to 15 per cent of the floor area is recommended. The exact areas will be dictated by the location and orientation of the particular building with respect to the sun, especially for buildings fully occupied during the summer season.

In buildings with large areas of openings for ventilation, these alone may suffice for natural lighting. For artificial illumination, one can recommend 250 lux for calving, treatment and calf pens, and 150 lux for the rest of the building. Reproduction can be affected by light. Considerable evidence exists to show that changes in light intensity and day length, reflecting changes in season, affect the reproduction of mammals. Allowing natural daylight into buildings will allow beef cattle to recognise such change. Solar radiation (sunlight) directly impinging on animals can warm them in cold conditions but may contribute to heat stress in hot conditions. Direct sunlight, through the biochemical and thermal effects of specific parts of its spectrum, can kill many biological organisms and hence promotes hygiene and health. Consequently, there are good reasons to make provision for the entry of daylight and sunlight, except when shade is required in hot conditions, into cattle buildings.

THE HERDSMAN

The welfare of beef cattle will be influenced by the treatment they receive from the herdsman (man or woman). It is important that the presence of humans does not cause fright or induce stress reactions. The good herdsman will adopt a caring, friendly and predictable attitude towards his animals. The herdsman will himself need good facilities to work with and will need to be relieved of laborious and tedious tasks, if he himself is not to be frustrated or stressed. If the herdsman is stressed, his frustration will often be vented on animals.

While a high level of mechanisation will lessen the burden on the herdsman, it can be counter-productive. In highly mechanised housing systems, for example, the animals may not regard the herdsman as the one, who brings the food but as the one, who carries out veterinary treatments that sometimes are painful for animals. In such situations it is important for herdsman to find other ways, in which his presence will elicit a positive response from the animals. If animals are on pasture, the herdsman will have to visit his animals every day to check the behaviour, the attitude and the health of each animal, and to maintain close contact with animals. He has to check the availability and quality of water. If there is a bull with the cows and the calves, he will have to take all the needed measures to prevent unexpected aggressiveness of the bull and also of the cows, which can act to protect the calves.

IMPORTANT POINTS

Beef cattle should have:

- Freedom of movement
- Sufficient light for normal behaviour and satisfactory inspection
- Sufficient water and feed to meet their requirements
- Complexity and change in their environment to avoid boredom

In loose housing systems:

- Dead end passages should be avoided
- There should be enough lying places or enough area for all animals
- Drinkers readily should be accessible, unobstructed and regularly checked
- Floors should not be slippery and should not cause excessive wearing

ANIMALS, BUILDINGS AND EQUIPMENT DIMENSIONS

BODY DIMENSIONS OF CATTLE

Basic Linear Dimensions

Space requirements for basic behaviours of young stock *e.g.* lying, feed intake or walking depend on body dimensions of animals. Size of animals is defined by the basic measurements H = height at withers, L = diagonal body length and W = width of chest according to *Figure.*

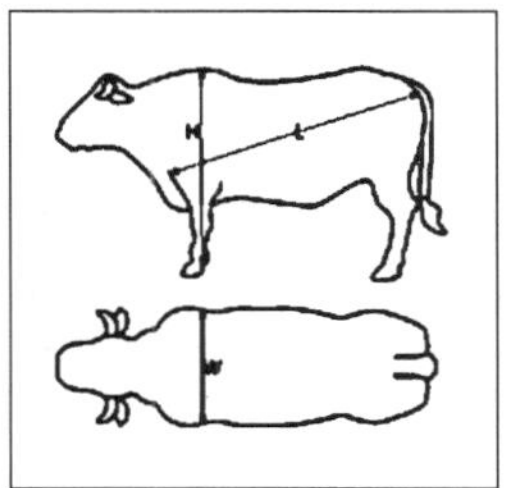

Fig. Body Dimentions of Cattle

Relationship between Body Weight, Age and Body Dimensions

When judging the space requirements of stock, the age of the animal is often used as the criteria for selecting dimensions. The animal's estimated or measured body weight can also be used. As animal's age is always known and their live weight is often known the relationship between age, body weight and body dimensions could be used to determine space requirements for the animals to be housed. However, these relationships considerably can vary between different breeds, different production procedures and between individual animals of the same breed. Accurate data of the body dimensions of beef cattle from all breeds are not available. The results of measurements of the dimen-sions of Brown Swiss heifers of different ages showed a wide range of dimensions, *e.g.* 300 kg heifer had an average bodylength of 1.26 m and a variation from 1.17-1.34 m.

The differences between breeds of equal weight show a larger variation, *e.g.* a Simmental heifer shows a minimum length of 1.14 m and a Holstein Friesian heifer a maximum length of 1.40 m. While the best way to provide recommendations that can be used for practical design work is to find out the body dimensions by measuring some of the animals, agreed standards can be adopted for practical purposes. *Table* gives animal dimensions of beef cattle that can be adapted for practical design work, taking into account that designs should be based on the dimensions of the larger animals in the herd.

Table. CIGR Standard Dimensions of Beef Cattle Related to Body Weight

Weight [kg] W [m]	H [m]	L [m]
200 0.34	1.09	1.17
300 0.40	1.19	1.31
400 0.46	1.27	1.42
500 0.51	1.33	1.51
600 0.55	1.38	1.59
700 0.60	1.42	1.65

In this section only loose housing is considered (because tied housing is not recommended). Loose housing systems provide more comfort for both stockmen and animals and thus improve productivity and welfare. In loose housing usually animals of equal line of production and similar age are kept in groups of at least four to five, usually up to twenty or, in large enterprises, even much more. Two major types of systems will be considered.

Loose Housing

Housing systems without cubicles provide an undivided lying area for all animals of a group. It is possible to design two-area or multiple area pens with littered lying areas or one area pens with deep bedding or without bedding. If no bedding is used, the pen floor will be designed as a fully perforated "slatted" floor or alternatively as a sloped area towards the dung removal system, so that faeces and urine of the animals are moved into or towards slurry tanks or channels by the walking activities of the animals.

Cubicle Housing

Male cattle deposit urine beneath their body thus wetting the bedding material of cubicles. This fact usually excludes male cattle from using cubicle housing systems. Thus cubicle systems are more suitable for female animals. It is important that each animal is provided with a reasonable clean, dry and resilient bed (upon which it can lie). For female beef animals properly designed, constructed and maintained cubicles can satisfy these requirements. Since cubicle houses can work with much or with very little bedding material, they can produce either solid manure or slurry. A disadvantage of the cubicle system is the inflexibility of the cubicles. Because of their fixed dimensions they can't take into account the changing body size of the animals.

LOOSE HOUSING

Beef cattle for practical reasons are usually kept at higher stocking density than cows. This can lead to reduced cleanliness, altered or aggressive behaviour and a higher risk of injury. Space available for bulls mostly is even more restricted especially in fully slatted floor pens. While the reduction of space for movement reduces fighting and mating behaviour, ethological sound systems avoid over crowded pens.

Terminology

One area systems are housing systems (pens) without division of the whole area into parts of different functions. All functions (lying, feeding, exercising, excreting) are carried out in one area. The floor can be fully slatted or solid with or without bedding.

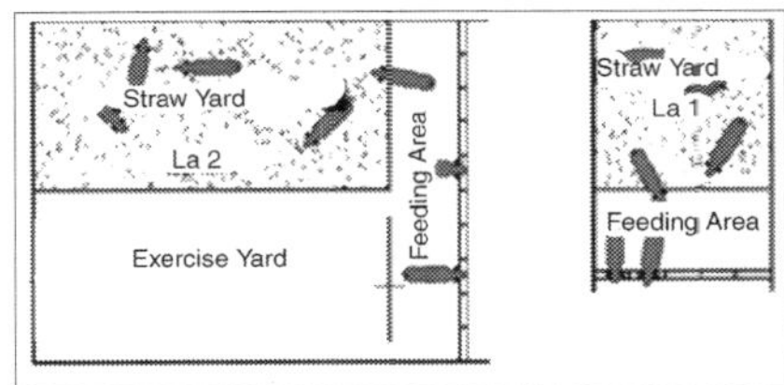

Fig. Three (a) and Two (b) Area Straw Yard Systems

Two area systems consist of the lying area and one other area, with unrestricted access, that provides sufficient space for feeding and exercise. Multiple area systems are those in which more than one area is provided for feeding and exercise. Any of the areas may be provided as uncovered outside yard. The lying area is separated from the other function areas.

Straw yards are unobstructed bedded lying areas for a group of cattle. Bedding is spread on top of the floor, with little (δ 2 per cent) or no gradient, and soiled bedding accumulates in a deep layer, which is removed as necessary. To keep animal clean 1 to 1,2 kg straw/m^2 day is required. Passages will be able to be slatted if the straw bedding is chopped or ground. The feeding area and the exercise yard could be divided or kept in one area.

Sloped floors are unobstructed lying areas for groups of cattle, that may be bedded or not. The floor has a gradient of 5 to 10 per cent and the activity of the animals causes movement of bedding and/or manure down to the bottom of the slope, where it is collected. Straw should be added daily to the highest part of the sloped floor and the cattle will spread it themselves. The feeding area and the dunging alley could also be divided.

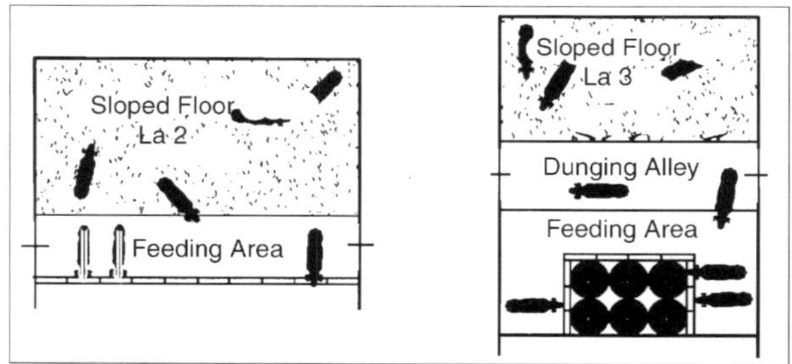

Fig. Two (c) and Three (d) Area Sloped Floor Systems

FLOORS AND WALKING SURFACES

The floor surface provides the interface between the animal and the house and it is of critical importance to the satisfactory performance of the facility as it is the part of the building, with which the animal comes into closest and continuous contact. Floors are multifunctional elements and this can lead to some compromises in their design. The floor must be strong enough to support all the loads from animals and equipment where applicable. In the case of the slatted floor the gap width should be limited to prevent hoof damage but the requirement for efficient drainage will impose minimum requirements on gap dimensions. Surfaces that are too rough can cause abrasions and a rapid wear of animal hooves. A surface, which is too slippery or which has too large a slope can cause injury resulting from falling or reduce the frequency of animal movement so affecting natural behaviour. Other factors such as environmental policies must also be considered *e.g.* the necessity to control ammonia emissions from livestock houses is influencing new floor designs in some countries.

FLOOR TYPES

Different functional areas can be identified in animal accommodation facilities including feeding areas, resting areas and cattle traffic routes Specific floor designs may be selected for the different functional areas *e.g.* solid unbedded feeding passage combined with a straw bedded resting or loafing area.

However, floor systems used in beef cattle houses can be broadly classified into two main types:

1. Solid, unperforated floors that are laid directly on the ground
2. Floors that are suspended above tanks or channels and which are perforated to assist in the drainage of liquids and the passage of faecal material.

Of the solid floors, those constructed of concrete are the most common and solid floors are typically provided with bedding material. For the suspended floors, reinforced concrete is the most common material in use. Pre-cast concrete slats above a slurry pit or channel are the commonest types of suspended floor design.

STRUCTURAL REQUIREMENTS

When specifying floors for beef cattle houses the designer must take into account a range of factors *e.g.* the loadings imposed by animals and equipment, the ability to provide a non-slip surface, the method of cleaning to be used, whether bedding material is available etc. Where concrete is used either as a solid cast insitu floor or as part of a pre-cast floor element, the aggressive nature of the environment imposed on the floor surface resulting from the chemical composition of manure and feed residues places extra demands on the quality of materials used.

In addition the mechanical impact of cleaning systems can place extra loadings of the structure. In response to the special structural demands placed of floor systems several countries have developed national standards for the specification of floor construction for use in cattle housing. These standards cover issues such as structural detailing and construction practice, reinforcement specification and concrete quality.

ANIMAL FLOOR INTERFACE

Many ailments in animals are multifactorial in nature and the floor can be considered to be amongst the causal factors contributing to problems associated with the health of the feet and legs of beef cattle. Flooring can contribute directly, through its physical properties, or indirectly, for example, by allowing (because of poor drainage) disease vectors to be harboured on the floor surface. Hoof disorders in cattle have been linked with the frequency of contact with faeces and urine. However, the predominant effect is through the floor's ability to cause physical injury through the destruction of the physical structure of tissue to the detriment of its functioning or by bone, muscle or ligament damage caused by the animal slipping. These effect sprimarily will be related to the important floor properties of friction, hardness (or softness), abrasive-ness, surface texture (roughness) and surface profile (slope).

Friction

This is measure of the friction between two surfaces, the higher the value the greater the slip resistance.

Normally two coefficients of friction are considered-static coefficient of friction when the body (foot) is at rest and kinetic coefficient of friction when the body (foot) is moving:

1. *Static Coefficient of Friction,* μ_s = The ratio of the resultant friction force (Fs) to the normal reaction (N) when slip is imminent
2. *Kinetic Coefficient of Friction,* μ_k = The ratio of the resultant frictional force in the plane of the interface (Fk) to the normal reaction (N) required to maintain a slip at a given velocity.

The ratio between the horizontal and vertical forces on the hoof, when a cow walks, is between 1:2 and 1:3 and this in turn means that a coefficient of friction of 0.33–0.5 is required. For hard materials the static coefficient of friction, μ_s, is accepted as being greater than the dynamic coefficient of friction, μ_k.

However, for elastic and visco-elastic materials, like rubber, the opposite is true. Indeed the interaction between the hoof and the floor is complicated by the fact that the animal's hoofs are flexible and they act more like an elastomer. For the interaction between a hoof and a floor it has been shown that kinetic coefficient of friction μ_k is the more relevant indicator of slip resistance of livestock floors.

Hardness

The hardness of floor materials may be unavoidable, if they are to perform other functions such as load bearing, resistance to corrosion and damage while being practical and economic in use. Hardness, *per se*, is not a problem. It is its association with other factors, such as high void ratios in slatted floors, which can increase the pressure on feet or other parts of the body, or slipperiness that causes problems. The covering of slats with materials providing a soft contact surface can be considered to alleviate the problem. In the case of solid floors the use of sufficient bedding material improves the animal floor interface. Where bedding material is not available or practical to use the fitting of appropriate mats can be considered.

Abrasiveness

All floors made of conventional materials will be abrasive to some extent.

Indeed for most hoofed animals, floors need to be abrasive to keep the hoof in good condition and prevent over growth. However, floors that are too abrasive can lead to abrasion injury to those parts of the body that come into contact with the floor, particularly knees, hocks and teats.

Surface Texture (Roughness)

The surface texture of the floor is a complex measure that dictates its anti-skid performance.

Occupational safety studies concerned with surface textures in the human working environment have identified two types of roughness vital to skid-resistance:

1. Micro-roughness
2. Macro-roughness

Micro-roughness covers all features less than 0. 5mm in a horizontal direction providing a safe frictional connection between the hoof and the surface. In concrete, micro-roughness is a function of the surface roughness of both the aggregates and the surface mortar. It is reduced over time by the grinding and polishing action of mechanical cleaning equipment and animal movements but these effects can be counteracted by using concretes with high strength and coarse and fine aggregates with a high polishing resistance.

Macro-roughness covers surface features greater than 0.5mm and the provision of adequate macro-roughness is necessary to establish a safe frictional connection between the hoof and the floor when the surface is soiled or wet. Anti-skid performance is particularly improved by features with a maximum size of 10mm. Macro-roughness in animal housing floors can be produced by making impressions in the fresh concrete or by milling/cutting the floor when the concrete has hardened. Animal's hoofs deform when they slide over a rigid surface.

This deformation means that hoof deforms around irregularities in the floor surface, giving rise to a total friction made up of two components. The first is the adhesion component of friction between the hoof and the surface and the second due to the delayed recovery, hysteresis, of the hoof after being deformed by an irregularity. On dry concrete floors, there is some conflict about whether it is smooth or rough surfaces that give the best slip resistance. However, since livestock floors, particularly those over which they are moving, are very likely to be wet, then this of little consequence. Wet floors are effectively covered in a lubricant that is likely to make adhesion component very small. Thus it is the hysteresis component that must be relied upon to give grip. On a smooth surface, a film of liquid (slurry or water) lies on the surface and the hoof cannot come into contact with the floor so slipping occurs.

If the surface has a texture or grooves that allow this liquid film to be squeezed away, rapidly, then the hoof will come into contact with the floor before a slip occurs. These effects are analogous with smooth tyres and aquaplaning in a motor car. A roughened surface, whilst it may allow rapid dispersal of the liquid film, may provide only a small hoof/floor contact area. This can lead to excessive contact pressure and in extreme cases puncturing of the sole of the foot. A surface with appropriate grooving, which allows rapid liquid drainage and provides hysteresis as the foot contacts the groove, is a more acceptable solution. This is analogous to the tread in a car tyre.

Surface Profile

While surface profile has been used in the past by others to describe some of the mechanisms affecting slip already considered above in the context of this exercise surface profile is taken as describing the slope or gradient of the floor. Slope will have obvious effects on drainage from the floor, on floor cleanliness and on the comfort of animals standing, walking and lying on the floor. Steep slopes will obviously allow liquids to drain rapidly from the floor and might prove an aid to cleanliness by ensuring that soiled bedding "flows" down the slope.

However, animals may not be able to stand, walk or lie comfortably on steep slopes. Floor slopes in passageways should not exceed 1:40 (2,5 per cent). In pens where animals lie the slope used will depend on the type of bedding and manure management system utilised. In sloped floor systems, which rely of the movement of animals to transfer soiled bedding to the manure collection area slopes of 1:10 (10 per cent) are required. In facilities where straw remains in the pen a slope of 1:20 (5 per cent) will ensure extraneous liquid is drained to appropriate channels.

FLOORING MATERIALS

All materials used in the construction of floors should be non-toxic to cattle and be resistant to or protected against:

- Chemical attack and deterioration
- Climatic conditions, *e.g.* extremes of temperature, frost, solar radiation
- The effects of pressure washers, etc.
- The effects of gnawing, digging or other animal behaviours

Concrete is the predominant material used for floor construction with the material being in direct contact with the animals where the floor is slatted or no bedding material is used.

Solid Concrete Floors

Concrete used for floors in cattle houses must be designed to be cater for the loads imposed by the animals and vehicles, which are used during feeding and cleaning operations. The surfaces must be resistant to mechanical damage (abrasion, chipping etc.) and chemical attack (manure, feed residues, cleaning chemicals and disinfectants). The floor must provide an impermeable barrier to ensure the safe collection of any effluents produced. There are various national standards regarding the specification of concretes for use in the floors of cattle buildings.

Typically these specify concretes with a characteristic 28 day crushing strength of 30N/mm2 with a minimum cement content of 280kg/m3 and a maximum aggregate size of 20mm. Where the concrete may come in contact with silage effluent the 28 day crushing strength requirement is increased to 40 N/mm2 and the minimum cement content increased to 350kg/m3. The concrete floor should be provided with mesh reinforcement and appropriate movement (expansion and contraction) joints in accordance with national standards.

Floors in areas used by vehicles should not be less than 150 mm thick. Where access is limited to animals the minimum can be reduced to 100 mm but this would not be a general recommendation as the use of the floor may change. Where bedding material is provided the actual animal interface with the floor is modified and the comfort and slip resistance characteristics are those of the bedding material.

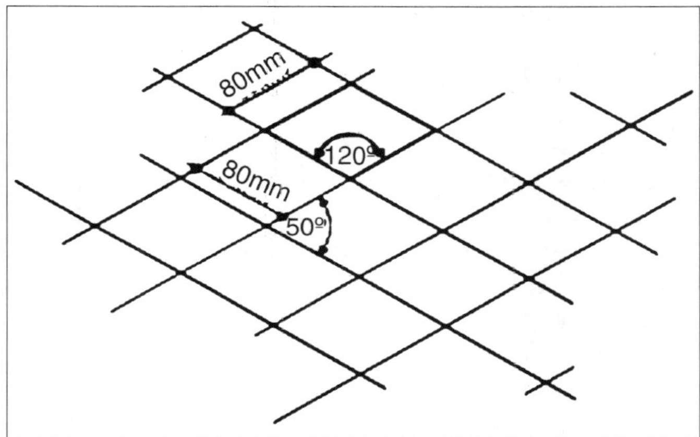

Fig. Grooves in Diamond Pattern

Where animals have direct contact with the surface the recommendations provided in CIGR Design Recommendations for Dairy Cow Housing should be followed. In order to provide slip resistance for cattle walking in all directions and to eliminate the risk of high pressure on the hoof, grooves should be formed in the solid concrete prior to setting in a pattern of rhomb with 80 mm sides as shown in *Figure*.

If this cannot be achieved then parallel grooves spaced at 40 mm between centres should be used. If the direction in which the cattle are likely to be walking is known then the grooves should run at right angles to this as shown in *Figure*. In all cases the grooves should be 10 mm wide and at least 6 mm deep.

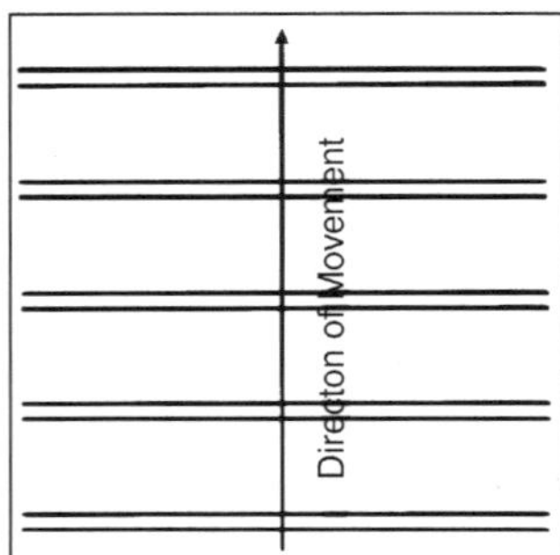

Fig. Grooves in Parallel

Slatted Floors

In areas where bedding material is not readily available combined with the need to reduce labour demands and the necessity to ensure manure is efficiently collected and safely stored has encouraged the development of beef cattle housing systems using slatted floors suspended over manure storage tanks or transfer channels. Slat design has improved and modern facilities are using multi-rib or "gang" slats rather than the single slats that were used in the original units. The resulting floors are more uniform level and provide a potentially better surface in terms of comfort for the animal. The length of slatted elements provided by manufacturers has increased over time and units are now available up to 4.8 m long.

There are variations within the range of slat types produced by different manufacturers in terms of void ratio and this will also influence the comfort aspect of the animal floor interface as well as the drainage characteristics and cleanliness of the animal. The latter is also influenced by feed type and the ventilation system used of the building. The nominal void ratio of different slats is presented in *Table*.

Table. Free Area of Different Slat (Rib and Gap Dimensions in mm)

Rib/Gap (Void Ratio)	125/25 (17)	125/30 (19)	125/35 (22) (24)	125/40 (27)	125/45
	135/25 (16)	135/30 (18)	135/35 (21) (23)	135/40 (25)	135/45
	145/25 (15)	145/30 (17)	145/35 (19) (22)	145/40 (24)	145/45
	150/25 (14)	150/30 (17)	150/35 (19) (21)	150/40 (23)	150/45
	170/25 (13)	170/30 (15)	170/35 (17) (19)	170/40 (21)	170/45

Several nations have developed standards for the design and manufacture of concrete slats for cattle houses *e.g.* British Standard, BS 5502; Irish Standard IS 249. Work is underway to establish an agreed European Standard-Precast Concrete Floor Slats for Livestock. This standard classifies slats according to the type of housed stock and load classes are given according to the animal mass.

Requirements are formulated for concrete mix components and concrete strength, size and position of reinforcement, floor slat geometry, surface characteristics and mechanical strength. As regards durability, the demands are that the water/cement ratio of the concrete should be no more than 0.45 and the cement content should be no less than 350 kg/m^3 at a concrete cover < 40 mm and 300 kg/m^3 at a concrete cover > 40 mm. The water absorption of the concrete (5 per cent quartile) should not exceed 6 per cent by mass. The concrete cover to be applied on the outer reinforcement should be at least 30 mm for reinforced concrete components and 40 mm for prestressed concrete components.

This value can be reduced by 5 mm, if the maximum aggregate particle size does not exceed 20 mm. These standards are still at a draft stage and are in fact exceeded by some present national standards which are presently in place. In some building designs slatted floors are located in areas, which are also accessible to tractors and other vehicles. Special heavy duty slats must be provided in these areas to cater for the axle loadings involved. The dimensions shown below are derived from a number of national standards including BS 5502. This standard gives further details including structural considerations, tolerances and opening details for these types of floors.

The definition of the terms used in the following tables is as follows:

- Preferred Width the width of a single slat or solid portion between voids in multi-rib slats (a panel consisting of parallel slats).
- Spacing the width of a single slat or solid portion between voids in multi-rib slats (a panel consisting of parallel slats).
- Spacing the unobstructed floor area through which waste can pass expressed as a percentage of the total floor area.

Table shows dimensions recommended for cattle floors. These floors are usually in the form of single or multi-rib slats.

Table. Dimensions of Slatted Floors for Cattle

Type of Animal	Preferred Width mm	Spacing "S" mm	Void Ratio %
Calves and young stock > 200kg	80-120	20-30	18-25
Beef animals > 550kg	100-160	30-40	18-25

The use of fully slatted floors for certain animals is limited or not recommended in some animal welfare codes, *e.g.* totally slatted floors should not be used for calving cows, cows with young calves or calves of less than 4 weeks of age. Manufacturers have developed slat covering systems where soft materials are fitted to the slat ribs to improve the animal floor interface. These products have been shown to be beneficial when used in fully slatted pens for beef animals with the improved comfort provided to the animals leading to improved performance. Concerns regarding the emission of ammonia emissions from cattle buildings have led to the development of some novel floor systems. One such design-"grooved floor system" has been developed in The Netherlands and is used at present for walking areas in dairy cow facilities.

The grooved floor system consists of solid level pre-cast concrete elements covering a manure pit. The floor is scraped with a mechanical scraper. The top surface of the floor consists of a series of parallel grooves 35 mm wide and 30 mm deep and placed at 160 mm centre to centre. The width of the solid flat area (*i.e.* area between the grooves) is 125 mm, which is similar to the rib width of a slatted floor.

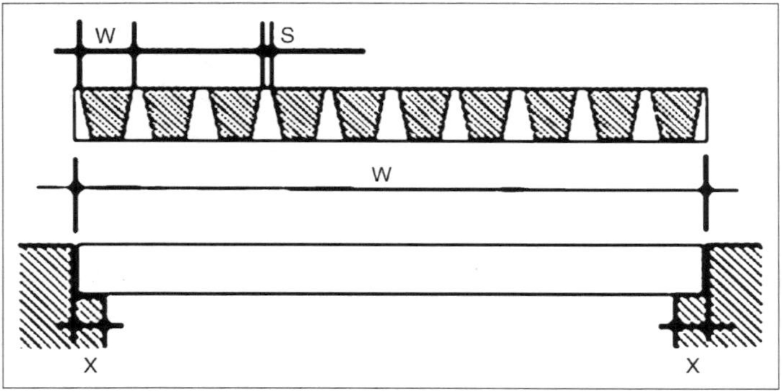

Fig. Slatted Floor

The floor elements are 1.1 m long and the adjacent edges of the abutted elements are tapered, which forms a self-discharging perforation at the base of the grooves for the urine deposited on the floor (total area of perforations is < 0.5 per cent of floor area). The faeces is removed by a mechanical scraper to an opening at the end of the passageway. To ensure the grooves remain clean and to prevent the perforations becoming clogged, the blade of the scraper is fitted with a tooth shaped rubber strip.

FACILITIES FOR FEEDING AND DRINKING

The following dimensions apply to loose housing systems, which permit indoor feeding so cattle can eat regardless of the weather. Maximum performance, particularly of heavier animals, can only be achieved by providing unrestricted access to the fodder, the availability of enough feed over the whole day of adequate quality according to type of animal, weight and production targets. Welfare aspects have also to be considered.

Stronger animals can disturb weaker ones in an aggressive way by inhibiting them from eating or drinking. A more or less unrestricted access to the feed should be possible for the hierarchically lower animals. Furthermore, it has to be considered that cattle are spending at the manger about six hours a day. Abnormal body posture of cattle during feeding can cause damage to legs, shoulder, neck and so on.

Feed handling is strenuous physical work for farmers and employees, both regarding working time requirement and ergonomic aspects. The building dimensions should offer enough space for the required feed processing equipment, feed transport equipment and free access to storage places.

FEED MANGER SPACE

Feeding management determines feed manger space requirement and two different feeding management systems are to identify:

1. *Limited Feeding:* With limited feeding, one feeding place for each animal is required. This involves the provision of adequate feed mangers, allowing large volumes of feed (oncedaily feeding) or frequently pushing the fodder against animal in flat alley. The space requirement of the manger depends on the age and weight of the animal.
2. *Unrestricted Feeding:* When feeding is available all the time, design can be based up to three animals for each feeding space, depending upon local animal welfare regulations. At a feeding place/animal ratio less than 1, feed must be offered ad libitum, in a constant quality and-as recommended-provided several times per day in form of feed mixtures.

The feed manger space requirements for one animal depends on the chosen feeding system, the age and weight of the cattle and their production intensity.

Feed Barrier Dimensions

Table. Feed Manger and Feed Barrier Dimensions (in m)

Weight (kg)	A	B [2]	C	×	F [3]	Neck Rail Height G
200	> 0,10	0,40	> 0,15	0-0,3	0,40	0.74
300	> 0,10	0,45	> 0,15	0-0,3	0,50	0.84
400	> 0,10	0,50	> 0,15	0-0,3	0,55	0.92
500	> 0,10	0,55	> 0,15	0-0,3	0,60	1.00
700[1]	> 0,10	0,60	> 0,15	0-0,3	0,70	1.10
900[1]	> 0,10	0,65	> 0,15	0-0,3	0,75	1.15

Notes:

[1] suckling cows, [2] max. value, [3] min. value

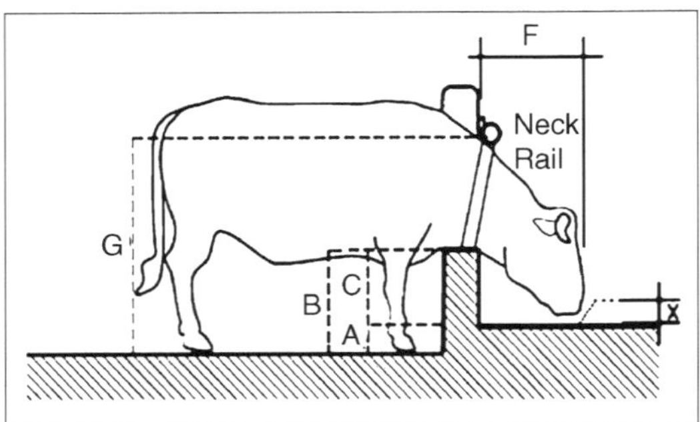

Fig. Feed Manger Dimensions

The feed barrier dimensions must allow an easy access to fodder and a natural feeding behaviour of the animal. Feeding barrier dimensions vary according to animal weight.

Manger Design

The usual manger type-feeding table-has a flat feed surface. One disadvantage is that the feed can be pushed away by the animals during feeding and must be brought back regularly into their reach. In smaller herds, this is done manually, for larger stock numbers it pays to use mechanical equipment (front- or rear mounted brushes, rotors, etc.). There is a range of acid proof coverings to protect the manger surface from corrosion *e.g.* plastic shells, stoneware shells, polyester-based coatings, stainless steel. Mechanical devices such as feed conveyors and flexible mangers (adjustable tarpulin or sheet) help optimize the delivery of the ration and reduce feed wastage and working time.

FEED ALLEY DESIGN

The feed alley and access dimensions are determined by the kind of mechanised feeding system used. The alley dimensions must be large enough for passing with different equipment. Transporting of feed using a two wheeled trailer or blockcutter and manual feed distribution.

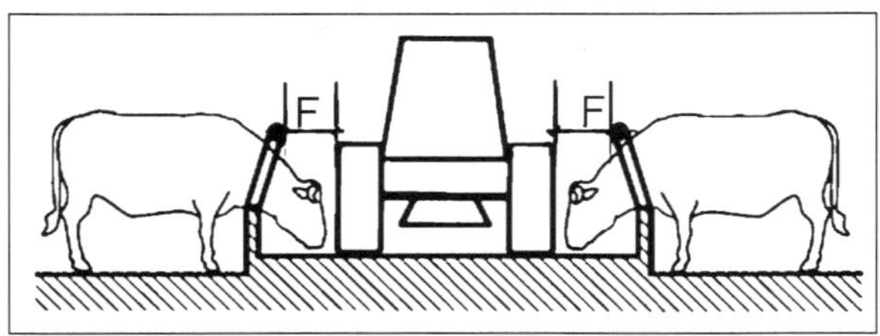

Fig. Feed Alley Dimension for Tractors, Block-cutter, Mixer Wagon

Transporting and distribution of feed using a mixer wagon (self-propelled or tractor-trailed). The turning radius plays an important role especially in trailed systems.

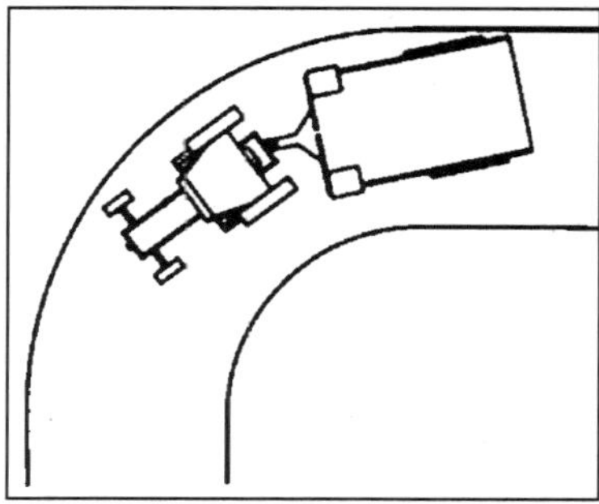

Fig. Turning Radius from Tractor with Mixer Wagon are Important

Feed Conveyor

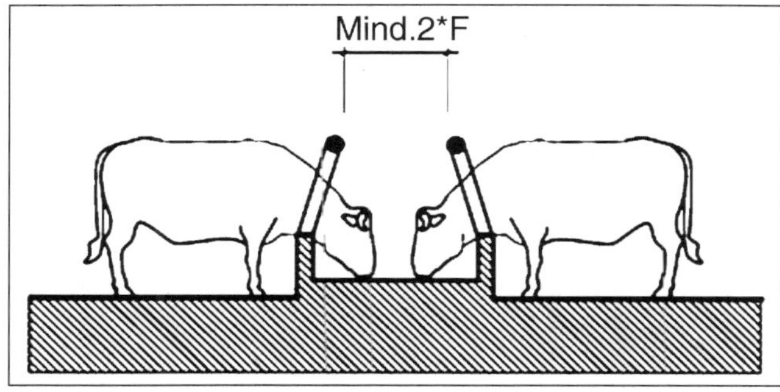

Fig. Feed Alley Dimension for Feed Conveyor

When using a feed conveyor, the required width is determined by the manger depth.

SELF-FEEDING FACILITIES

The importance of self-feeding systems is decreasing. Two different systems are possible: self-feeding of silage (*e.g.* maize silage) accounting for a substantial part of the ration, or the use of hay feeders for supplementary feeding of roughage (hay, straw) inside the building or on the pasture.

Self-feeding in Horizontal Silos

The height of the silage pile must not exceed the animals' reach. The silo width depends on the group size of the animals. A range of barrier designs are used in practice to restrain the animals. Unrestricted access to silage allows more than one animal to be kept per feeding place. Individual concentrate distribution being impossible, this system is recommended only for extensive fattening.

Hay Feeders

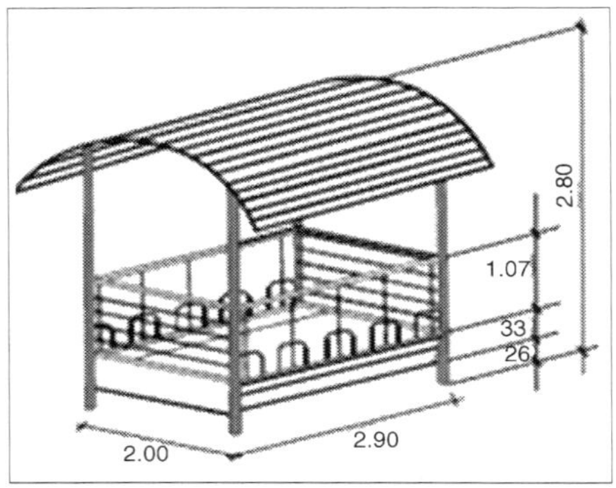

Fig. Hay Feeders

The feeding place width is determined by the animal weight. Feeders must be large enough to hold big bales. Hay feeders are suited for supplementary feeding of roughage in intensive fattening or grazing systems. A variety of feeding racks are available on the market.

DRINKING FACILITIES

Beef cattle must have free access to water, both indoor and on the pasture. Water requirements depend on the animal weight, the dry matter content of the ration and the ambient temperature.

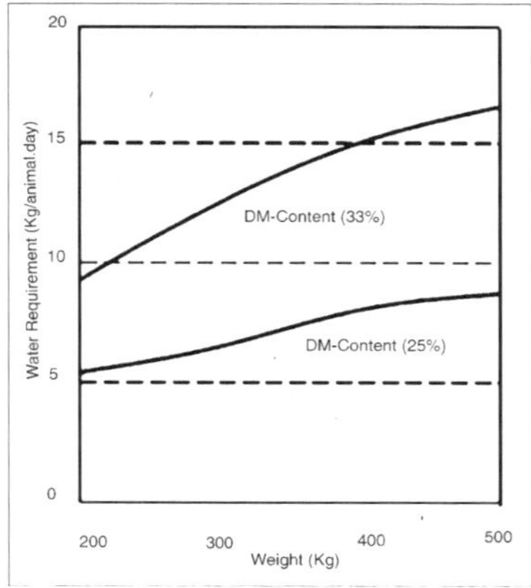

Fig. Water Requirement

In general the requirements are as follows:

- Drinker designs must take into account the cow's natural drinking position, *i.e.* they must allow the animals to immerse their muzzles a few centimeters in the water.

- Drinkers must be at least 0.1 m deep. Diameter of the bowl: 0.25 m. Water should be supplied at a minimum water flow rate of 8 l/min.
- Since beef fattening is performed mainly in cold housing systems, the drinkers and supply pipes must be protected from frost.
- When using drinking facilities on pastures the natural subsoil must be stabilized and drained in order to prevent water logging.

Number and Location of Drinkers

- One water bowl per 10 animals, one water trough per 15-20 animals.
- 2 drinkers for each group
- *Height above the Floor*: > 0. 55 m.
- Drinkers should not be located in the manger area, but in a separate area of the fattening pen.
- Integration of the drinker in the partition between adjacent pens allows two groups of animals to be watered with the same drinker.
- For bigger groups it is recommended to adapt the size of the water troughs.
- Enough space around the drinking place should be provided.

Drinker Types

Water Troughs

The recommended width and depth are 0.40 m each. The length depends on the group size and the type of trough and should be at least 0.40 m. The trough should allow easy cleaning (inlet nozzle, water stop valve). A distance barrier helps reduce soiling of the trough.

Ball Drinkers

The container is made of a sandwich-wall. A float is used to control the inside water level. The supply pipe is placed sufficiently below the ground surface and the ascending pipe is insulated in order to prevent freezing The water quality has to be controlled regularly. This type of drinker is not recommended in cattle fattening.

Water Bowls

Water bowls are generally made of cast iron with a corrosionresistant inside coating. Water is supplied by pushing down the trigger. The inflow rate can be adapted to a given water pressure by varying the inlet nozzle size. Water inflow rates of up to 20 l/min are possible. Electric heating of the supply pipe, valve, and bowl ensures functioning at temperatures as low as-25°C.

Nipple Drinkers

These are not recommended for ruminant because they do not allow a drinking style appropriate to this species. Reduced water intake and false behaviour such as urine drinking will result.

Frost-proof Water Supply

In cold and open housing systems, the water-supply pipe of the drinker must also be functional during winter.

This can be assured by the following three methods:

1. Laying of the water-supply pipe in a frost-proof area, depending on climatic conditions (location of the housing system), at approximately 0.50 to 1.00 m deep. For a failure-free operation, the connections to the drinkers (water trough, drinking bowl) must be heated and/or insulated (according to the climatic conditions and flow rate).
2. Wrapping the supply pipe by means of a heating cable and insulating material. The heating cable assures a minimal water temperature. The heating capacity is automatically regulated according to outdoor temperature. In the area where the animals stay, the heating cable and insulation have to be protected against damage.
3. Connecting the drinker to a closed circuit. The temperature sensor records the water temperature. If it drops below a certain reference value, the circulating pump will produce a cycle. If the value continues to decrease, *i.e.* below the reference value in the temperature range of freezing, the water within the circuit will be heated by a water heater. In addition, it must be assured that the water-supply pipes outside the circuit do not freeze (accompanying heating system, insulation).

VENTILATION (ENVIRONMENTAL CONTROL) OF LIVESTOCK BARNS

Wide range of air temperatures if proper consideration is given to their surroundings. In cold weather, young calves and older cattle alike will be able to adapt to very low temperatures if a deep and dry litter is provided along with abundant fresh air without excessive draughts and high humidity. In hot weather, shade and fresh air help to avoid excessive temperatures that lead to heat stress. Rapidly moving fresh air (1-3 m/s) over the body of the animal increases the rate of convective heat transfer to the ambient air.

VENTILATION

Ventilation-directly and indirectly-impacts many aspects of animal health. Good ventilation assures that animals breathe quality air, important to respiratory health. Good ventilation helps to keep bedding dry, a factor in favour of good animal health. Good ventilation along alleys helps to keep walking surfaces dry, a condition that contributes to healthy feet.

Good ventilation may lead to greater productivity; *e.g.*, maintaining air movement in the area of the feed manger makes the cattle more comfortable, especially important during hot weather as an aid to maintaining dry matter intake. A comfortable, well-ventilated stall area encourages animals to lie down, an important contribution to many aspects of animal health.

The ventilation process brings outside air into the barn where it collects moisture, heat and other contaminants. Air is then exhausted to the outside. Ventilation is an air exchange process-contaminated air inside the barn is exchanged for fresh outside air. To determine ventilation rates, we focus on the moisture content of the air, measured by relative humidity. But moisture is only one aspect. Ventilation removes other undesirable contaminants as well.

Air Quality

Animal health and disease are influenced by air quality. Air quality, in turn, is related to ventilation and its impact on reducing concentrations of contaminants in the air. Empirical observations and field trials suggest that the aerosol spread of pathogens between animals and the influence of air pollutants on pulmonary defence mechanisms are important, especially to respiratory health. Excess moisture, gases and other contaminants in the air are considered to be problematic as well.

The term air quality itself is not easily defined. With respect to animal spaces, good air quality generally implies that the characteristics of ambient air bear no harmful effects on the animals in the space. Ambient air is a mixture of clean, dry air (a mixture of gases, chiefly nitrogen and oxygen) and varying amounts of water vapour. At high concentrations, even moisture in the air in an animal space is considered to be a problem and is then considered an air contaminant. Other contaminants may include pathogens, harmful gases, dust and undesirable odours. The contaminant itself does not give rise to concern.

Rather, it is the concentration of a contaminant above some predetermined level that causes concern and is considered when assessing air quality. In hot weather, ventilation improves the environment for animals by removing heat and other contaminants from the animal space. Higher air velocities (1-3 m/s) over the body of the animal increase the rate of convective heat transfer from the animal's body to the ambient air.

The Dilution Effect of Ventilation

Ventilation is truly a process of dilution. Air moved through a barn serves to dilute the inside air and, very importantly, to dilute all of its components. Dilution reduces concentrations of moisture and heat. Dilution reduces concentrations of airborne disease organisms, harmful gases and dust, and undesirable odours as well. Reducing ventilation below recommended levels-usually in a misguided effort to warm the barn using animal heat-results in less moisture being removed.

If substantial quantities of heat are added to the air, relative humidity may remain in an acceptable range, as measured, and air quality may be deemed to be satisfactory. But even though excess moisture may not be apparent, the reduced dilution does indeed result in increased concentrations of airborne disease organisms, harmful gases and dust, and undesirable odours. If these increases are ignored, animal health problems are inevitable. Air quality is more than just measuring relative humidity. Through ventilation the air inside the barn is continually diluted, assuring that the air available to the animal has low concentrations of all contaminants that threaten the animal's health.

Minimum Continuous Winter Ventilation

A minimum rate of ventilation is required in animal housing in the winter regardless of outside temperature, whether the barn is designed to be a warm barn or a cold barn. In addition, the minimum ventilation should be continuous. Continuous dilution of inside air acts to maintain concentrations of contaminants in the air at minimal levels. The minimum rate depends on outside weather design conditions, number and type of animals in the barn, age and size of animals, and whether the barn is intended to be cold or warm.

Deciding between warm and cold housing is critical to the design and subsequent management of the ventilation system. Understanding the differences between the two types of environments is especially important as related to the need for maintaining the minimum continuous ventilation for winter in either situation that is in the best interest of animal comfort and health. Cold housing with natural ventilation is preferred for beef animals. Natural ventilation depends upon thermal and wind forces to provide air exchange.

VENTILATION DESIGN AND OPERATION FOR CATTLE BARNS

Uninsolated Barns with Natural Vent

In a cold barn, indoor temperatures are allowed to fluctuate with outdoor temperatures. In winter, ventilation must be sufficient to maintain indoor temperatures within 3-5°C of outdoor temperatures. During summer, ventilation should be sufficient to maintain indoor temperature at or slightly below outdoor temperature. Moisture naturally present causes the barn itself to act as an evaporative cooler.

A cold barn with natural ventilation has these general characteristics:

- No insulation,
- Open ridge and eaves, and
- Sidewalls and endwalls that open.

Providing an open ridge and open eaves has long been recognized as a mean of creating a stack effect to cause air exchange, especially for controlling moisture in winter. Provide a ridge opening of 5 cm per 3 m of barn width and equivalent open area divided between the two eaves. Raised ridge caps are to be avoided. Spaced roof sheeting (gap between sheets 2cm) can also be effectively used to provide a uniform air escape pathway over the complete roof structure.

However, care must be taken with this form of construction in areas where snow may cause blockage of the ventilation openings. Summer ventilation mainly depends on the wind. Factors affecting ventilation rates due to wind include area of building openings, local obstructions (hills, vegetation, nearby buildings) and wind speed and direction. To obtain maximum air exchange rates due to wind forces, maximize inlet and outlet openings and site buildings for maximum exposure to existing winds. Orienting buildings perpendicular to prevailing warm weather wind is preferred.

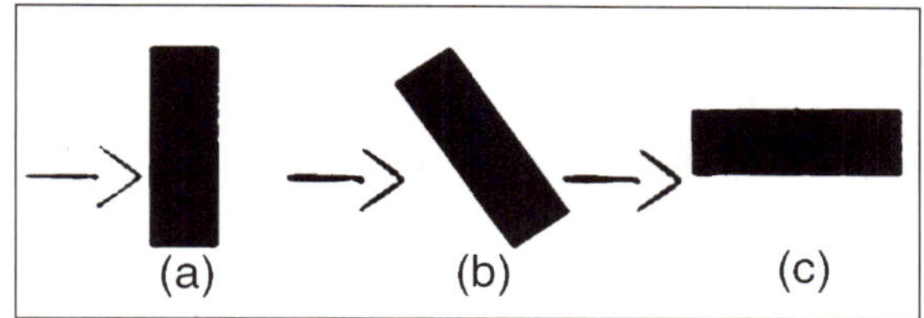

Fig. Orientation of a Building According to Wind Direction (Perpendicular to the Wind, at an Angle to the Wind, Parallel with the Wind)

Although, if sidewalls and endwalls are completely open and the barn is not long, say less than 30 m, orientation will be less critical. If a wind is blowing, a combination of thermal and wind forces will provide air exchange,

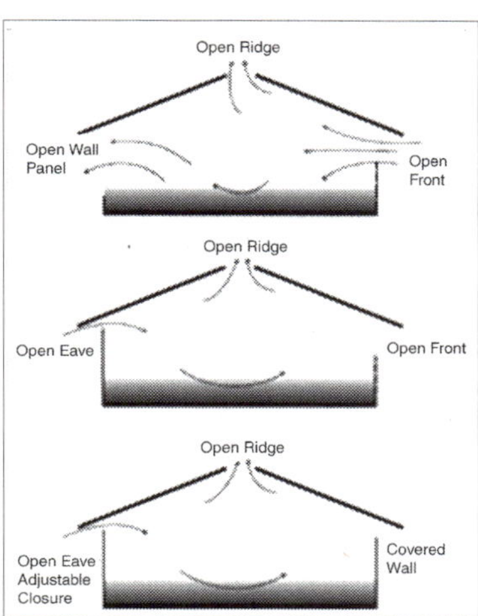

Fig. Airflow in Naturally Ventilated Buildings. Air Flow Patterns Vary with Wind Direction and Velocity

Fresh air enters through eave and sidewall openings, *Figure*. Air containing heat, moisture and other contaminants exists through the open ridge and downwind sidewall openings. Even with sidewalls closed on calm days, some air exchange occurs as a result of the chimney effect. Various materials and methods may be used to cover sidewalls for colder weather.

Automatic control or even frequent manual adjustment of air inlets is unnecessary. Cattle can tolerate usual diurnal fluctuations in environment and even fluctuations during the season, especially in summer. The simpliest and cheapest method of covering sidewalls uses a fabric covering over the full sidewall. For summer, the fabric is manually rolled up as a rug and tied.

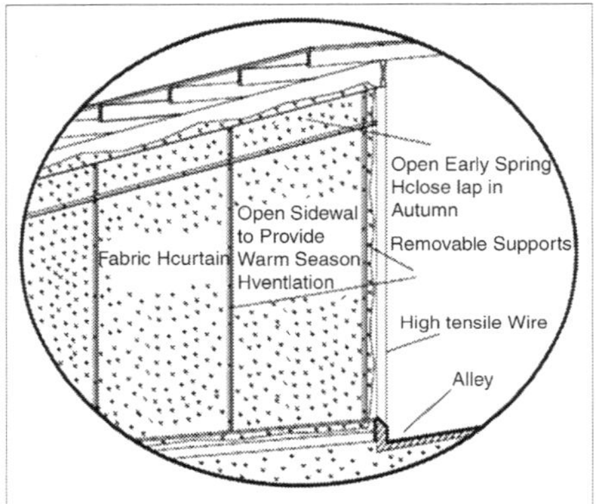

Fig. Full-wall Ventilation Provided by Removing Fabric Curtain. Nailing Strips are Removed and Curtain is Rolled to the Horizontal Member Near the Top of the Wall and Tied in Place during Warm Weather

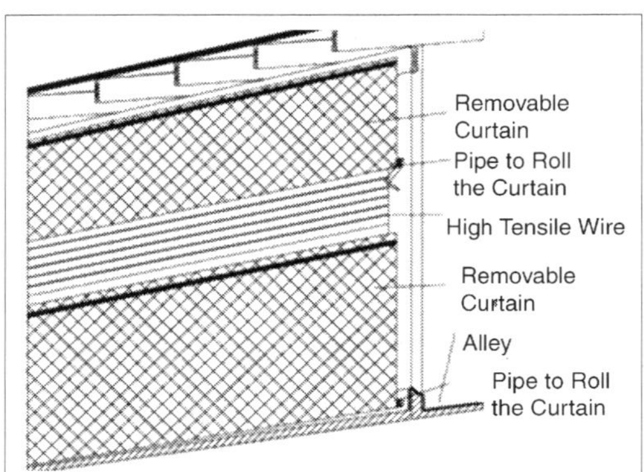

Fig. Full-wall Ventilation with Curtains on the Upper Half and Lower Half of the Wall Operated Separately. Curtain Operation is Accomplished with a Small-diameter Metal Pipe Installed in the Hem at the Bottom Edge of the Curtain and a Simple Crank at the End for Turning the Pipe.

To close the sidewall, ties are released and the hanging curtain is then fastened in place using a vertical nailing strip at each post and horizontal nailing strips all along the bottom. A variation on fabric covering is shown in *Figure.*

Fabric curtains to cover the top half and the bottom half of the sidewall are operated independently. A curtain is rolled up by fitting a crank to the small-diameter metal pipe installed in the hem at the bottom edge of each curtain. In regions that do not experience high temperatures or where animals will not occupy barns in summer, permanent "porous" sidewall construction is used. This can take the form of spaced boarding (*e.g.* 5-15 cm wide timber laths with 1.5-3.0 cm gaps) with height depending on the free area required.

Alternatively proprietary ventilated sheeting or flexible material can be used and manufacturer's data for free area of different types should be used for design purposes. The combination of the open ridge and eaves may be viewed as the sole source of ventilation only during the most severe winter weather-during periods when temperatures reach the lowest levels or times when especially windy, stormy conditions are present. During all other times in winter, additional ventilation must be provided.

Typically, doorways are left open for this purpose. Or, sidewalls away from prevailing winter winds may be left open. Then, as temperatures rise into spring and summer, sidewalls and endwalls are fully opened. As a general rule, too much ventilation is preferred over too little. In winter, suspend a thermometer inside a cold barn. If the temperature inside is more than 3-6° C above outside temperature, more ventilation will be necessary.

Also, persistent condensation on the underside of the roof is a further indication that additional ventilation openings must be provided. In summer, barns with open sidewalls and endwalls have improved ventilation resulting in lower average temperatures inside the barn. But, the real advantage to the cattle has to do with the extremes; specifically, during the heat of the day and the cool of the night. Cattle are not only exposed to lower temperature peaks during hot weather, they are exposed to these peaks for shorter periods of time. In addition, inside temperatures closely follow outside temperatures as they lower at night, allowing cattle to take advantage of whatever cooling effect may result from lower nighttime temperatures.

Insolated Barns with Mechanical Ventilation

In an insolated barn, indoor temperature is maintained substantially higher than outdoor temperature during winter, at 5°C or higher to keep water lines from freezing or, as in the case of a calves nursery, at about 10-15°C with the addition of supplemental heat to meet the needs of the animals. These buildings are well insulated. Fans with thermostat controls automatically regulate the ventilation rate as outside conditions change, diurnally and seasonally.

Three levels of ventilation, using fans, must be provided if cattle occupy the barn year-round. Summer ventilation rates of 60 to 90 air changes per hour are not uncommon, requiring several fans. These levels are on the order of ten times the minimum continuous rate for winter.

Warm Barns with Natural Ventilation

Well-regulated, naturally ventilated warm buildings, relying on stack and wind effects, have been successful. Natural ventilation for warm barns lowers investment and operating costs. Insulation and a warm environment in winter are the same as with mechanical ventilation. Adjustable openings provide for modulating both the stack effect and the wind effect as necessary, depending upon outside conditions. Because frequent adjustments in ventilation openings, sometimes several times per day, are required to compensate for changes in outside conditions-wind velocity or direction, temperature, solar radiation, ventilation openings are usually opened and closed automatically by various types of actuators controlled by thermostats. Natural ventilation for warm housing has been described by Choiniere for buildings that are temperature-controlled in winter.

CONSEQUENCES OF MISMANAGED VENTILATION IN WINTER

Reduced Dilution of Ambient Air

A major reason for air quality problems in barns in winter is adjusting natural ventilation for the worst case-severe winter weather-and not readjusting to allow increased ventilation when milder winter weather appears. Ventilation openings that are closed in anticipation of a windy, cold, blustery night must be opened the next day when, although the temperature may still be cold, the wind subsides and the sun shines. Reduced ventilation due to no wind reduces ventilation, reducing air exchange and reducing the positive effects of dilution. Problems are likely also during winter, spring and autumn, especially during rainy weather and warmer days coupled with cold nights. Ventilation reduced by manually closing ventilation openings for conditions at night is inadequate for warmer days that follow, unless openings are again uncovered. Closing ventilation openings to restrict airflow to keep manure from freezing in winter can result in too little ventilation and poor environmental conditions. To assure sufficient dilution of inside air and healthy conditions for animals, maintain a maximum temperature difference between inside and outside of no more than 3-6° C.

Building Components Affected by Poor Ventilation

Besides adversely affecting the animal environment, the design and operation of naturally ventilated barns influence moisture related deterioration in wood members and metal fasteners. American specialists studied 10 naturally ventilated dairy free stall barns located in Michigan. In barns where air exchange in winter was defeated by blocking ventilation openings, average wood moisture contents exceeding 30 per cent dry basis (capable of supporting wood decay and corrosion in metal fasteners) were found after 2-3 months of cold weather operation. Moreover, restricted air movement in these barns inhibited drying and allowed wood moisture contents to remain elevated even into warm weather. Warm, moist conditions favour growth of mold, bacteria and decay fungi and accelerate metal corrosion. The presence of insulation under the roofing in these problem barns fostered this situation. Even if free water from precipitation and condensation causes slightly elevated moisture contents, adequate air exchange, especially as weather warms, will promote drying of wood truss components so that deterioration will not be a problem.

Misguided Use of Insulation in Cold Barns

If insulation is installed under the roof, a potentially cold barn may not be operated and managed as a cold barn. Insulation suggests that the barn is something other than a cold barn and that an available option is to close or block ventilation openings during extreme weather conditions to restrict ventilation. The most serious deficiency associated with this approach is the lack of proper control to restore ventilation rates when extreme weather has passed. Barns with insulation under the roof are often underventilated because evidence of a moisture problem doesn't appear. Besides contributing to problems with animal health, underventilation can lead to the premature deterioration of structural components in buildings. Condensation on the underside of the roof of a cold enclosed barn can be considered a management tool or signal for the farmer that excess moisture buildup is occurring and additional ventilation openings must be provided for better air exchange. The presence of insulation can take away this important indicator resulting in a potentially unfavourable environment.

SUCKLER COWS AND CALVES

During the last twenty years, a number of changes have occurred in the management of suckler cows. These include the concentration of calving period during winter/spring time, the move to the use of feeding of silage instead of hay, the increase of the herd size and the reduction of labour requirements. These new tendencies, the design of buildings for suckler cows housing has evolved as well as working practices with the animals.

This chapter tackles the topic of "classic" suckling, which means the timing of calving is during winter/spring, and that the young animals stay with the cows until weaning time. This method of production requires the housing of cows and calves together. There are several types of housing design, which can be used for suckler cows and calves with the choice depending on a range of factors. This report describes the common systems, which are in practical use. In certain instances it is possible to operate with no housing system and such "open-air systems" constitute an economical solution in some cases even in cold climates because of the rusticity of suckler cow breeds. Such systems are possible with special environmental conditions, and imply for the farmer, the obligation to accept some constraints in his working conditions. This type of production is not a part of this document, which is devoted to buildings for beef production. Suckler cows can be accommodated in a wide range of housing systems.

The main housing systems in common use are:

- Bedded house
- Sloped floor house with bedding
- Cubicle house
- Slatted accommodation

Numerous variations of these main housing types exist in practice. Before detailing the specific organization of these systems, with their advantages and disadvantages, it is necessary to speak about the area requirements for the calves, and the size of the groups of suckler cows. The area requirements for the calves are in a strict relationship with the calving period. An autumn born calf needs more area than a spring born calf, because the calf weight and the calf dimensions are proportional to the housing period duration. The *table* gives some examples of area requirements in bedded court and bedded sloped floor systems.

SIZE OF THE GROUPS

In the housing facility the herd is typically divided into several groups for ease of management. Generally, the size of a group is between 8 and 16 cows. For each group of suckler cows, it is necessary to have a creep area to accommodate the calves. The dimensions of the creep area are to be defined according to the number of cows calving at the same period.

LOOSE HOUSING SYSTEMS (NON-CUBICLE)

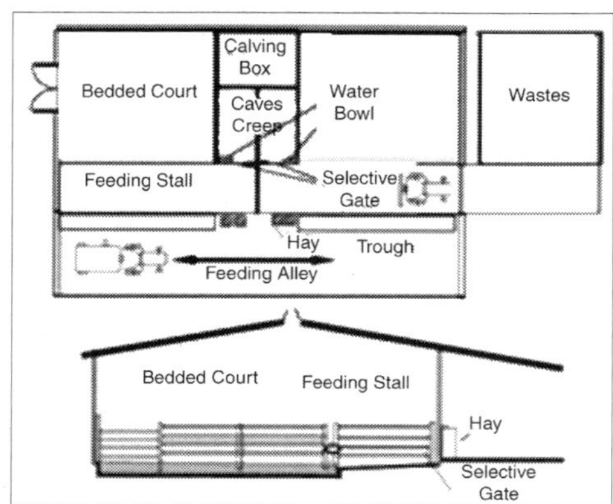

Fig. Layout and Cross Section from a Bedded House with a Concrete Exercise Court and Calves Creeps between Cow Pens

Outline designs are provided for a range of loose housing systems which do not use cubicles. A subsequent section deals with cubicle based systems.

Bedded Houses with a Concrete Exercise Court, and Calves Creeps between Cow Pens

Feeding:

- Concrete exercise court of 3.7 m2/cow
- Possibilities to distribute silage and hay together in the trough
- *Frequent Variant*: A separated access to the trough for the calves, and no hay rack for the mothers.

Rest Area:

- A number of 16 cows per section, with an area of 6.5 m2/cow.
- Calves creeps designed in order to have an area between 1 m^2/calf and 1.6 m^2/calf, with the possibility to use the calving box as part of the calf creep area, when the calving period is finished.
- A straw requirement of 5 to 7 kg/couple (cow+calf)/day, with an increase to 6 to 8 kg during the calving period.

Ventilation:

- Most of the time this kind of building is designed with a free open side along the straw bedded court and is orientated to give this side protection from the direction of the prevailing wind. If required this open side can be protected with a synthetic wind-break. Such a wind-break should be fixed so that it can be dismantled easily as required in order for example to be able to scrape out easily the manure.

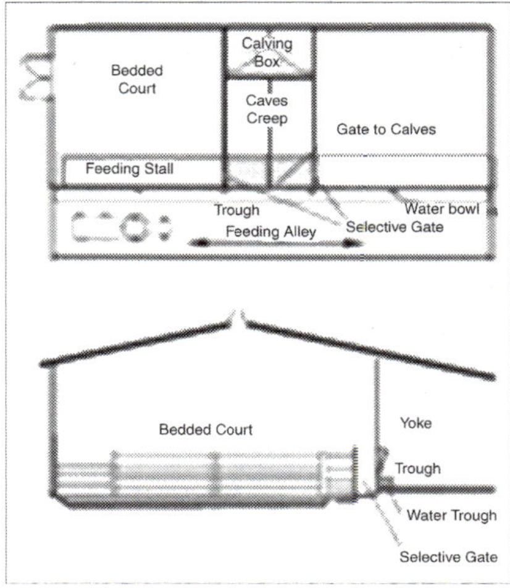

Fig. Layout and Cross Section from a Bedded House with Straw Yards and Calves Creeps between Cow Pens

Straw Yards and Calves Creeps between Cow Pens

Organization of the life area:

- Rest area and feeding alley merged into a mixed-function area
- An adequate standing stall in order to avoid an excessively dirty area near the trough by spoiling litter too much. This allows to keep clean a theoretical rest area of 6.7 to 7 m^2
- *A Calving Box between the Two Pens of Cows*: It can be used by all the calving cows
- A requirement of 7 to 10 kg of straw per couple (calf and mother) per day
- A requirement of 10 to 12 kg during the calving period.

Feeding:

- The main diet is based on silage, but a small quantity of hay (2 to 3 kg/cow. day) can be distributed in the trough at the same time as the silage

Ventilation:

- *Specific Requirements*: Be careful to avoid a "corridor effect" in the building. Same comments as for 1 A possible variant: bedded court and calves creeps between cow-yards, with a *separate hay rack*

Feeding:

- For the herds with a mixed feed (silage and hay), including more than 4 to 5 kg of hay/cow. day, it is practically necessary to provide the hay separately.

Rest Area:

- In this variant accommodation for the cows is similar to the previous system, but the area for the calves is reduced to only 1.2 m^2 per calf as calving takes place close to the end of the housing season.

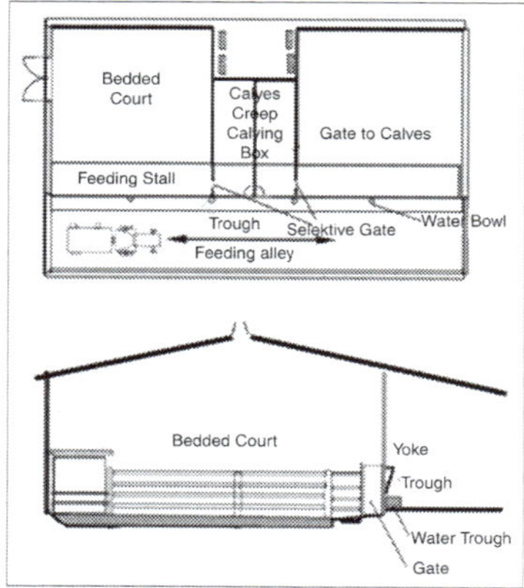

Fig. Layout and Cross Section from a Bedded Court and Calves Creeps between Cow-yards, with a Hay Rack

Comments on the Disadvantages of that Solution of "Feeding Stall"

The self cleaning function reduces labour requirements as it is not necessary to scrape the area. However, the area requires a sufficient slope to allow the manure to slide down (3 per cent), and this can possibly lead to the animals adopting a bad posture during the feeding period. Other consequences are: a lot of manure between the area and the bedded court, wet litter, dirty animals and problems with animal health.

Bedded Court on Sloped Floor with Calves Creeps at the Rear Part of the Straw Bedded Court

Feeding

- Concrete exercise court with an area of 2.40 m^2 + 1.35 m^2 for the standing stall, whose secondary function is in simplified systems, the immobilizing of the cows in order to treat the animals. We recommand to have in addition, a specific restraining device to allow some security to the farmer and the veterinary surgeon.
- Feeding of the calves separated from the feeding of the mothers. The access to the calves creeps is given by the service alley.
- Watering with a big water bowl on the standing stall.

Rest Area

- Sixteen cows per pen, with an area of 4.90 m^2/cow
- Calf creeps designed in order to have an area between 1.25 m^2/calf and 1.90 m2/calf, with the possibility to use the calving box as part of the calf creep area when the calving period is finished.
- A slope of about 6 per cent, which limits the height of the straw bed at a level of 0.30 m.
- A straw requirement of 4 to 6 kg/couple (cow+calf)/day, with an increase to 5 to 7 kg during the calving period.

A possible variant: bedded court on sloped floor, and calves creeps between cow-yards, with a specific hay rack

Changes in Feeding

- Hay and silage separated for the cows
- Access to the trough for the calves with a specific diet, which is easy to distribute in this part of the manger.

Changes for the Rest Area

- *A Little more Surface Area for the Cows:* 5.20 m^2
- A very good system for the regions with a short housing period (less than 130 days), and with a dry climate.

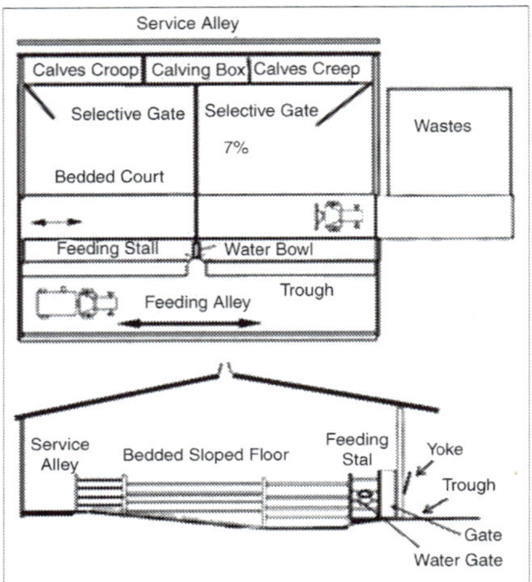

Fig. Layout and Cross Section from Bedded Court on Sloped Floor with Calves Creeps at the Rear Part of the Straw Beeded Court

FREE STALLS/CUBICLES

Outline designs are provided for a range of loose housing systems, which use cubicles.

Head to Head Cubicles with Calves Creeps between Cubicles Rows

Feeding

- Possibilities to give forages separately.
- Calves feeding independently in the creep areas (access by the extremities)
- Minimum one water bowl per section.

Rest Area

- A head to head design with a calf creep area between the two rows.
- Length of the cubicles ranging from 2.30 m to 2.50 m. It is necessary to put some tubes at the front side of the partitions, not only to fix the parti-tions, but also to be able to confine the calves in the creep area if required.
- *Straw Requirements for the Cubicles*: A minimum of 0.50 kg/cow. day for animal welfare (synthetic mats can also be used but straw must be prefered if available).
  - 3 kg/cow/day in order to obtain a soft to solid manure
- Straw requirements for the calves:
  - 1 to 2 kg/calf/day for the calves creep
  - 6 to 8 kg/day during calving period for the calving box.

Ventilation

- Like in other kinds of buildings, there is very often a free open side. In order to be able to supply easily the hay racks with big bales, the open wall is located at the side of the feeding alley, and not at the opposite side.
- This free open wall can obviously be protected by a wind-break material, with the same precautions to avoid draughts on the animals.

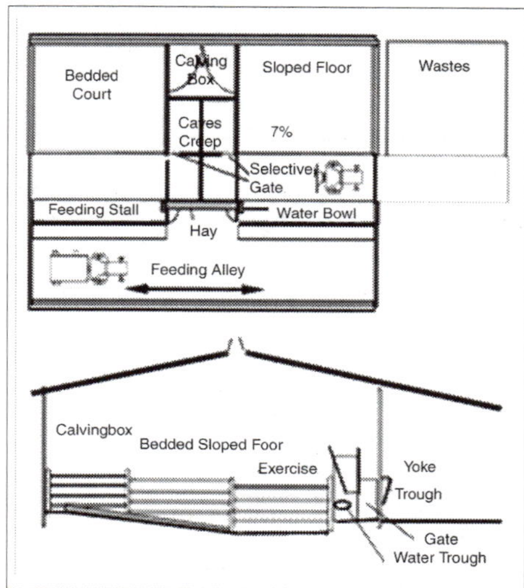

Fig. Layout and Cross Section on Bedded Court on Sloped Floor and Calves Creeps between Cow-yards, with a Specific Hay Rack

Head to Head Cubicles with Calves Creep and Calving Box at the Extremities

Changes in feeding:

- Possibility to give a specific feeding to the calves in front of their boxes.
- Same possibility for the cows using the calving boxes.

Changes for the rest area:

- Cubicles shorter than in the variant 4.1 because of the possible crossing of the cow-heads in the front part of the cubicles, designed in a head to head position, each row close to the other one.
- Limits of the calves creeps and the calving box in the continuation line of the cubicles rows, giving an area of 1.65 m2 to 1.90 m2 [depending on the duration (organization) of the calving period].

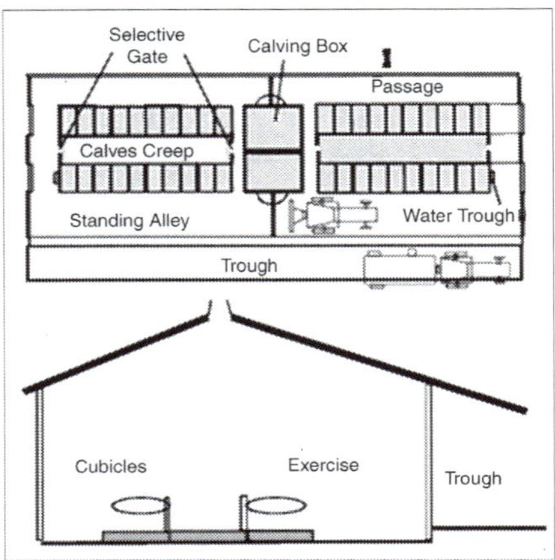

Fig. Layout and Cross Section from Head to Head Cubicles with Calves Creeps between Cubicles Rows

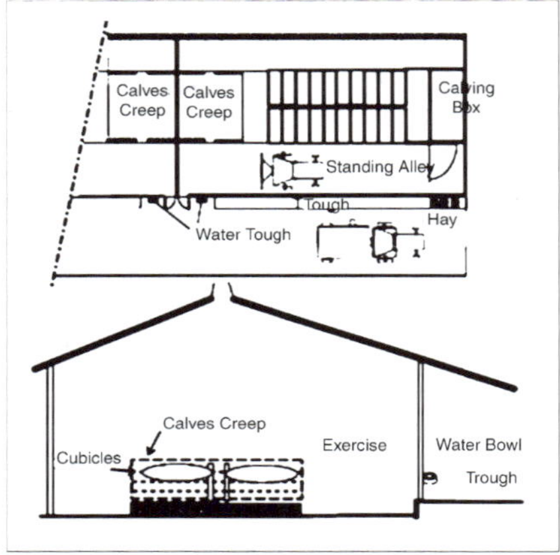

Fig. Layout and Cross Section from Head to Head Cubicles with Calves Creeps and Calving Box at the Side

Back to Back Cubicles with Calves Creeps and Calving Box at the Extremities

Feeding:

- Same organization as for the variant 4.2

Rest Area:

- Separation between resting area and feeding area.
- Length of the cubicles designed like in the case of a front wall (long cubicles).
- Straw spreading not easy to realise.
- Frequent need of two calves creeps for each pen.

Ventilation:

- One must pay attention to the position of the cubicles row near the wall, exposed to cold draughts coming down from the inlets. The height of these inlets must be sufficient to avoid this risk.
- The other side, generally free open can be protected by a windbreak material.

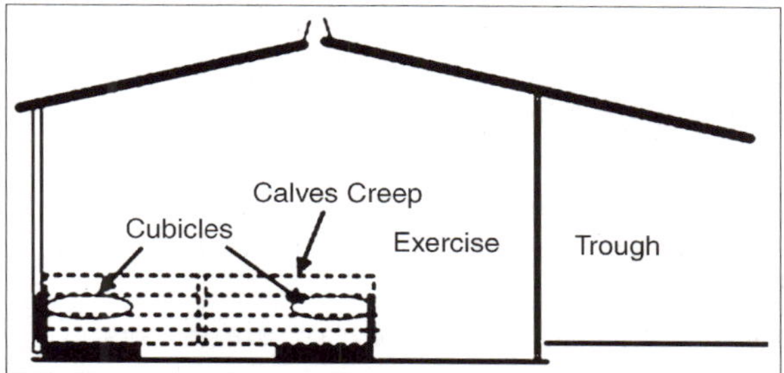

Fig. Cross View from Back to Back Cubicles with Calves Creeps and Calving Box at the Extremities

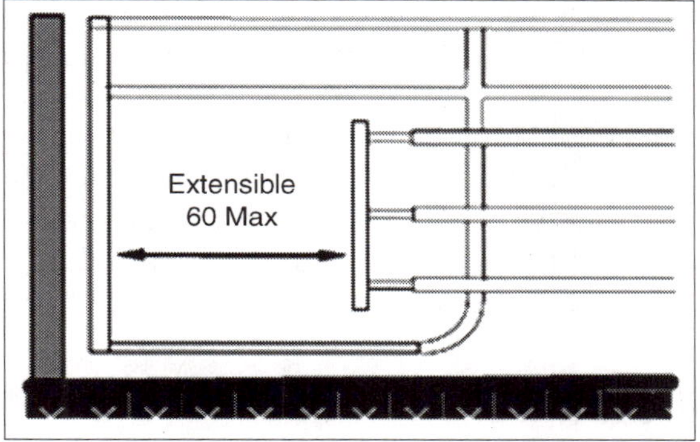

Fig. Back to Back Cubicles with Calves Creeps and Calving Box at the Extremities

HOUSING FOR CALVES FROM BIRTH TO 6 MONTH

This chapter deals with calves that are weaned (separated from their mother) close to the birth. The calves will be housed either individually or in group according to the management system chosen by the farmer. The individual housing can last for a few days or for several weeks (2 to 8 weeks). The European Union has taken measures (EEC Directive 91/629, EU Directive 97/2) in which are laid down the minimum terms with respect to housing that are to be met with by farm buildings and their equipment for veal calves.

The most important features of this directives are:

- Individual housing is forbidden after the age of 8 weeks, excepted for veterinary reasons;

- The width of individual cage must be equal to the height at the withers and the length equal to the length of the animal multiplied by 1.1;
- Partitions between cages must be open to permit sight and tactile contacts between animals;
- For groups of animals, the free area per animal must be 1.5 m2 with a live weigh less than 150 kg, 1.7 m2 with a live weigh above 150 kg but less than 220 kg and 1.8 m2 with a live weigh above 220 kg,
- The stable and the equipment must be built so that each animal can stretch, rest, stand up and groom without any difficulties,
- Litter must be provided for animals younger than 2 weeks;
- Calves are not tied except in groups only for one hour during the milk distribution;
- If artificial ventilation is used, an alarm system will have to be installed;
- Keeping the animals permanently in the dark is forbidden. Natural or artificial lighting must be provided;
- Calves must be fed twice a day;
- Calves must receive adequate fibre and enough iron in their diet;
- Calves older than 2 weeks must have permanent access to fresh water.

This regulation is not enforced on farm with less than 6 calves and where the calves remain with their mothers to receive milk. All the other farms are subject to this regulation. All existing buildings must be satisfied the regulation by 31.12.2006. New buildings for veal calves must be built according to the EU regulation and existing buildings must be adapted to comply with the EU regulations.

INDIVIDUAL HOUSING

Hutches

The hutches are frequently made from a synthetic opaque material to prevent the green house effect inside the hutch (heat stress) and from reflective material (light colour material) to reflect sun rays that might otherwise overheat the inside part of the hutch. They may also be built in wood, panels, plywood. The opening must not be oriented in the direction of the prevaling wind, considering dominant wind direction and rainfall.

In many areas of Western Europe a southeast orientation is most suitable. Generally, the size of the hutches is as follows: length 2.0 m, width 1.5 m (+/-3 m^2), height 1.5 m. In addition, the hutches have an outdoor run of more than 2.0 m^2 surrounded by either metal wire netting or by welded tubes. There is also a milk bucket support, a dry feed recipient support and a hay rack.

Litter may be provided as straw, wood shavings, sawdust, newspapers...and should be thick enough to provide a favourable lying environment. It must be dry and clean. Litter must be removed immediately after the calf has left the hutch. Hutches should be placed on well drained ground according to the water legislation. This may mean placing on soil with a sand layer of 15 cm. After use, the sand should be removed to suppress the risks of contamination or on concrete floor.

If the hutches are placed on concrete to make cleaning and disinfecting easier, it is necessary to collect urine and disinfectant in a storage facility to prevent the pollution of the environment and to respect the local regulations. If the weather is hot, it will be advisable to shade the hutches in order to avoid the negative effects of high temperatures. During the winter it could be useful to take measures to prevent the consequences of very low temperatures

Pens

It is recommended to put the calves into individual pens until weaning. Individual pens are either dismountable or made from hard material with concrete walls. Dismountable pens are either bought from a tradesman or made by the farmer himself with plywood panels for the walls and hardwood (tropical wood) for the (perforated) floor, which is covered with a litter (thick enough, dry and clean). Bucket supports are provided for on the front. It is recommended to prolong the partition between two pens to the front part to reduce disease transfer from noseto-nose contact.

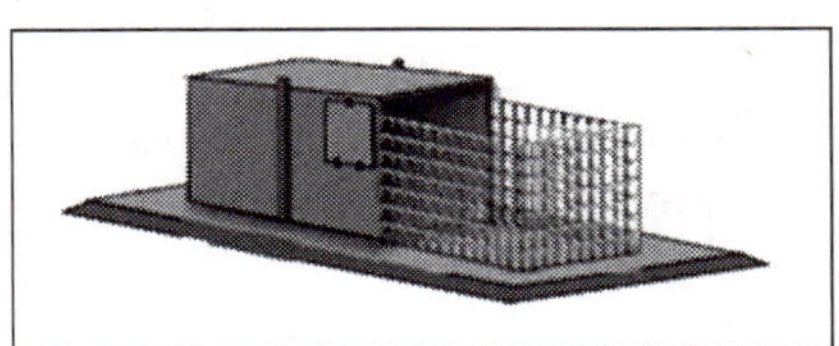

Fig. Calf Hutch

The 0.90-1.00 m × 1.50-1.60 m pen can be put 300 mm above the ground with a view to draining and the removal of urine, and to allowed regularly cleaning of the floor during occupation. In cold barns, the thickness of the litter must be increased to prevent draughts around the calves.

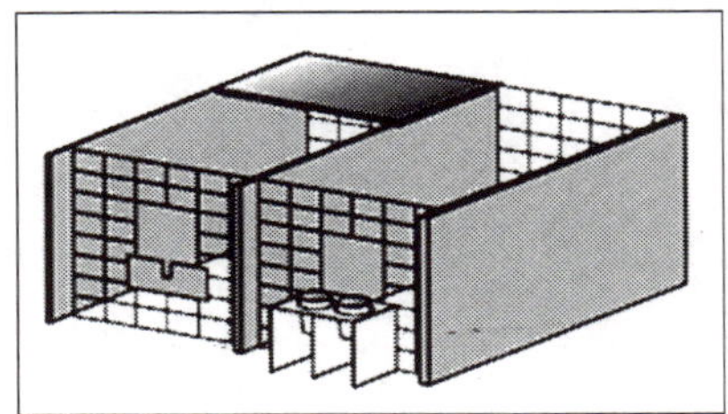

Fig. Individual Calves Pen

GROUP HOUSING

Group housing gives the opportunity to calves to learn living with comrades and to develop relationships with other animals.

It also gives the possibility to the calves to increase their immunity against a wide range of micro-organisms:

- *Collective Hutches:* The collective hutches are designed typically to house a group of between 2 and 6 calves. The hutches are made of synthetic materials or wood and have, for example, for 4 calves an indoor area of 10 m2 and an outdoor run of 10 to 15 m2. The inside of the hutch is provided with litter and some hay may be put in a rack. Roughage is distributed at a feeding barrier and anti-freeze drinking device is recommended. With collective hutches fastened on concrete, the outdoor run should have a non slippery surface. The outside run must be cleaned 1-2 times a week. Manure and spent bedding have to be removed manually or the collective hutch has to move over a few metres distance by means of a tractor and guide-blocks.
- *Bedded Sloped Floor*: Sloped floor systems are not recommended for calves younger than 6 months.
- *Straw Yard with Bedded Lying Area*: These facilities will be extremely suitable for young animals if sufficient straw and proper ventilation is provided. If the calves stay there for several months it will absolutely be necessary that a passage on slippery free concrete is provided that their hooves remain strong and wear out regularly. Moreover the floor of this passage should be quite rough to prevent slipping. With respect to labour costs the concrete floor may be replaced by a slatted floor provided that the spacing between slats agrees with the age of the animals and the local regulations.
- *Cubicle House:* Cubicles are not recommended for calves younger than 6 months.
- *Fully Slatted Floor*: Concrete fully slatted floors are not recommended for calves younger than 6 months.

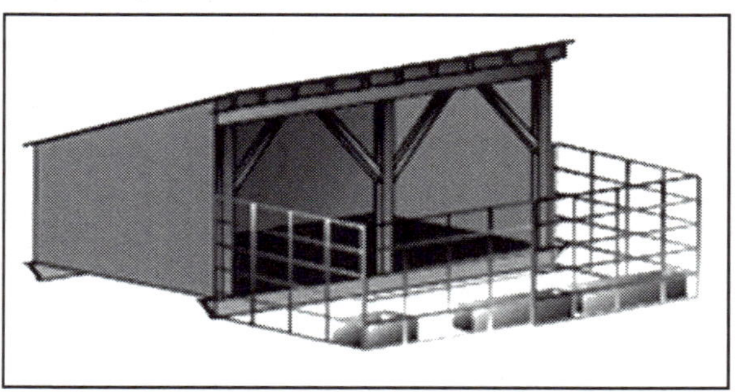

Fig. Collective Hutch

TIED STALL BARN

Tying stalls are forbidden by a EU directive and are not recommended in the countries where they are not forbidden.

VEAL CALVES

In the European Union, regulations have been adopted to improve the housing conditions of veal calves according to the wishes of groups of persons dealing with animal welfare.

The New Buildings

The new buildings must be equipped to house calves in groups. The calves are fed manually with a hose or by an automatic milk feeder. In the case of manual feeding, the calves are housed in groups of 8 to 10 and they are fed twice a day. There are partitions in the front of the pen to avoid situations in which one calve drinks the milk of other calves. In the front of the pen, cages can be placed to maintain the calves separately during one hour after the distribution of milk to prevent comrade suckling. After one hour the calves are free to move around.

In the case of automatic milking feeder, the calves are housed in groups of about 30. The calves can be housed on a bedded court (straw on the whole pen or straw for the lying area and concrete or slatted floor for the rest of the pen) or on a fully slatted floor (wood, concrete or concrete covered by a rubber). The required surface depends on the weight at slaughter. For calves slaughtered at the weight of 180-200 kg live weight the surface requirements are at about 1.7-1.8 m2 per animal in the EU regulation but are frequently increased to 2.8 m^2 per calf.

Existing Buildings

In existing buildings, the single pens are replaced by group pens that are put on the place formerly occupied by the single pens and by the passage between the pens and the wall; as a result each calf gets an area of approximatly 1.9 m2 which is larger than the requirements of the EU regulation. The front doors of the single pens are replaced by a feeding barrier especially made to supply the liquid milk replacer in buckets. Each calf has a feeding place of about 0.72 m. The calves are brought together in groups of 8 to 10.

Partitions between the calves can be placed in front of the pen to improve the distribution of the milk replacer. There must be a sufficient supply of daylight so that the animals may see each other and be watched by the farmer. If necessary provision for light entry must be made in the walls. The wooden slatted floors (hard wood) are replaced by concrete slats covered with rubber mats of the same shape or by a new wood slatted floor. The artificial ventilation must be adapted to obtain an optimal air quality.

Veal Calves and Automatic Milk Feeder

Automatic milk feeding systems are increasingly being used for veal calves. Each automatic milking feeder is made to manage 2 milking dispensers, and each milking dispenser can be used for about 30 fattening calves. The calves are assembled so as there is a limited age difference between the animals so as to prevent hierarchic and health problems within the group.

Calves remain together until slaughter and they receive milk replacer according to their needs or ad libitum. If calves are fed according to their needs, they will be identified by the system by means of a collar with a transponder or by means of a transponder inserted in an ear tag or injected under the skin.

Type of Lying Area and Ventilation

Natural ventilation and cold housing are recommended for raising calves. In some cases (calves on fully slatted floor) warm housing is the most suitable system to provide a good environment to the calves and to prevent diseases and mortality.

Bedded Pack

For calves housed on a deep litter of straw (bedded pack, 2.3 to 2.8 m^2 per calf) cold housing is the recommended system to provide a good environment to the calves. An open front with adequate orientation based on prevailing wind and exposition to the sunrise is recommended. Movable curtains on the opposite wall are necessary to prevent drafts during the cold months and heat stresses during the summer. An insulation of the roof is not required.

Slatted Floor

For calves housed on a fully slatted floor, warm housing, heating and mechanical ventilation are necessary to provide a good environment to the calves. Insulation of the walls and the roof, heating during the cold months and mechanical ventilation are required to prevent too low temperature of the air and too high relative humidity of the air. During the hot days, mechanical ventilation and thermal insulation help to maintain a normal temperature in the housing.

HOUSING FOR FINISHING ANIMALS

The provision of accommodation systems for finishing beef animals is essential for efficient herd management. The type of housing provided will depend on a range of factors including geographic location, availability of straw, size of the unit and on the traditional methods of fattening in the particular region. Depending on the finishing system animals may remain in the house until slaughter or return to pasture following the winter period. In the latter case these animals may be finished outside or spend a subsequent period in the accommodation prior to being slaughtered. Loose housing systems predominate for beef cattle. When designing accommodation facilities for fattening cattle consideration should be given to labour availability, feeding system, type of diet, group size, drinking system, and facilities for handling and storage of the manures produced.

The requirement for housing during the finishing period may be due to land conditions that do not facilitate outdoor feeding due to soil type and climatic factors. In certain situations housing is provided to facilitate the structured feeding of the animals under controlled management conditions. Also, housing facilities should provide a suitable working environment for the farmer and any employees involved in taking care of the animals.

HOUSE TYPES

Traditionally, beef cattle were housed in straw bedded facilities. The unavailability of straw in some areas (combined with its increased cost), the need to reduce labour requirements and the necessity to ensure manure was efficiently managed to avoid pollution risks, has encouraged the development of housing systems utilising liquid manure storage.

Variations in the design have evolved including houses with partially slatted floors, houses with sloped floors inclining towards narrow slurry channels and houses with slats over shallow tanks from which the slurry flows by gravity to an adjacent storage facility. Cubicle houses can also be used for finishing animals where no straw is available but such facilities are not recommended for male animals because, they foul the lying area with urine.

Where straw is avail-able for bedding typical systems include fully bedded pens, facilities with bedded lying areas and solid unbedded or slatted feeding stands and facilities with sloped floors, which depend on the animals to move the fouled bedding down the slope for collection. Tethering of animals in stalls is still used as a management system in some beef units but this method of housing is not recommended.

Bedded House

Such houses consist of bedded pen(s) with the total living area covered in bedding material, which normally is straw. The facilities are roofed but are sometimes referred to as "straw bedded yards". Cattle should be housed in groups of not more than 20 to aid management. This type of house requires 4 to 6 kg of straw per animal per day which equates to approximately 1 (metric) ton straw per animal for a winter housing period.

The completely bedded system does not prepare the hooves of the animals for subsequently walking on harder surfaces such as concrete. Sometimes the hooves may become overgrown and misshapen, which may lead to lameness problems. Although the systems are relatively cheap to construct the high straw requirement with associated labour costs must also be taken into account when making comparisons with other systems.

The manure/bedding mixture is allowed to build up over the housing period and is normally removed once at the end of the season. Depending on the length of the housing season the accumulated material may rise up to greater than 1m above floor level. It is necessary to take this into account when installing gates, partitions and feeding barriers and troughs. A typical layout of such a facility is presented in *Figure.*

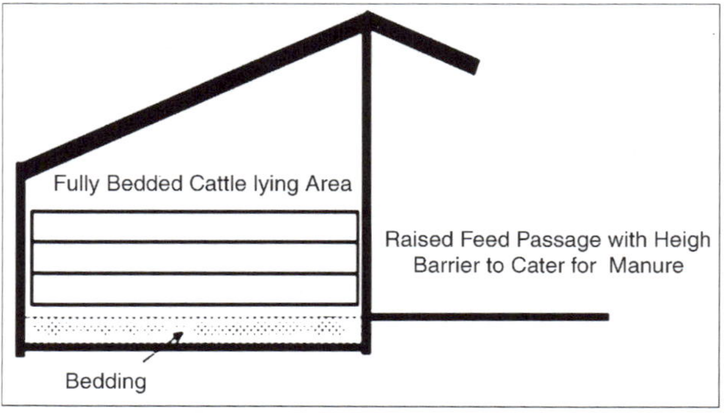

Fig. Straw Bedded Facility Cross-section Showing Raised Passageway

Bedded House with Concrete or Slatted Feeding Stand

In this type of facility the animals come to feed on an area of solid concrete or an area covered with slats. In the case of solid concrete the area is cleaned by an electric, hydraulic or tractor powered scraper. Where a tractor is used additional gates are used to close off the feeding stand from the bedded area during cleaning.

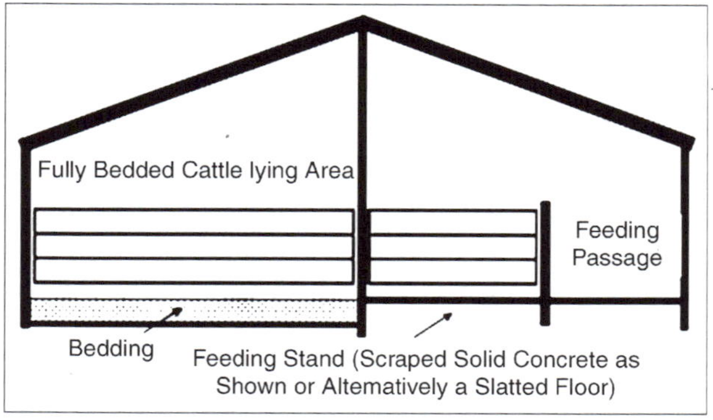

Fig. Bedded House with Concrete Feeding Stand

The design has the advantages that lower quantities of straw are required and that the geometry of the feeding stand does not change as the manure builds up over the housing period. Straw usage is in the order of 2 to 3 kg per animal per day. However, both a liquid and solid manure is also produced with the system. If slats are used in the feed stand it is important to minimise the quantity of straw entering the tanks to avoid problems with slurry agitation. A cross sectional view is shown in *Figure*.

Bedded House with Sloped Concrete Floor

This housing system involves the frequent removal of manure but daily straw requirements can be as low as 1 to 3 kg per animal per day. The floor is laid with a slope of 5 to 10 per cent. The system operates on the principal that the movement of the animals will transfer the manure down the slope where it is removed by scraping. A cross section of a typical layout is shown in *Figure*.

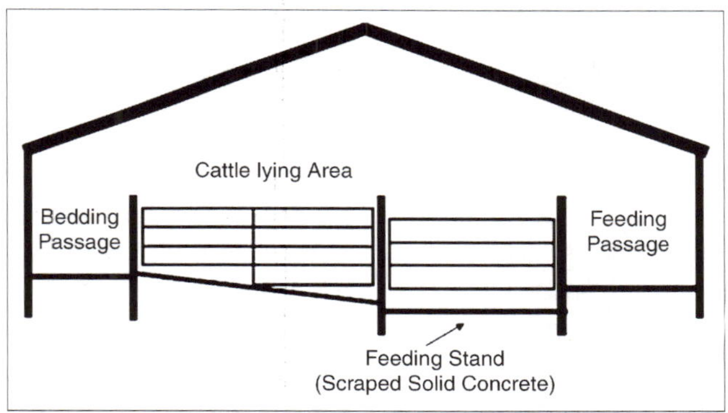

Fig. Bedded House with Sloped Concrete Floor

Cubicle House

A cubicle house provides an animal with an individual safe lying area. The system is widely used in the dairy industry for cows and the house type provides a clean lying area without the requirement for bedding material. Sometimes a little straw is used on the beds, which are normally constructed with concrete. Artificial mats are widely used in the dairy industry to improve the lying environment in cubicle beds.

Major limitations with cubicles for beef finishing animals are:

- The fact that as animal size is changing it is difficult to optimise the dimensions of the cubicle
- Male cattle foul the cubicle bed with urine
- Animals may only be housed for a relatively short period *e.g.* one winter season and often it is difficult in these situations to train animals to use the facilities

Slatted Floor House

The development of housing systems for beef animals utilising liquid manure storage has been promoted in order to overcome the unavailability of straw in many areas (combined with its increased cost), the need to reduce labour requirements and the necessity to ensure manure is efficiently managed to avoid pollution risks. The majority of such systems use concrete slatted floors with the liquid manure or slurry falling through the floor perforations into a below ground concrete tank.

The depth of the tank is such so as to provide adequate waste storage capacity for the housing period and is now typically about 2,5 m. A central covered feeding passage is typically used with confinement pens on each side. Silage can either be fed independently from concentrates or in combination. Feed face length is typically 0.3 m per adult animal for silage only feeding; 0.45 m where complete diets are fed and 0.6 m where concentrates are separately fed from silage.

The ratio of pen depth to width can be manipulated at the design stage to ensure adequate lying area and feeding space is provided. The superstructure is typically constructed from steel stanchions, steel trusses and timber purlins. Portal frame configurations are also used. Roof sheeting and cladding is typically galva-nised steel or fibre cement sheeting. Ventilation openings are provided at the sides of the building and at the ridges.

The size of the opening is dictated by the exposure of the site. More recently spaced roof sheeting has successfully been used and it has the advantage in that it provides a more uniform removal of stale air from over the animals throughout the buildings. To improve the interface of the floor with the animal the ribs of the slats can be covered with rubberised materials to provide cushioning for the animals. A cross sectional view of a typical unit is shown in *Figure*.

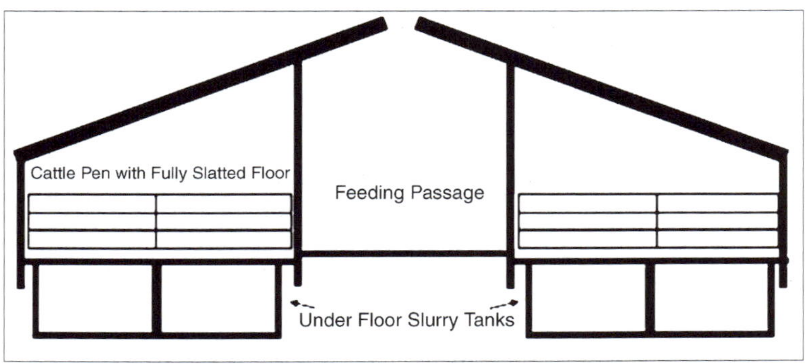

Fig. Cross Section of Slatted Floor House

Sloped Floor System without Bedding

This design is based on solid floors, which slope towards narrow manure collection channels covered with slats. The optimum length of the sloping floor section to avoid manual cleaning is approximately 1.5 m. The slope should be 1:12 (8 per cent). The manure channels should be 300 mm wide and at least 300 mm deep and up to 450 mm deep for long channel runs.

A flushing system or mechanical scraper can be used to effectively remove the manure from the channel to an outside storage facility. While the system offers the advantages of the slatted system (no straw costs and effective collection and management of liquid manure) the animal's hides will be dirtier, resting behaviour of the animals disturbed and the risk for pressure injuries on the animals will increase with this design of facility.

SAFETY AND ANIMAL HANDLING

Stockmen working in animal housing and associated handling facilities are exposed to a number of potential risks and health hazards. Many stockmen work alone, handling big, sometimes dangerous animals as well as large groups of animals.

Several work tasks involve daily lifting, carrying of heavy loads and awkward working postures, which may cause overload injuries on the worker's musculo-skeletal system. Other potential risk factors contributing to accidents as well as to physical health problems and physiological stress for the worker is the fact that they operate in an environment where they are exposed to airborne particles, gases, noise.

The work environment is partly the same environment, which is provided for the animals, and it should be noted that there is a strong relationship between the animal welfare issues and the handling of the work environment problems in cattle houses.

HEALTH AND INJURIES AMONG LIVESTOCK FARMERS

Accident Agents

In an accident situation there is a complex interaction between man and injury agents. In animal husbandry the human is subjected to a high degree of exposure to a large number of factors that singly or in combination can be accident provoking, such as animals, equipment and building structures. Risky situations are often due to wet and slippery floors as well as systems for material and animal handling.

Prevention of Accidents

With reference to accident statistics some accident preventing facilities and measures can be listed.

- Good cattle handling and handling facilities
- Pens from which the herdsman can easily escape if necessary in case of for instance frightened cattle and aggressive bulls
- Personnel passages through yard fences, properly placed
- Wide feeding passage or possibility to shut out the cattle from the feeding area
- Non slip flooring
- Satisfactory lighting considering quality and quantity
- Well designed ladders and stairways
- Protective railings around the fodder hay-chute in two storey houses
- Handles and bolts that do not stand out in alleys and pathways
- Protectors for the knuckles on barrows
- Emergency stops on machinery

Table. Recommended Illumination Level for Different Work Areas in Buildings Used for Beef Production. Lux Values Refer to the Work Plane. In Addition to the Quantity, the Quality of Light must be Considered

Building or Work Area/Task	Intensity of Illumination, Lux
Animal housing area	150
Animal handling area	250
Veterinary treatment	1,000
Feed processing, feed alley	250
Silo, feed storage	100
Ladders and stairs	250

Ergonomics

Any normally fit adult person, regardless of sex, physical strength and body dimensions should be able to work comfortably in livestock buildings. Despite an increasing degree of mechanisation and automation many jobs in animal husbandry are still associated with lifting heavy loads, moving and carrying equipment, feed and other materials with manual methods. An important step towards improved human welfare within cattle housing is to eliminate unnecessary loads on the human musculoskeletal system.

Health Aspects Related to Air Quality

It has been known for decades that farm workers suffer health risks due to inhalation of gases and airborne particles commonly referred to as dust. The particles may be liquid droplets or solid. Several respiratory disorders have been reported, which are associated with dust and work in confined livestock buildings such as hypersensitivity, pneumonia, acute inflammation, chronic bronchitis, occupational asthma and toxin fever. The respiratory problems connected to gases range from mild irritations of the respiratory tract to lethal effects. For the most frequent components in the air environment in livestock buildings there are statutory threshold limit values, which differ from country to country. It should be noted that threshold limit values in connection with animal welfare in many countries often are lower than the work environment legislation.

Dust and Dust Reducing

Dust in animal houses is generated inside the building and arises primarily from the animals and bedding and feed material. The airborne particles are often carriers of biologically active material like endotoxins, pathogens and allergens that can highly be disease provoking. Of special interest is the concentration (*i.e.* number of particles per air volume) of respirable particles with a diameter less than 5 µm that can be inhaled and deposited in the lung.

The smaller particle the higher possibility that the particle reaches the lower respiratory tract and the deeper the particle is deposited the higher is the risk for illness. Even if "common dust" can be seen by human eyes (larger diameter than 100 ìm), the very small respirable particles cannot be, so we are indeed dealing with a danger our senses are not able to detect.

There are basically four approaches that can be used for airborne dust reducing:

1. Prevent particle formation
2. Prevent particle release
3. Remove suspended particles from enclosed workspaces
4. Isolate workers from dust clouds in workspace.

Of course the best approach in this matter is to have the cattle and the working sites outdoors or in open barns. In the cattle barn the most effective way to obtain a low dust concentration level is to prevent formation by always using hygienically perfect forage and bedding material. Providing an effective ventilation system in a barn is a good practice to remove suspended respirable particles as well as gases.

Gases and Reduction of Gas Levels

In animal buildings over 150 different gases and volatile compounds have been identified. Most of the volatile compounds originate from biodegradation of animal excreta or are produced by the animals themselves such as carbon dioxide (by the respiration of the animal). The gases that are found in the highest elevated concen-trations are ammonia, carbon dioxide, hydrogen sulphide and methane.

It must be emphasised that it is dangerous to enter any manure tank without either using a self-contained air supply or combining several measures: testing the air, constant and adequate ventilation of fresh air and using an harness and lifeline on the person entering the tank. As well, human and animals positioned over a slatted floor with manure storage underneath are at risk during agitation, mixing or pumping of manure due to the gases, especially hydrogen sulphide. A good strategy is to evacuate dangerous zones during these manure-handling actions.

Ammonia

Ammonia is the most common polluting gas in the atmosphere of the cattle barn. Animal manure is the main source of ammonia. The gas together with hydrogen sulphide a major component in what is termed odour, noticeable at ammonia concentrations of 5 ppm or more.

Higher concentrations than that cause irritation to the respiratory organs and can aggravate the negative health effects of high dust concentrations. Many factors affect the emission and concentration of ammonia such as air flow rate, manure and air temperature, manure surface area, density of animals, the degree of mixing of urine and faeces, time intervals between manuring, the pH-value, carbon/nitrogen ratio, mois-ture content and type of bedding.

Consequently, many measures can be taken such as: proper ventilation and sufficient number of air changes, low air temperature in the barn and good urine drainage characteristics of the floor.

Hydrogen Sulphide

Hydrogen sulphide is the most toxic gas in animal confinement houses and 200 ppm and more are lethal for humans. The presence of the gas is of concern in buildings with liquid manure systems particularly. During slurry clearing operations concentrations in the range of 1,500 to 2,000 ppm have been reported. Since hydrogen sulphide is lethal the aim should be to keep it below detectable concentration at all working sites.

Special care has to be taken when pumping or agitating the manure. During emptying a slurry cellar the workers and the animal should be evacuated from the barn. In mechanical ventilated, closed animal houses continuously evacuation of the gases in an indoor slurry pit through a perforated duct under the floor and along the pit can reduce the gas concentrations above the slatted floor. By removing the slurry daily from the cattle barn to an outdoor storage it is possible to hold the concentration at an acceptable level.

Methane

Methane is generated when manure is stored under anaerobic conditions. This occurs in all non-aerated manure storages. Primarily, methane is dangerous because of its flammability. If methane is mixed in a proper proportion with oxygen a spark will be able to set off an explosion.

Carbon Dioxide

Carbon dioxide is present in all air, indoor as well as outdoors. Only extremely high concentrations (70,000 ppm or 7 per cent and over) could have severe health effects. Mostly, incidents and accidents involving carbon dioxide are connected with asphyxiation due to oxygen deficiency rather than the direct effect of carbon dioxide itself. For instance, it is dangerous to enter a haylage silo during storing. In animal buildings the gas is more an indicator of ventilation efficiency than a health risk.

Noise

Noise can be defined as "unwanted sound, rapid, annoying pressure vibration in the surrounding air". Ventilation fans, grinders, vacuum pumps and mechanical feeding and manure systems generate noise. High sound levels are a real stress factor.

Exposure to noise will be able to cause temporary deafness and permanent hearing loss after a variable period if the level is over 85 dB(A). The unit, dB(A), is exponential and the human sense of hearing will perceive the sound level as halving if a reduction of 10 dB(A) occurs.

It is fairly easy to reduce the sound level of ventilation fans and other mechanical noise generators. Maximum noise level recommendations and regulations differ from country to country. Furthermore, it is important to reduce noise when handling cattle in order to improve animal movement and to make cattle handling safer.

Cattle are more sensitive to high frequency noise than human. Animals will be calmer and easier to handle, if noise level is reduced. Clanging and banging metal parts should be silenced with rubber pads. Equipment operated with hydraulics should be engineered for quietness.

CATTLE HANDLING AND CATTLE HANDLING FACILITIES

Handling facilities are an essential part of a safe, easy and rapid handling of cattle. Appropriate handling and handling facilities remove much of the stress and frustration of the workmen, which inevitably occurs with excited, stubborn or aggressive animals. Properly constructed facilities confine cattle safely and efficiently with minimal animal stress and risk of injury to both cattle and workers.

Animal Behaviour and Improving Animal Handling

Understanding cattle behaviour can help farm workers to avoid dangerous situations and minimise accidents to handlers, as well as to design the handling facilities appropriately. Animals have natural boundary called the Flight Zone.

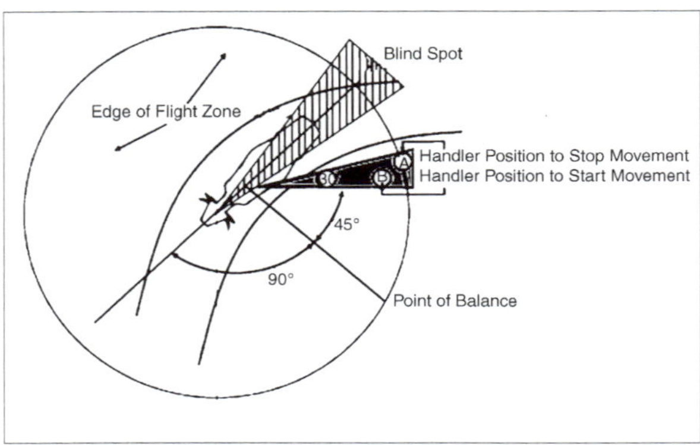

Fig. The Flight Zone of Animals

Deep penetration into the Flight Zone can cause panic and escape attempts. Handlers should have the possibility to remove, and should remove themselves from the Flight Zone, if the animal becomes aggressive. To move an animal forward: stand in the shaded area position B, behind the Point of Balance at the shoulder. Keep out of the Blind Spot at the rear of the animal. To stop movement: back off to position A. To make an animal back up: stand in front of the Point of Balance. To make an animal turn left or right: approach the animal head on. Factors reducing an animal's Flight Zone size: frequent contact with people; history of gentle handling; calm environment. Factors enlarging the Flight zone: infrequent contact with people; history of rough or abusive handling; excitement.

To improve animal handling and animal movement, many technical measures can be taken such as:

- Appropriate handling facility design.
- Animals tend to move from a dark to a more brightly lighted area. The light should illuminate the chute up ahead. Eliminate shadows and patches of light and dark, which may confuse animals. An approach is to illuminate the entire working area. Lamps should not shine into the eyes of approaching animals because glaring and blinding light impedes movement. Illumination should be uniform and diffuse.
- Prevent distractions, such as a chain hanging down in an entrance. Avoid sparkling reflection in a puddle, a moving reflection on a sheet of metal or bars of shadow across an otherwise sunlit alleyway. Dark colours can create shadow effects. Bright colours such as white and light yellow have been proven satisfactory.
- Reduce noise
- Animals might refuse to move, if they can see people ahead. Install shields to prevent animals from seeing farther ahead. Gates can be rigged with motor controls so a handler standing behind the cattle can open them.

- Solid sides that prevent the cattle from seeing outside the fences should be provided in the races and crowding pens. The crowding gate on the crowding pen should be solid as well, preventing animals from attempting to turn back to were they come from.
- Cattle are sensitive to changes in type and texture of floors and fences. Changes in type of flooring can cause balking. Use the same type of flooring throughout a facility, if possible. Use non-slip flooring. Drains should be located outside main drive alleys, chutes and crowd pens.

Cattle Handling Systems

A handling system has three main purposes: to sort, handle and treat cattle.

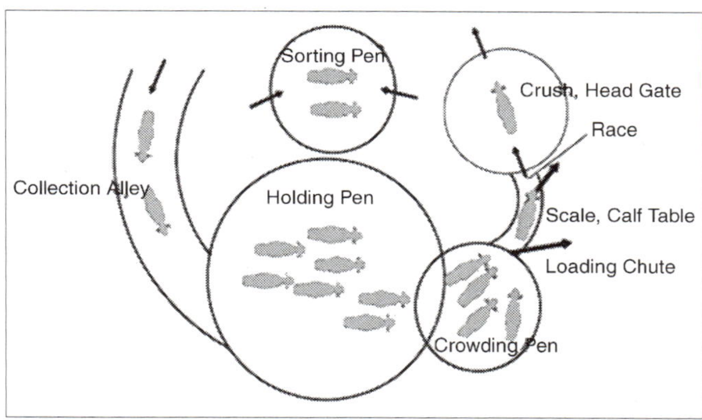

Fig. Components of a Cattle-handling System

The parts and the requirements of a system are:

- Collection alley to move cattle from the cattle house, pasture or feedlot to the holding pen
- *Sorting Pens*: Opening off the collection alley or holding pens, or after the working area
- Holding pens to hold either the whole herd or groups of 30-50 heads
- Crowding pen to move small groups of 8–10 cattle into the working area
- Single file race, at least 6 m long to hold 3–4 cattle at once
- Loading chute
- Crush, preferable type "walk-through" and with a self-locking head-gate
- Options such as scales, calf crush or table, belly clipping crush, crush equipped for claw-trimming, access kiosk for artificial insemination

and gynaecological examinations, shelf near the crush for veterinarian's equipment and materials, the availability of hot and warm water near the crush

The current trend in the design of cattle working facilities is to use circular crowding areas and working chutes.

If the single file race is bent too sharply where it joins the crowding pen, the cattle may refuse to enter, because it looks like a dead end. Cattle standing in the round crowding pen must be able to see a minimum of three body lengths up to the single file chute before the curve begins

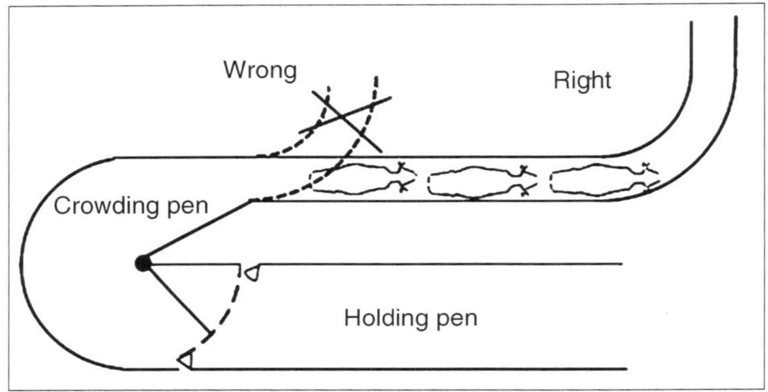

Fig. Layout for a Curved Handling System.

The circular designs take advantages of cattle's tendency to circle and crowd towards the outside of a curved passage.

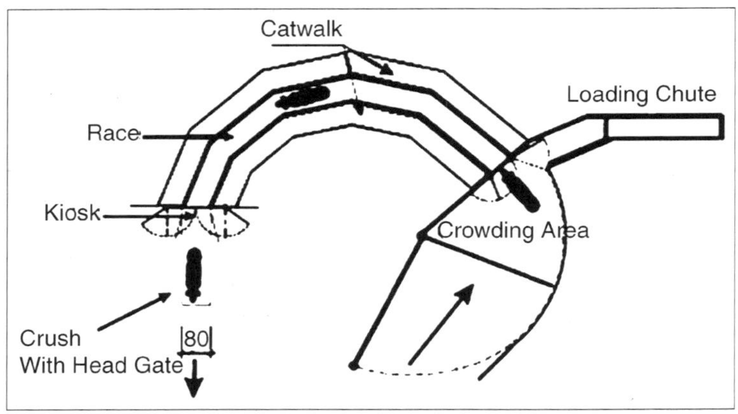

Fig. Basic Layout for a Working Unit

Cattle can normally be worked in less time with a round crowding pen and a curved race than a straight one. Round crowding pens should be laid out so the cattle make a 180° turn as they move though the crowding pen.

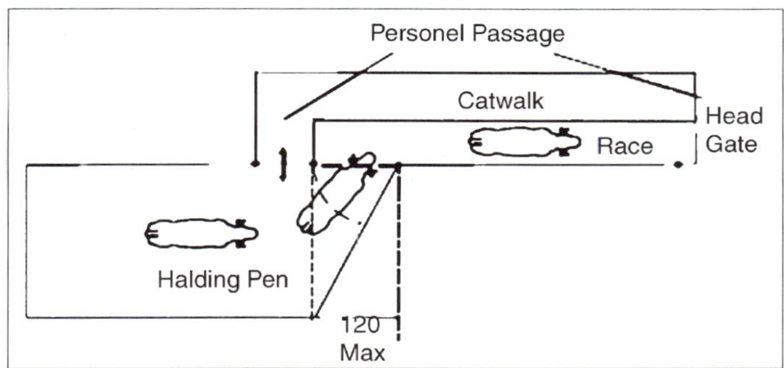

Fig. A Straight-line Designed Working Unit

However, a straight-line designed as well as a corner located working unit are area saving alternatives, especially valid for small herds of cattle and indoor, respectively.

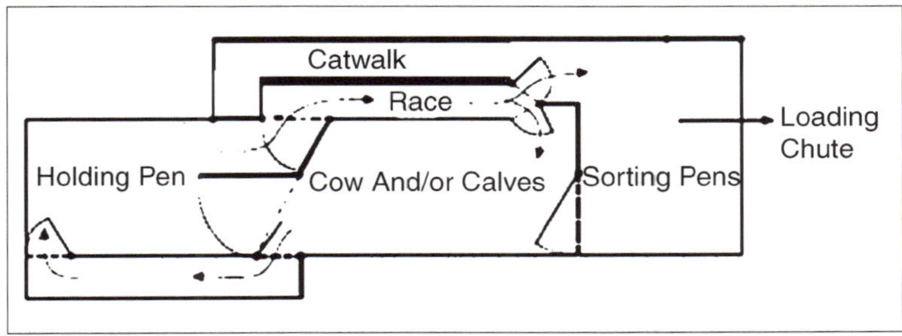

Fig. A Sorting Unit, for Instance for a Suckler Herd

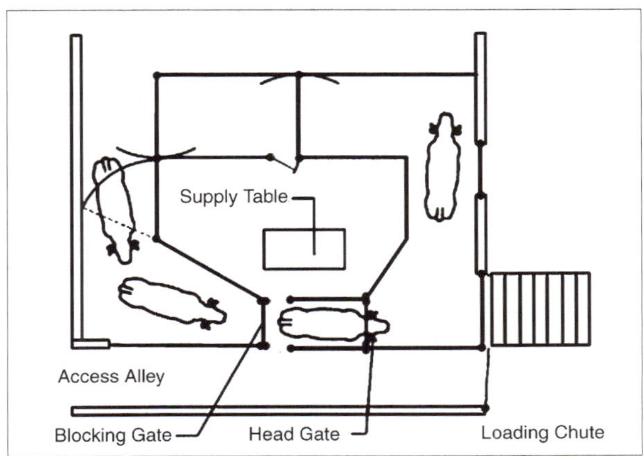

Fig. A Corner Located Working Unit

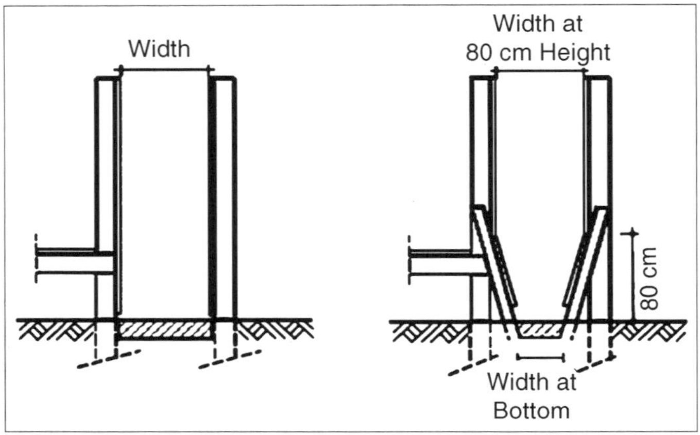

Fig. Straight Sided (Left) and Half Tapered (Right) Race Design

Some corral and working facility dimensions are given in *table.*

Table. Corral and Working Facility Dimension. L, W and H, Respectively in the Equations Correspond to Body Dimensions of Beef Cattle. Dimensions of Facilities Related to Animal Size are Calculated from CIGR

		Animal Size, kg					
	Equation	**200**	**300**	**400**	**500**	**600**	**700[a]**
Pen Space							
Holding pen, held overnight, m²/head	HAon= 6*L*W	2,4	3,1	3,9	4,6	5,2	5,9
Catch or holding pen[b], m2/head2,3	HA = 2,3*L*W	0,9	1,2	1,5	1,8	2,0	
Crowding pen, m2/head	CA = 1,4*L*W	0,6	0,7	0,9	1,1	1,2	1,4
Race with vertical sides							
Width, m	WR = 1,3*W	0,44	0,52	0,60	0,66	0,71	0,78
Length (minimum), m	LR = 4,2*L	4,9	5,5	6,0	6,3	6,7	6,9
Race with sloping sides							
Width at bottom inside clear, m	WRb = 0,85*W	0,30	0,35	0,40	0,43	0,47	0,51
Width at 80 cm height inside clear, m	WR = 1,3*W	0,44	0,52	0,60	0,66	0,71	0,78
Length (minimum), m	LR = 4,2*L	4,9	5,5	6,0	6,3	6,7	6,9
Race fence							
Height (minimum), m	HR = 1,15*H	1,25	1,36	1,46	1,53	1,59	1,63
Corral fence							
Height, m	HC = 1,25*H	1,36	1,49	1,59	1,66	1,73	1,78
Loading chute							

Width, m	WL = 1,4*W	0,48	0,56	0,64	0,71	0,77	0,84
Length (minimum), m		3,7	3,7	3,7	3,7	3,7	3,7
Rise (maximum), m/m		0,25	0,25	0,25	0,25	0,25	0,25

Notes:

[a] including cow-calf operations

[b] worked immediately

Some facilities and detailed solutions improve the human safety in cattle handling systems:

- Catwalk around the crowding pen, and working and loading chute allows the handler to see over a high, solid fence, follow the cattle and manoeuvre animals while avoiding direct animal contact. The catwalk should be minimum 60 cm wide, or wide enough to provide a comfortable surface. The catwalk height should be 90–110 cm below the top of the fence or at belt buckle height, if one stands on the catwalk. With any less, there is a danger of toppling into the pen or race. Access to the catwalk should be provided by steps. Catwalks and walkways that are more than 60 cm off the ground should have handrails for worker safety.

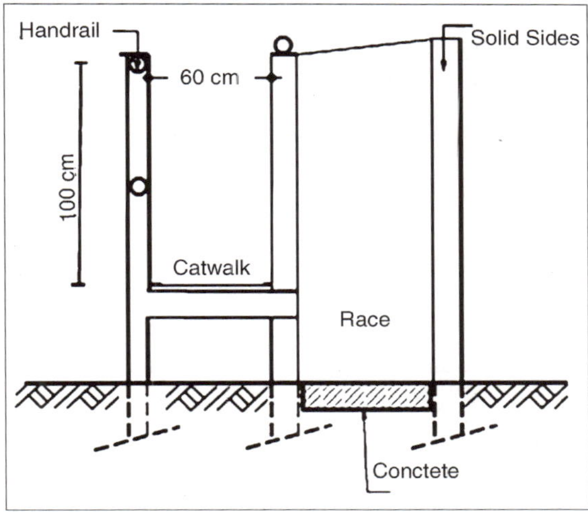

Fig. Cross-section of a Catwalk with Handrails

- Optional footholes/toe slots or escape boards/rails along solid sides inside pens at a 60 cm height will make toe ledges, if one has to make a quick exit from the pen. High solid fences (over 180 cm high) should have grab rail to facilitate the escape.
- Personnel passages, 36 cm wide, well placed in yard fences for hasty retreat. The two plank pieces in *Figure* in the gap are intended to keep calves inside the fold, but the planks can be designed to be removable.

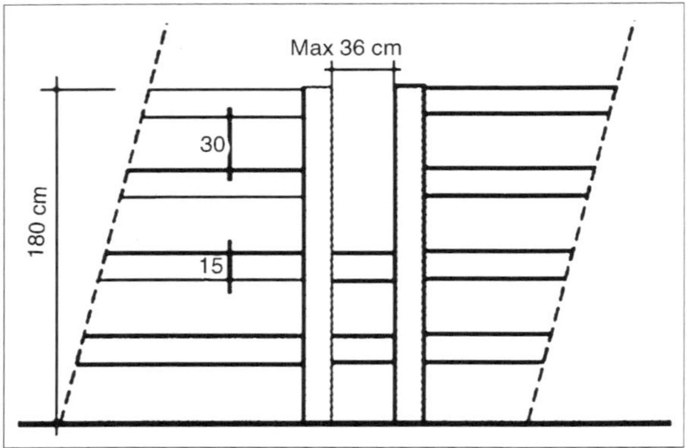

Fig. A Personnel Passage of a Wooden Yard Fence

- Personnel gates, 45 cm wide, spring loaded, no latches, open inward towards the cattle. Personnel escape gates are especially important in confined areas with solid fences such as the crowding pen where the handler may be deep in the animal's flight zone.

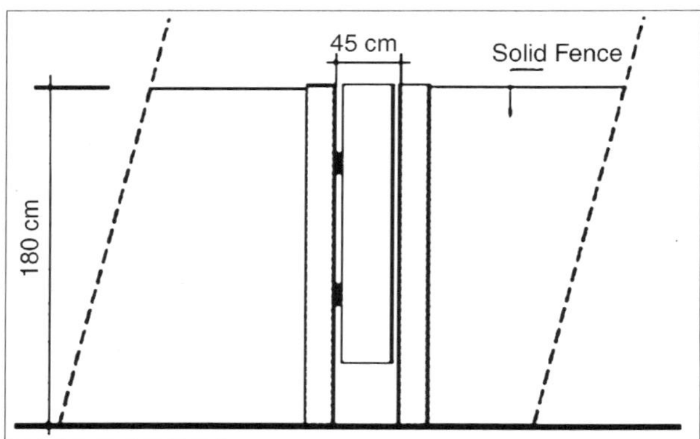

Fig. A Personnel Gate in a Solid Yard Fence

- One-way gates, to prevent cattle backing in the race are a safer alternative to pipes placed behind animals in the race. If backstops are not installed and pipes must be used, be sure the pipe is between the cattle and worker. If not, a worker can be caught between the pipe and the chute or fence if the animal backs up before the pipe is extended through the race. One-way gates should be adjusted to block an animal 15–20 cm below the top of the tail head. How-ever, too many backstop gates may cause balking and stop cattle movement through the facility. Install the one-way gate at least two body lengths up the race beyond the crowding pen, or let the oneway gate at the entrance be either tied open or remote controlled so it can be open as the animals enter.

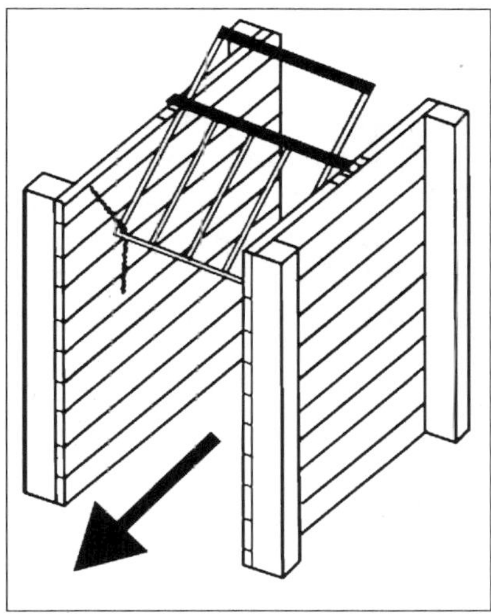

Fig. One Type of a One-way Gate

- Special bull pen with several personnel passages

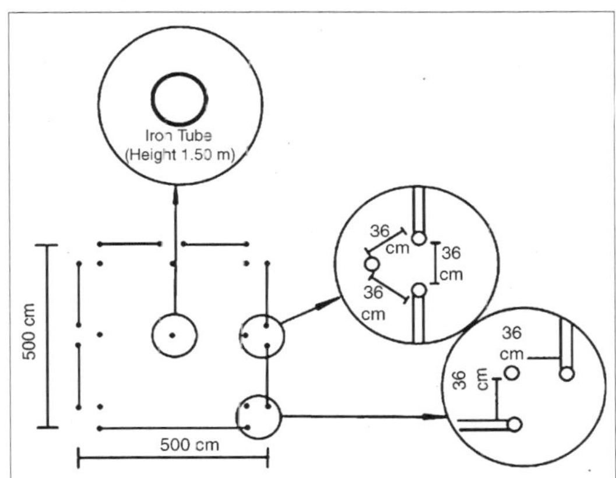

Fig. Bull Pen with Personnel Passages and a Central Column

- Hydraulically powered restraint equipment often is safer than manually operated facilities, because protruding lever arms are eliminated. In addition, a well-designed hydraulic crush takes less effort to use, is faster and sturdier than a manually operated crush. However, the pressure relief valve must correctly be set. Extreme pressure can cause severe injuries to both people and animals.
- Latching devices and protruding lever arms cause many injuries and are commonly described as "head-knokkers" and "jaw-breakers". To decrease the accidents, it is important to keep the latching devices well maintained and to avoid lever arms that protrude too long.

- Veterinarians performing rectal palpation might be injured, if a cow lies down and jams veterinarians arm. Use restraining methods that help circumvent this problem, *e.g.* types of head gates that reduce the risk of animal choking and going down.
- Accidents occur when treating animals, which are caught around their hips by the head gates. To reduce the temptation of working on an animal that is half out of the crush, install a sorting gate in front of the crush and a separate holding pen. Then the animal is easily moved back through the crush for reworking.

11

Agricultural Practices and Animal Husbandry

We all need food to survive. Food is the basic need for all living beings, as it provides energy for doing work, and raw material for building and repair of various parts of the body. You know that our country has a large population, and therefore, we need to produce a lot of food. You also know that to produce such a large amount of food we need a large area of land.

However, our land availability is limited. Indian scientists have experimented and researched and suggested ways and means by which more food can be grown than before, on the same piece of land. Improved methods of agriculture have led to the production of about 360m tonnes of plant food products and about 88m tonnes of animal food products.

HUMAN DEPENDENCE ON PLANTS AND ANIMALS FOR FOOD

Our food items are either plant products, such as grains, vegetables and fruits or animal products like milk, egg, mutton, chicken etc. We eat various parts of plant as food. For example, grains of rice, wheat and corn are seeds; radish and carrot are roots; potatoes and ginger are the stem. We also eat leaves and stem of spinach and plenty of fruits. Thus, human beings depend on plants and animals for food.

AGRICULTURE AND AGRICULTURAL PRACTICES

The branch of science which deals with methods of food production is known as agriculture. Besides studying the new methods of food production, in this branch of science we also study about how new and better varieties of crops can be grown, how animals and birds like cows, hens, etc. can be reared well and made to give more milk or better quality eggs? All these new methods which scientists develop come under agricultural practices. We need vegetables, fruits, cereals, pulses, etc. as food. For our clothes, we need the fibre of plants or animals. We get all these foods and fibres by farming or agriculture.

Example: Make a list of things which you use every day. Categorise those items which you get directly or indirectly from agriculture. Does your list look like the one given below?

For easy reading, agricultural products have been divided into the following groups as given in the table.

Table. Various Categories of Food Items

Category	Examples
Millets	Sorghum (Jowar), Ragi (finger millet) and Bajra (pearl millet)
Pulses	Arhar (*Tur*), Black gram (*Urad*), Green gram (*Moong*), and Bengal gram (*Channa*)
Beans	Peas, Soyabean, Cowpea, Lentil
Oilseeds	Mustard, Groundnut, Soyabean, Sunflower, Linseed,
Castor and	Cotton seed
Root crops	Carrot, Turnip, Sweet potato
Tuber crops	Potato, Tapioca, Ginger and Turmeric
Sugar crops	Sugarcane and Beet root
Plantation crops	Coffee, Tea, Rubber and Coconut

HORTICULTURE

Did you observe that something is missing from the list of food items which we eat every day. What is it that we have not listed here in table? Yes, we have neither included vegetables nor fruits in this list. Vegetables and fruits are essential items of our diet and their growth and production are studied under a branch of agriculture called horticulture.

Horticulture is derived from two latin words:

1. *Hortus* which means garden, and
2. *Culture* which means cultivation.

Horticulturists research to find new ways by which better varieties of fruits and vegetables can be grown in large quantities.

STEPS IN RAISING IMPROVED AGRICULTURAL PRODUCE

To increase our food production we can sow good quality seeds and improve the methods of sowing. We can make the soil more rich and even use better techniques for harvesting the crops. Some of the agricultural practices which scientists have developed and which our farmers have started are explained here.

PREPARATION OF SOIL

This is an important practice which helps to enrich the soil and make it more fertile and aerated. It involves addition of manure followed by turning, loosening and levelling of the soil, using agricultural implements like spade, plough or mechanical farm implements.

SEED TREATMENT

Seeds can easily be attacked by micro-organisms. The crops that grow out of diseased seeds will also be unhealthy. So farmers treat these seeds by dipping them in certain chemicals like *cerosan* or *agrosan*. These chemicals do not allow the microorganisms to attack the seeds and damage them. Such chemicals are called Fungicides. Once the seeds are treated, they can be sown.

PREPARING THE SEED BED AND CARE OF THE SEEDLINGS

In certain crop plants like paddy and some of the vegetables, seeds are not sown directly in the main field. First these seeds are sown in a nursery bed. Once they grow to a certain age they are transferred and planted in the main field. These small plants are called seedlings.

When the farmers prepare a nursery bed they take care of the following:

- The soil of the bed should be soft and loose so that the tender roots of the seedlings can grow well. This can be achieved by digging or ploughing the field well.
- The seed bed or where the seedlings are planted should be even so that when we water the plants, the water distributes itself uniformly all over the field.
- All weeds or unwanted plants in the field must be removed. Do you know why? It is because these weeds also take water and nutrients from the soil and as a result the desired plants cannot get enough of the nutrients. The seedlings also need to be protected from diseases and pests. This is done by spraying chemicals like *Parathion, Sevin, Dimecron* and *Rogor* on the seedlings.

TRANSPLANTING

The process of removing the seedlings from the nursery bed and planting them in the main field is called transplanting. When we transplant, we must select those seedlings which have 4 to 5 healthy leaves. These are sowed at proper distance from each other. The main field must be ploughed and manured before transplanting.

Generally rice and vegetables like tomato and brinjal are sown by transplanting. Transplanting of seedlings is a very important practice. This enables us to select good and healthy seedlings and get a better crop. Besides, when we transplant seedlings, their roots are able to go deep into the soil and get more nutrients. When seedlings get good food, they grow into healthy plants and give a better yield.

ADDING FERTILIZERS

Crops need nutrients like phosphorus, calcium, nitrogen etc. for their growth and pick up these nutrients from the soil. It is very important to add fertilizers to the soil. They provide nutrients to the soil and help to obtain a better crop yield. Depending on the type of soil and the crop to be grown, we use different fertilizers. The way we use a fertilizer also depends upon what type of fertilizer is being added to the soil.

A fertilizer which contains nitrogen (nitrogenous fertilizer) is generally given in two or three doses. Other fertilizers are phosphatic and complex fertilizers. Some fertilisers are added to the soil before transplanting. You must have heard about the most commonly used fertilizer 'NPK'. The letter N stands for nitrogen, P for phosphate and K for potassium. While fertilizers are manufactured from chemicals in factories, manure is made from organic substances and contains nutrients in small quantities.

Some of the commonly used manure are:

- *Farmyard manure,* as the name suggests is a mixture of decomposed cattle dung (excreta) and urine, left over fodder (cattle feed) and litter (bedding provided to cattle in the farm).
- *Compost* is manure made from vegetable and animal refuse collected from domestic waste, straw, weeds etc., dumped in a deep pit to decompose.
- *Vermicompost* is compost broken down by earthworms. Like fertilizers manures too add nutrients to soil.

USE OF PLANT GROWTH REGULATORS

Plant growth regulators are certain chemicals which regulate the growth of plants. All plants have growth regulators which determine how tall the plant would be, how big its fruit will be, etc. We can now add some plant growth regulators like *auxins, gibberellins, cytokinins, abscisic acid* etc. to get a better yield of crops. You will learn more about these plant growth regulators in higher classes.

IRRIGATION

Irrigation is necessary for proper development of plants. Roots fail to develop and penetrate in the dry soil. The crop is irrigated according to its requirement and soil characteristics. Irrigation is essential during the seedling, flowering and grain filling stages of the crop. Rice crop needs standing water.

HARVESTING

Harvesting machines have now replaced the back breaking job of hand harvesting with the sickle and scythe. Harvesting machines cut or dig out the plant or its parts as required. The machines gather the plant parts, separate desired parts and eliminate parts not needed. Certain harvesting machines may even load the crop for transport. However, the above mentioned functions of harvesting machines depend on kind of crop, plant parts to be harvested, crop use, stage of maturity, etc.

SOME OTHER DIFFERENT AGRICULTURAL PRACTICES

ROTATION OF CROPS

If you stay in a village you must have seen that the wheat crop is planted during the month of November and harvested in March and April. The rice crop is planted in June-July and harvested in October and November. The land that lies fallow in between these two cereal crops, can be used by the farmers for sowing a leguminous crop at this time.

A leguminous crop does not take as long as wheat or rice to grow. So by the time the farmer has to plant the cereal crops (rice, wheat etc.) the pulse is ready to be harvested. Leguminous crops include pea, beans, grams and pulses. They harbour nitrogen fixing bacteria in nodules of their roots. These bacteria convert free nitrogen from atmosphere into usable form. Thus, after the leguminous crop is harvested, the soil is left fertile for other crops.

The process of growing a different crop preferably a leguminous crop in between raising of two similar crops is called rotation of crops.

Crop rotation has a lot of benefits:

- The land gets utilized,
- The pulse crop uses up different nutrients from the soil but it fixes the nitrogen from the air and makes the soil richer in nitrogen and so more fertile.

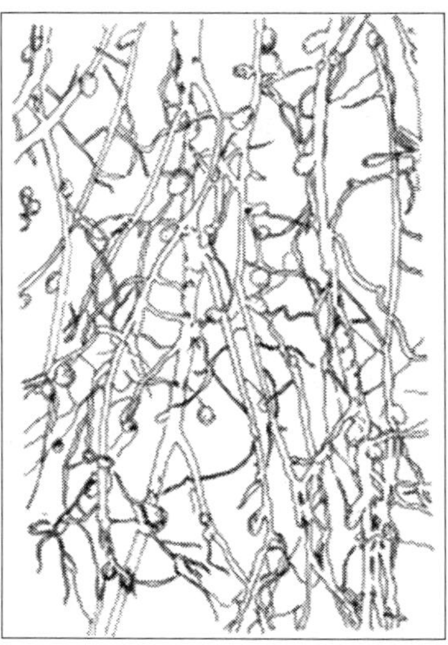

Fig. Nitrogen Fixing Bacteria in the Root Nodules

This way the next cereal crop gives a better yield. If we do not practice crop rotation by growing different crops on a piece of land, but continue to grow the same crop, year after year, they will keep on using the same nutrients from the soil till all the nutrients in the soil get used up.

The newly grown plants get poor nourishment from the soil and grow up to be weak and of bad quality. When plants are weak the insects can easily attack them and destroy them. Thus, crop rotation restores the fertility of the soil, it gives better yield, prevents crop from diseases and pests and reduces the dependence on chemical fertilizers.

MULTIPLE CROPPING

Growing two to four crops one after the other in a year in the same field is called multiple cropping. Multiple cropping is possible, when we make use of crop varieties that grow for a short period of time. However, to get best results there must be a properly managed field. In fact, multiple cropping is the best solution for a country with food problem because same piece of land is used to grow different kinds of crops.

Example: Here is something you can do. Visit a nearby agricultural farm or vegetable garden. Observe and note down the agricultural practices being used there.

All the above mentioned practices are meant to ensure that plants have a healthy growth and yield a good crop. Along with these developments in our country we have also brought under cultivation more and more land. The increased cultivation of agricultural crops is in order to meet requirements of a growing population.

IMPROVING THE VARIETY OF SEEDS

You must have often heard or read advertisements which encourage farmers to buy new and better varieties of seeds. Some of these new varieties are resistant to diseases and give a very good crop. Some of the improved high-yielding crop varieties which our scientists have developed are given in table.

Table. Improved High-yielding Varieties of Crops

Crop	Variety
Rice	I R-8, Jaya, Padma, Bala
Wheat	Sarbati sonara, Sonalika, Kalyan sona, Hira-moti, RR-21 and UP 301
Maize	Ganga 101, Rankit and Deccan hybrid
Lady's finger (*Bhindi*)	Pusa savani
Brinjal	Pusa purple, Pusa kranti and Muktabeshi

Do you know what name is given to scientists who develop such new varieties of seeds? They are called plant breeders. Plant breeders have not only raised better quality seeds but also better quality fruits. Mango has been named the 'king of fruits' and in our country we grow many varieties of mangoes.

Some of them are:

- Alphonse,
- Langra,
- Chausa,
- Saroli,
- Dussehri,
- Himsagar,
- Safeda,
- Sinduri,
- Mulgoba,
- Amini.

PROTECTION OF CROPS IN THE FIELD

As crops grow in the field, they have to be protected such that they produce a healthy yield. The weeds growing along with crops have to be removed and growing crops have to be saved from the attack of pests especially insects pests.

WEED CONTROL

The undesirable plants that compete with the main crop for sunshine, water and space in the field are called weeds. Weeds must be removed as they use up the nutrients in the soil and thereby make them unavailable for the crop itself.

Weeds can be divided into two groups:

1. Graminaceous (Monocotyledonous), and
2. Nongraminaceous (Dicotyledonous).

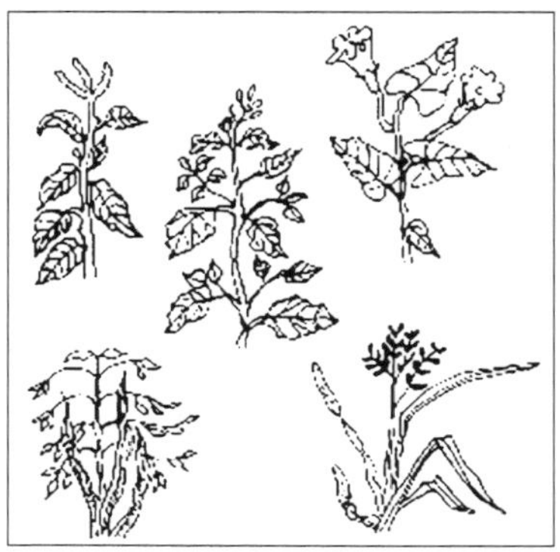

Fig. Some Common Weeds

Hariali or *Doob* grass is a graminaceous weed, while *Choulai* is a non-graminaceous weed. Before sowing or transplanting seedlings, weeds are removed by hand or with the help of a plough or harrow. If some of these weeds start growing again during the crop growth they must be removed. They can be removed by hand or by spraying weed killing chemicals called weedicides like 2, 4-D; MCPA and Simazine.

CONTROL OF PLANT DISEASES AND PESTS

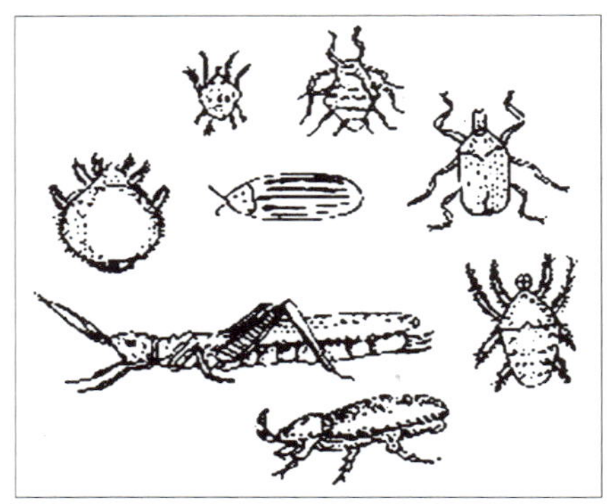

Fig. Some Insect Pests of Crops

A lot of plants die due to some diseases and pests which attack and damage them. Generally plant diseases are caused by fungi, bacteria, and viruses. These diseases are transmitted either through the seed itself (seed-borne) or by air (airborne) or soil (soil-borne).

Rust of wheat and Blast of rice are two common fungal diseases of plants. Insects are generally pests which eat and destroy crops. To control plant diseases and pests we can spray fungicides and pesticides on the crops or on the soil. Apart from chemical methods, biological control methods are also used. For example aquatic weeds are eaten up by certain fish. Some insect pests are controlled by introducing their predator insects.

PRESERVATION AND STORAGE OF AGRICULTURAL PRODUCTS

Once harvested, food grains have to be safely stored. They have to be saved from being attacked and eaten up by rodents, birds or insects. Also they have to be protected from spoilage due to improper temperature and moisture in the storage place or due to growth of fungi.

Some of the methods to prevent loss and spoilage of agricultural products are as follows:

- *Drying*: The grains can be dried in the sun or by blowing hot air on them.

- *Maintaining Storage Containers*: Godowns or gunny bags or tanks or earthen pots used for storage should be free of the cracks and holes and should be clean.
- *Chemical Treatment*: Spraying or fumigation (insecticide solution converted into fumes) of godowns and containers with insecticides and fungicides should be done before storage. Care should be taken to ascertain that the grains for consumption by human beings are not treated with chemicals poisonous to human beings. Grains are often treated with neem kernel powder or pepper or mineral oil which prevent laying of eggs by insect pests.
- *Use of Improved Storage Structures*: Structures which are airtight, rat proof, moisture proof and can maintain a steady temperature are now used for storage. Few of them are named Pusa bin, Pusa cubicle and Pusa kothar. Fig. shows a type of of storage structure called 'silos'.

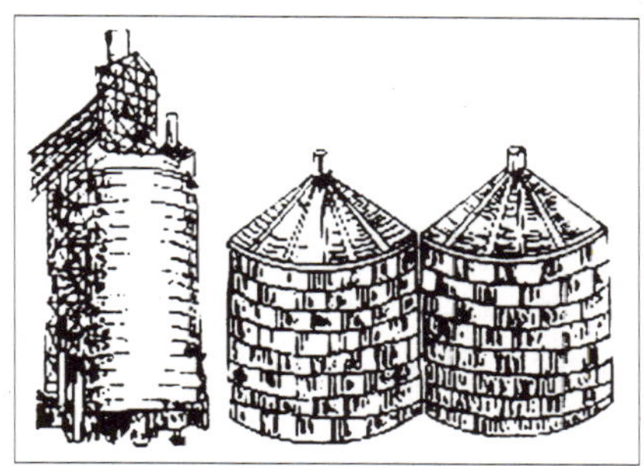

Fig. Silos

GREEN REVOLUTION

A general improvement in crop yield and food production occurred in our country between 1960 and 1980 and marked a turning point in Indian agriculture. This is commonly referred to as the golden era of agriculture or the *green revolution*. As a result of this we have become self-sufficient in food. In fact we are able to have surplus crop to stock and use in natural calamities like drought and floods. The credit for green revolution goes to a great agricultural scientist of our country, Dr. M.S. Swaminathan. He is the recipient of World Food prize for fighting against hunger.

Thus, we find that modern agriculture needs the support of:

- Industries to produce farm implements, pumps, fertilizers and pesticides;
- Irrigation and power projects to provide timely supply of water and power; and
- Research and development institutions to breed newer, sturdier, pest resistant and better yielding varieties of crops and animals.

ANIMAL HUSBANDRY

The branch of science, which deals with the study of various breeds of domesticated animals and their management for obtaining better products and services from them is termed animal husbandry (the term husbandry comes from 'husband' which means one who takes care).

- *Milk Giving (Milch) Animals:* Cows, buffaloes and goats who give us milk.
- *Meat and Egg Giving Animals:* Pigs, cattle, goat, sheep, fowls and ducks which are the main source of meat. From hens and ducks we get eggs.
- *Working (Draught) Animals*: Bullocks, buffaloes, camels and horses are draught animals used for doing work in the field and for transportation of goods and human beings. Mules are also used especially by the army to take things from one place to another in the hilly areas.

We also get horns, feathers and leather from some of these animals which can be used for making various things. Their urine and droppings help to make the soil fertile by acting as manure.

NEED FOR ANIMAL HUSBANDRY

We have a large number of animals in our country. Yet we do not get as much food from these animals as we possibly can and need for our large population. Besides the food, which we get from animals, we need them to do a lot of our work. In India, we have about 80.4 million cattle, which work in the fields. If we take the ratio of working cattle to the area of land, which is being used for cultivation we find that only two individuals of cattle are available to plough 3.8 hectares of land. You all know that cattle wastes like urine and faeces are natural manure which enrich our soil. Unfortunately, in India we do not use all the cowdung available and a lot of it goes waste. Gobar gas plants have been developed so that we can make use of the cattle dung both for fuel as well as to make manure. Thus, we find that animal husbandry is a very important field which helps us to improve our livestock and other useful animals and make the maximum use of them.

MANAGEMENT OF LIVESTOCK

When we study about improving our livestock we learn how they must be sheltered, fed, and mated, what kind of drinking water should be given to them and how the sick and diseased animals ought to be treated? This way we learn to manage our livestock for better production and utilization.

Feeding of Animals

All animals must be fed properly. The food should contain the requisite nutrients i.e. carbohydrates, proteins, fats, minerals, vitamins and water.

The food which is given to cattle can be divided into two categories:

1. Concentrates like cotton seeds, oilcakes, cereal grains, bran etc. They are very rich in most of the nutrients.
2. Roughage includes fibrous and rough food like straw and stems of cereal crops. Generally roughage has a low nutrient content.

An average Indian cow eats about 15-20 kg of green fodder and 4 to 5 kg drygrass, which is mixed with a sufficient amount of grain. A cow drinks about 32 litres of water. Goat and sheep eat grass, herbs and waste products from the farms. Pigs are usually given cereals and their products to eat. Poultry birds are given a mixed feed consisting of cereals, bone meal, minerals and vitamins.

Housing of Animals

We must protect our animals from too much heat, rain and cold. We must, therefore, be careful where we house them. Their houses should have proper sanitation and ventilation. Too many animals should never be kept in a small space. Different animals require different types of houses. Hens and fowls are kept in cages while sheep and goats stay in open yard, which is partially covered with roof made of straw. This open yard should have a hedge of iron wires all around to prevent the animals from running away.

Water and its Supply

To keep these animals healthy they should be given clean water to drink and in sufficient quantities. For example, on an average a cow consumes about 27-36L of water, pigs require 5-23L, camel 8-90L and poultry birds require about 240mL of water. Besides this we must also bathe the cattle with clean water.

Some Common Diseases of Animals and Vaccination

Sometimes domestic animals may be afflicted by diseases.

Some of the common diseases of animals are listed below:

- *Viral Diseases*: Pox in cattle, goats, sheeps, and fowls; dermatitis in goats and sheep; foot and mouth disease in cattle.
- *Bacterial Diseases*: Tuberculosis in cattle and poultry birds; cholera in fowls; diphtheria in calf; diarrhea in chicks; foot rot in sheep.

Most of these diseases can be prevented by proper sanitation, a controlled diet, proper housing and also by vaccinating the animals against these diseases at the proper time and age.

Animal Breeding

Breeding means to reproduce. In case of animals, breeding is done to obtain animals with desired characters. The two individuals of desirable characters can be selected as parents. These are then crossed to obtain new breeds of animals, e.g. by cross breeding a cow of low milk yielding breed, we can get breeds of cow which produces more milk.

Artificial insemination is an important and effective method of breeding. The process involves injecting the semen obtained from desired bull belonging to high milk yielding breed into the reproductive tract of female during heat period. It generally gives important breeds, and is widely used to improve the qualities of cow, buffaloes, poultry, horse and goat etc.

Important Breeds of Cow

In India, improved breeds of dairy cows have been developed at National Dairy Research Institutre (NDRI), Karnal, Haryana.

Some examples are:

- Karan Swiss (Crossbreed of brown Swiss and Sahiwal)
- Karan Fries (Crossbreed of Tharparkar and Holstein- Friesian)
- Frieswal (Crossbreed of Holstein-Friesian and Sahiwal)

Over the last two decades, improved practices of raising animals have resulted in the development of new breeds of dairy animals, poultry and pigs. This has substantially increased our milk, egg and meat production.

Fig. High Yield Breeds of Cows

There is no dearth of milk, the most wholesome food in the country. The credit for increased milk production goes to Dr. V. Kurien. Dr Kurien is the founder chairman of National Dairy Development Board which designed and implemented "Operation flood"–the programme which led to the "white revolution" or self sufficiency of the country in dairy products.

12

Animal Reproduction

INTRODUCTION

Reproduction is one of the most characteristic features of living organisms. Life would not exist on Earth if plants and animals did not reproduce to make their offspring. By reproducing, a living organism can be sure that there is another individual of its kind to take its place when it dies. In this way a species of organism guarantees its survival.

A species is a particular type of organism. For example, a horse is a species and a zebra is another species. A species which cannot reproduce enough offspring will disappear for ever from the face of the Earth - it will become extinct. This has happened many times in the past. The best known example of animals which have become extinct is the dinosaurs. The dinosaurs were a group of reptiles which mysteriously became extinct 60 million years ago. Fortunately there has always been another type of living organism to replace those that become extinct. In the case of the dinosaurs they left the Earth to the group of animals that we belong to, the mammals.

HOW ANIMALS REPRODUCE

Animals can be grouped into those which give birth to living offspring and those which lay eggs that eventually hatch into offspring. Those animals which give birth to live offspring are called live-bearing or viviparous.

Those animals which lay eggs are called egg-laying or oviparous. The difference is in the place where the offspring develops before it is born. Below is a table of the vertebrates which shows which groups are viviparous and which groups are oviparous.

Group	Oviparous (Egg-layers)	Viviparous (Live-bearers)
Mammals	Only a few primitive egg-laying mammals exist. They live in Australia and New Guinea. *e.g.* spiny	Nearly all mammalssss *e.g.* mouse, human, cat, dog, bear, kangaroo and dolphin.

	anteater and duck-billed platypus.	
Birds	All birds. *e.g.* robin, penguin, parrot, sparrow and eagle.	None.
Reptiles	Most reptiles are egg-layers. *e.g.* crocodile, turtle and cobra.	Some lizards and snakes are live-bearing. *e.g.* vipers.
Amphibians	Nearly all. *e.g.* frog, toad and living in South America	A few species of frogs and West Africa are live-bearers.
Fish	Most species. *e.g.* herring, salmon and trout.	Quite a few species are live-bearers. *e.g.* sharks and guppies.

Amongst the invertebrates there are many which are oviparous but a few are viviparous such as sea anemones and aphids.

SEXES AND SEX CELLS

A species of animal usually exists in two types or sexes called males and females. Each sex has its role to play in reproduction. When an animal gives birth or lays eggs we notice that it is always the female which does this. In some cases, such as the sea horse and the midwife toad, the male appears to give birth to the offspring. In these exceptions the male has been given the eggs to look after but it is still the female animal that lays the eggs in the first place. To produce an offspring two special cells are needed. A cell is a microscopic part of an organism's body. The bodies of animals are made of millions of cells. There are many different sorts of cells in a body, each having specialized functions. Some are found in the blood transporting oxygen, others are found in the walls of our stomach producing juices to digest our food. To reproduce, animals make special sex cells. In the male animal these sex cells are called sperm cells or sperms and in the female animal they are called egg cells or eggs.

Sperm Cells

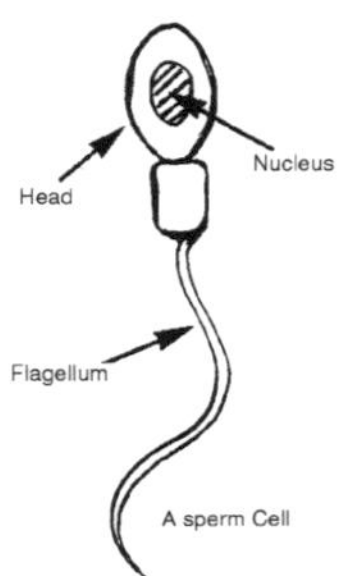

Fig. Sperm Cell

Sperm cells are very small but they are very specialized too. The sperm cells of different species of animal are all about the same size, about 60μm long (μm = micrometres; This is a thousandth of a millimetre). Over 11 000 sperm cells could fit on a pin head! All sperms have a head and a tail called a flagellum.

They use the flagellum to swim through liquids. The head of the sperm is very important because it contains the nucleus. The nucleus of the cell is the control centre.

In sex cells the nucleus carries half of the information needed for reproduction (like the plans needed to construct a house). Sperm cells are made in very large numbers by special organs in the male's body called testes (sing. testis). In most animals the testes are carried inside the male's abdomen but in mammals they are kept in a sack of skin called sperm duct the scrotum outside the abdomen.

Egg Cells

Egg cells are produced by female animals in special organs called ovaries (sing. ovary). These are found inside the abdomen of all female animals. Egg cells are much bigger and simpler than sperm cells in their structure.

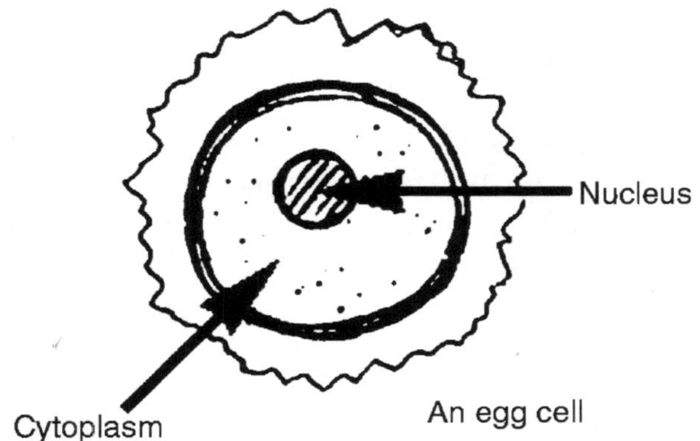

Fig. Egg Cell

They do, however, vary a lot from one species of animal to another. For example the egg of a human is only 0,1 mm wide but the egg of a chicken is 20 mm wide.

Animal	Number of Eggs Produced At One Time
Cod	5000000
Frog	1500
Viper	12
Human	1

Even so the human egg cell is still nearly 50 times wider than a sperm cell. The reason for the difference in size is that the egg has a large food supply stored inside it called yolk. Yolk is the yellow part of a chicken's egg.

The egg also has its own nucleus which carries the other half of the information needed for reproduction. Because eggs are bigger than sperms they are not produced in such large numbers. Even so animals which do not take care of their offspring, such as fishes and frogs, will lay a large number of eggs. Animals which take care of their offspring, such as mammals and birds, will produce less eggs.

ASEXUAL REPRODUCTION

Reproduction is a marvelous culmination of individual transcendence. Individual organisms come and go, but, to a certain extent, organisms "transcend" time by reproducing offspring. Let's take a look at reproduction in animals.

WHAT IS REPRODUCTION?

In a nutshell, reproduction is the creation of a new individual or individuals from previously existing individuals. In animals, this can occur in two primary ways: through asexual reproduction and through sexual reproduction. Let's look at asexual reproduction.

ASEXUAL REPRODUCTION

In asexual reproduction, one individual produces offspring that are genetically identical to itself. These offspring are produced by mitosis. There are many invertebrates, including sea stars and sea anemones for example, that produce by asexual reproduction. Common forms of asexual reproduction include:

Budding

- In this form of asexual reproduction, an offspring grows out of the body of the parent.
- Hydras exhibit this type of reproduction.

Gemmules (Internal Buds)

- In this form of asexual reproduction, a parent releases a specialized mass of cells that can develop into offspring.
- Sponges exhibit this type of reproduction.

Fragmentation

- In this type of reproduction, the body of the parent breaks into distinct pieces, each of which can produce an offspring.
- Planarians exhibit this type of reproduction.

Regeneration

- In regeneration, if a piece of a parent is detached, it can grow and develop into a completely new individual.
- Echinoderms exhibit this type of reproduction.

Parthenogenesis

- This type of reproduction involves the development of an egg that has not been fertilized into an individual.
- Animals like most kinds of wasps, bees, and ants that have no sex chromosomes reproduce by this process. Some reptiles and fish are also capable of reproducing in this manner.

ADVANTAGES AND DISADVANTAGES OF ASEXUAL REPRODUCTION

Asexual reproduction can be very advantageous to certain animals. Animals that remain in one particular place and are unable to look for mates would need to reproduce asexually. Another advantage of asexual reproduction is that numerous offspring can be produced without "costing" the parent a great amount of energy or time. Environments that are stable and experience very little change are the best places for organisms that reproduce asexually. A disadvantage of this type of reproduction is the lack of genetic variation. All of the organisms are genetically identical and therefore share the same weaknesses. If the stable environment changes, the consequences could be deadly to all of the individuals.

Asexual Reproduction in Other Organisms

Animals are not the only organisms that reproduce asexually. Yeasts, plants and bacteria are capable of asexual reproduction as well. Bacterial asexual reproduction most commonly occurs by a kind of cell division called binary fission. Since the cells produced through this type of reproduction are identical, they are all susceptible to the same types of antibiotics.

MATING AND FERTILIZATION

The sperm cell carries half of the information needed for reproduction and the egg cell carries the other half. To produce an offspring the sperm and egg have to meet. This means that the male and female animals have to come together. This is called mating. Because the sperms can swim on their own, aquatic animals such as fish can simply release the eggs and sperms into the water. Amphibians, which return to water to reproduce, also release their eggs and sperms directly into the water.

The sperm cell is microscopic and only lives for a short time, so the eggs and sperms need to be released close together. Fish, such as herring, which live in the open sea will shoal at certain times of the year. Shoaling occurs when the males and females gather close together, usually near the surface of the sea. The females release their eggs and the males release their sperms at the same time and in the same place. Therefore, the sperms do not have far to swim. Fish, such as salmon, trout and sticklebacks, build their nests in the mud and gravel on the bottom of shallow rivers and lakes. The male usually builds the nest and then he guards it. When a female enters his territory he will try to encourage her to lay her eggs in his nest. This sometimes involves quite a complicated mating display. If the female decides to lay her eggs in his nest he will release his sperms over the eggs.

Amphibians

Animals which live on land have a problem sperm cells cannot walk or fly! For the amphibians the answer to this problem is to return to the water to mate. Frogs and toads will migrate to the ponds and lakes where they were born. They do this usually in Spring. Sometimes they cross roads on their migration route in such large numbers that they can cause accidents! In France the motorway which runs through the Sologne, south of Orleans, has special tunnels constructed underneath it.

These tunnels allow the amphibians, which are very numerous in this region, to cross underneath the road safely. These tunnels are called crapauducts! When the frogs arrive at the water the males and females call to one another. This helps the amphibians to identify one another, as many different species may be mating at the same time and in the same place.

The male holds the female round the waist so that as she releases her eggs he will release his sperms close to them in the water. The mating calls are very important for some species because the males will try to mate with any object floating in the water, including fish or pieces of wood!

Mating on Land

Vertebrate animals such as reptiles, birds and mammals, and invertebrates, such as spiders and insects, do not return to water to mate, so the male must place the sperm cells directly inside the female's body. The male often has a special organ to place the sperms inside the female and the female has a special opening to receive the sperms. This kind of mating is called copulation and it has two advantages. First, the sperms are released in a liquid called semen which is made by the male. The sperms can swim in this liquid towards the eggs inside the female.

The second advantage is that the sperms cells inside the female are more certain to meet the egg cells. Animals which mate in this way do not produce so many eggs because only a few of them are lost. Copulation is so effective that many aquatic animals use it too, even though they are surrounded by water in which the sperms could swim. Getting closer to the female can have its disadvantages. If the animal is a carnivore, such as a spider, the female may think that the male is a meal to be eaten rather than a mate! The result is that land animals have developed complicated mating behaviour which involves dances, smells and often very colourful mating displays. It is usually the male which is colourful in the animal world, even amongst the herbivores. This is very apparent amongst birds; the peacock, for example, has brilliant tail feathers. The female (peahen) by comparison is quite drab.

Fertilization

When a sperm cell meets an egg cell, the head of the sperm fuses with the egg. The flagellum of the sperm is lost, its work is finished. The information in the nucleus of the male's sperm can combine with the information in the nucleus of the female's egg to produce an offspring. This important event is called fertilization. If fertilization takes place inside the female's body - as it does in mammals or birds - it is called internal fertilization. Only one sperm cell will fertilize one egg cell successfully. It is possible, however, for two sperms to fertilize two eggs.

Species	Litter Size
Bat	1
Dolphin	1
Chimpanzee	1
Lion	3
Hedgehog	5
Red Fox	6
Rabbit	6
Black rat	11

This will result in two offspring. This is not at all unusual in the animal world. Foxes give birth to litters of between four and eight puppies. A litter is a group of babies born from the same mother at the same time. The table below gives some examples of different mammals and their average litter size

REPRODUCTION IN BIRDS

The egg cell of a bird is really what we call the yolk. In the chicken's egg this yellow ball of yolk is about 20 mm in diameter. The yolk is the food supply for the developing embryo. The nucleus of the bird's egg can be found in the middle of a white spot which is found on top of the yolk. You need a microscope to see the nucleus itself but the white spot is visible to the naked eye. The egg that a hen (a female bird) lays is covered in layers of albumen (a material like jelly), two membranes and a hard shell. The shell and the membranes protect and support the egg.

The albumen feeds the developing embryo with water and protein. The albumen, membranes and shell are added to the yolk layer-by-layer as it passes down a tube called the oviduct inside the hen's body. The oviduct carries the egg from the ovary out of the hen's body. The last layer to be added is the shell. If a bird's egg is to be fertilized, mating must take place so that the egg will meet a sperm cell in the oviduct before these layers are added. The shell of a bird's egg is often coloured or patterned to help camouflage it from predators.

This is especially important for birds which nest on the ground, such as plovers. A hen bird may lay from 1 to 19 eggs in her nest. A group of eggs laid by a hen is called a clutch. It does not matter whether the hen bird lays 2 or 20 eggs in her clutch, she will only lay one egg per day. This is important because birds' eggs are very large. If the hen bird were to lay all her eggs at once she would have to produce smaller eggs or fewer eggs. The hen bird usually lays her egg for the day early in the morning. This is so that she can be free to hunt for food during the morning and in the middle of the day.

Taking Care of the Eggs

Birds take great care of their eggs. Usually the eggs are laid in a nest. Sometimes the nest can be a simple scrape in the ground or it can be a very elaborate nest. For example the mallee fowl of eastern Australia builds a huge nest of decomposing vegetation which helps to keep the eggs warm.In most cases it is the body heat of the parent bird which keeps the eggs warm. Keeping the eggs warm is called incubation or brooding. If the eggs get cold the embryo developing inside will die.

In some types of birds the hen develops a patch on her breast without feathers. The eggs that she is incubating will be in contact with the skin and so they will be close to her body temperature. The hen must go and feed from time to time, so the cock (the male bird) may take over. This is particularly important for one species of bird, the emperor penguin. This is the largest species of penguin, it has a mass of 16 kilogrammes and it lives on the continent of Antarctica. Antarctica is mostly covered in solid ice but it is there that the emperor penguin breeds.

It is the male bird that looks after the egg to begin with. The hen lays only one large egg per year. She uses up a lot of her food reserves to make this egg, so she must go to sea to fish for food to replace these reserves. The male stays on the ice and keeps the egg on his feet covered by a fold of skin. Obviously the emperor penguins cannot build a nest from the ice, so the male keeps the egg on his feet for eight weeks through the fierce Antarctic winter. The temperatures can drop to - 60° C. The chick hatches at about the time when the hen returns with food. At last the cock can go and hunt for food. He will return about two weeks later with more food for the chick.

Reproduction of Dog

In domestic dogs, sexual maturity (puberty) begins to happen around age 6 to 12 months for both males and females, although this can be delayed until up to two years old for some large breeds. Adolescence for most domestic dogs is around 12 to 15 months, beyond which they are for the most part more adult than puppy. As with other domesticated species, domestication has selectively bred for higher libido and earlier and more frequent breeding cycles in dogs, than in their wild ancestors.

Dogs remain reproductively active until old age. Most female dogs have their first estrous cycle between 6 and 12 months, although some larger breeds delay until as late as 2 years. Females experience estrous cycles biannually, during which her body prepares for pregnancy, and at the peak she will come into estrus, during which time she will be mentally and physically receptive to copulation.

Dogs bear their litters roughly 56 to 72 days after fertilization, although the length of gestation can vary. An average litter consists of about six puppies, though this number may vary widely based on the breed of dog. Toy dogs generally produce from one to four puppies in each litter, while much larger breeds may average as many as 12 pups in each litter.

Spaying and Neutering

Neutering (spaying females and castrating males) refers to the sterilization of animals, usually by removal of the male's testicles or the female's ovaries and uterus, in order to eliminate the ability to procreate, and reduce sex drive. Neutering has also been known to reduce aggression in male dogs, but has been shown to occasionally increase aggression in female dogs.

Animal control agencies in the United States and the ASPCA advise that dogs not intended for further breeding should be neutered so that they do not have undesired puppies. Because of the overpopulation of dogs in some countries, puppies born to strays or as the result of accidental breedings often end up being killed in animal shelters.

Neutering can also decrease or eliminate the risk of hormone-driven diseases such as mammary cancer, as well as undesired hormone-driven behaviours. However, certain medical problems are more likely after neutering, such as urinary incontinence in females and prostate cancer in males.

The hormonal changes involved with sterilization are likely to somewhat change the animal's personality, however, and some object to neutering as the sterilization could be carried out without the excision of organs.

It is not essential for a female dog to either experience a heat cycle or have puppies before spaying, and likewise, a male dog does not need the experience of mating before castration.

Female cats and dogs are seven times more likely to develop mammary tumors if they are not spayed before their first heat cycle. The high dietary estrogen content of the average commercial pet food as well as the estrogenic activity of topical pesticides may be contributing factors in the development of mammary cancer, especially when these exogenous sources are added to those normal estrogens produced by the body.

Dog food containing soybeans or soybean fractions have been found to contain phytoestrogens in levels that could have biological effects when ingested longterm. Gender-preservative surgeries such as vasectomy and tubal ligation are possible, but do not appear to be popular due to the continuation of gender-specific behaviours and disease risks.

According to the Humane Society of the United States, 3-4 million dogs and cats are euthanized each year in the United States and many more are confined to cages in shelters because there are many more animals than there are homes.

Spaying or castrating dogs helps keep overpopulation down. Local humane societies, SPCAs and other animal protection organizations urge people to neuter their pets and to adopt animals from shelters instead of purchasing them. Several notable public figures have spoken out against animal over population, including Bob Barker.

On his game show, The Price Is Right, Barker stressed the issue at the end of every episode, saying: "Help control the pet population. Have your pets spayed or neutered." Dogs are susceptible to various diseases, ailments, and poisons, some of which affect humans in the same way, others of which are unique to dogs.

Dogs, like all mammals, are also susceptible to heat exhaustion when dealing with high levels of humidity and/or extreme temperatures. Infectious diseases commonly associated with dogs include rabies (hydrophobia), canine parvovirus, and canine distemper. Inherited diseases of dogs can include a wide range from elbow or hip dysplasia and medial patellar luxation to epilepsy and pulmonic stenosis.

Canines can get just about anything a human can get (excluding many infections which are species specific) like hypothyroidism, cancer, dental disease, heart disease, etc. Two serious medical conditions affecting dogs are pyometra, affecting unspayed females of all types and ages, and bloat, which affects the larger breeds or deep chested dogs.

Both of these are acute conditions, and can kill rapidly; owners of dogs which may be at risk should learn about such conditions as part of good animal care. First generation hybrids (such as this terrier mix) often are healthier than either parent due to the genetic phenomenon of heterosis or "hybrid vigour". Common external parasites are various species of fleas, ticks, and mites.

Internal parasites include hookworms, tapeworms, roundworms, and heartworms. See also CVBD (Canine Vector-Borne Diseases). Some breeds of dogs are also prone to certain genetic ailments, such as hip dysplasia, luxating patellas, cleft palate, blindness, or deafness.

Dogs are also susceptible to the same ailments that humans are, including diabetes, epilepsy, cancer, and arthritis. Gastric torsion and bloat is a dangerous problem in some large-chested breeds.

The typical lifespan of dogs varies widely among breeds. Based on questionnaire surveys of owners in the UK, Denmark, and the USA/Canada, the median longevity of most dog breeds is between 10 and 13 years.

The breed with the dubious distinction of the shortest lifespan (among breeds for which there is a questionnaire survey with a reasonable sample size) is the Dogue de Bordeaux with a median longevity of about 5.2 years, but several breeds, including Miniature Bull Terrier, Bulldog, Nova Scotia Duck Tolling Retriever, Bloodhound, Irish Wolfhound, Greater Swiss Mountain Dog, Great Dane, and Mastiff, are nearly as short-lived, with median longevities between 6 and 7 years.

On the other end of the spectrum, the longest-lived breeds, including Toy Poodle, Border Terrier, Miniature Dachshund, Miniature Poodle, and Tibetan Spaniel, have median longevities between 14 and 15 years. The median longevity of mixed breed dogs (average of all sizes) is one or more years longer than that of purebred dogs (all breeds averaged).

As a rule of thumb, small breeds are longer-lived than large breeds, but some of the longest lived large breeds have median longevities nearly as large as those of the shortest lived small breeds, and some of the breeds with the shortest longevities are medium-sized.

"Median longevity" refers to the age at which half the dogs in a population have died and half are still alive. Individual dogs, even in breeds with low median longevities, may live well beyond the median. The dog widely reported to be the longest-lived on record is "Bluey," purportedly born in 1910 in Australia. He died in 1939 at the age of 29.5 years.

Bluey is usually identified as an Australian Cattle Dog, but the first Australian Cattle Dog breed standard was written in 1902, only eight years before Bluey's birth. It is unclear how closely Bluey was related to the breed as it exists today. The Bluey record is anecdotal and unverified. The longest verified records are of dogs living to 24 years.

Reproduction of Goats

Reproduction is considered a primary trait of economical importance in animal production systems. Within this context, there is a need to adequately manage the reproduction of bucks and does to increase reproductive efficiency and herd production.

Through reproductive management, goat herds may improve production levels. In order to understand and manipulate the reproductive processes of goats, it is important to be aware of their reproductive systems and functions.

Ovaries

Ovaries are almond-shaped, paired, and located on each side of the pelvic cavity. They produce the ova or female gametes and sex steroid hormones such as estrogen and progesterone. Estrogens are responsible for the development of the secondary sex characteristics of does and the physical and behavioural changes that does display during heat. Progesterone is responsible for changes in the uterine environment for embryo implantation, as well as for maintaining pregnancy and promoting mammary gland growth and development during pregnancy.

Oviducts

Oviducts are tiny, convoluted tubes located on each side of the uterus that connects the ovary to the uterine horns. The oviducts are divided into three distinct segments that transport the ova and spermatozoids in opposite directions. Once the ova are released from the ovary during ovulation, they are captured in the oviduct. The oviduct is the site where the ova are fertilized. In a segment known as the ampulla. The oviduct is the site where further capacitation of the spermatozoa occur.

Uterus

A doe's uterus is bicornuate, which means that it has two long cornus or horns that connect the uterine body to the oviducts. Does are known to have a small uterus, generally 3 cm in length and 2 cm wide. The uterus is a smooth, muscular organ that stretches during the pregnancy along with the growth of a fetus or fetuses. The uterus protects and provides nourishment to the embryo and fetus during pregnancy. The uterus is also the site where the sperm cells reach maturation or capacitation, and where the embryo migrates and develops throughout the pregnancy until parturition. The endometrium, or internal layer of the uterus, is formed by glands that secrete endometrial milk that nourishes the embryo. The endometrial glands also secrete prostaglandin F2a or PGF2a, a hormone responsible for the luteolysis or degradation of the corpus cycle or days before parturition. The uterus separates itself from the vagina through a cartilaginous structure named the cervix.

Cervix

The cervix is a fibro-cartilaginous-like structure composed of three or four cartilage tissues named rings. The cervix connects the uterus with the vagina. The cervix has an anterior and a posterior opening or OS. The cervix remains closed; however, it opens during heat under the influence of thehormone estrogen to facilitate the penetration of the sperm cells. The cervix is also opened during parturition for the passage of the fetus. During pregnancy, the cervix enlarges like the uterus. The inner layer of the cervix has secretory cells that produces a thick mucus, or "plug," that accumulates during pregnancy to protect the uterine environment against pathogens or infectious agents and foreign bodies.

Vagina

The vagina is a large and tubular elastic structure 9 to 15 cm in length. It is located between the cervix and vulva. The vagina is the copulation organ of the female, receiving the penis during mating, and it expands during birth.

Vulva

The vulva is the external genitalia consisting of the vestibule and the labia. The vestibule, generally 3 cm in length, is common to the urinary and genital tract. The vestibule joins the vagina with the urethral orifice.

The labia consists of the labia majora and minora, the outer and inner folds of skin outside the vagina. The labia majora is homologous to the scrotum in males, and it is the visible external portion of the female tract.

Clitoris

The clitoris is located in the lower portion of the vulva. It is the excitatory organ of a doe's reproductive tract.

Supporting Structures

The female reproductive tract is located in the pelvic cavity, and is supported by the broad ligament. This ligament supports the ovaries, oviducts, and uterus. Blood vessels and nerves pass through the broad ligament to supply blood to the female tract.

Testes

The testes or testicles are oval-shaped and paired. They are the main reproductive organs of a buck. The testicles are housed in the scrotum. They are symmetrical in shape and size, elastic to firm in consistency, and mobile in the scrotal sac. The primary functions of testicles are to produce spermatozoa or male germ cells in the seminiferous tubes, and to secrete steroid hormones (testosterone) by the Leydig cells. A buck within 8-14 months of age should have 25 cm of scrotal circumference.

Scrotum

The scrotum is the sack-like pouch formed by the skin that is responsible for protecting the testicles and the epididymis that is located in the inguinal region between the legs. The scrotum also aids in the thermoregulation of the testicles.

Epididymis

This is the first external duct of the testicles that is divided into three parts: the head, body, and tail. The epididymis transports, matures, nourishes, and stores spermatozoa produced in the testes. It is the site where the spermatozoa acquire motility.

Spermatic Cord

The spermatic cord is composed of muscles and fibre tissues and a portion of the vas deferens. The cord connects the testicles to veins and arteries that irrigate the testicles in conjunction with the scrotum to position the testicles outside the body, and to help regulate the temperature of the testicles.

Vas Deferens

The vas deferens, or ductus deferens, are a pair of ducts tied to the tail or cauda of the epididymis. They pass along the spermatic cord to the pelvic cavity where they merge with the urethra. The vasa deferentia transport spermatozoa from the epididymis to the urethra.

Urethra

The urethra is a duct common to the urinary and reproductive tracts. A distal portion of the urethra is connected to the urinary bladder. The distal portion is inserted in the penis and serves in discharging urine and semen.

Accessory Glands

The accessory glands are located next to the urethra and consist of the vesicular, prostate, and bulbouretrals glands. The accessory glands are responsible for producing seminal fluid that nourishes, serves as a buffer, and provides other substances needed for the motility and fertility of spermatozoa. The spermatic fluid and spermatozoa combined form the semen. Accessory gland fluids empty into the urethra.

Penis

This organ is responsible for male copulation and deposits semen in the female tract. The corpus spongiosum and cavernosum are expandable tissues that enlarge and fill with blood when arousal occurs. In this excitatory state, the penis is erect, facilitating copula and the ejaculation of semen in the female genital tract.

Prepuce

The prepuce is the sheath or foreskin that protects the penis.

Thermoregulation

The temperature inside a testicle is 2°C below body temperature. In cold weather, the testicles rise near the abdominal cavity; in hot weather, the muscular relaxation permits testes to swing and hang down from the body. Structures responsible for thermoregulation are the muscles cremaster, dartus and the plexus pampiniform.

This relaxed state maintains optimum temperature for the spermatogenesis to process and the spermatozoa to survive. A buck's low fertility rate is attributed to environmental conditions and the incapacity to regulate the optimum testicular temperature.

Hormonal Control of Reproductive Process and Doe Cyclicity

The reproductive process is complex and regulated by hormones. Hormones are chemicals produced by endocrine glands and secreted and released in the bloodstream that act directly on target organs, or indirectly through the regulation of other hormones. These hormones can be classified as peptides and proteins or steroid hormones.

In temperate regions such as in the United States and Canada, goat breeds are seasonal or "short-day breeders." This means that the period of cyclicity is regulated by the photoperiod. Thus, the decrease in day length triggers neuro-endocrine and ovarian interaction that occurs during late summer and continues on through the fall and winter months. Seasonality can be a limiting factor in the reproductive process because it reduces the annualbreeding season and limits the opportunity for producers to market their kids year-round.

The phenomenon of photoperiod is regulated by melatonin, a hormone produced by the pineal gland. The pineal is an endocrine gland located in the brain. The reduction in daylight exposure stimulates the optic nerve of the retina, which, in response, stimulates the cells of the pineal gland to secret melatonin. Higher levels of melatonin trigger a sequence of positive and negative feedback involving several endocrine glands and the gonads.

The increased levels of the gonadotropin-releasing hormone (GnRH) generated from the hypothalamus, a gland located in the brain, triggers doe cyclicity. The GnRH stimulates the cells of the anterior pituitary, or hypophysis, located at the base of the brain to secrete the follicle stimulating hormones (FSH) and the luteinizing hormone (LH). The FSH supports the development and growth of primordial follicles into secondary and tertiary follicles. These follicles produce estrogens. The increase in hormone estrogens will induce the production of LH surges, triggering ovulation or the release of the ova from the graffian follicles. After ovulation, the ova are captured in the oviduct, where in the presence of spermatozoa, they will be fertilized to generate an embryo.

After ovulation, the cells of the ruptured follicle will be transformed by luteinization to form a new ovarian structure called the corpus luteum (CL). The luteinization process is promoted by the action of LH. During the fifth day of formation, the CL is active, secreting progesterone to maintain a possible pregnancy. The maintenance of the CL is determined by the presence of an embryo. In case of pregnancy, the CL remains active, secreting progesterone to maintain the appropriate uterine environment for fetal development during pregnancy. In the case of a non-pregnancy, the CL will suffer luteolysis or regression. Luteolysis is caused by the action of prostaglandins F2a secreted by uterine glands. The prostaglandin PGF2a is transported from the uterus to the ovaries through the arteries and uterine vein connections to promote luteolysis or regression of the CL. The regressed CL will allow the ovary and other endocrine glands to prepare for another cycle.

In bucks, the main class of androgens is the testosterone that is produced in the testicles by Leydig cells. Testos-terone is responsible for a buck's secondary sex characteristics, to maintain the libido, and to promote the function of the accessory glands and spermatogenesis among others. Testosterone regulates the release of hypothalamic and anterior pituitary hormones like progesterone in does.

Reproduction of Horse

Pregnancy lasts for approximately 335-340 days and usually results in one foal (male: colt, female: filly). Twins are rare. Colts are usually carried 2-7 days longer than fillies. Females 4 years and over are called mares and males are stallions. A castrated male is a gelding. Horses, particularly colts, may sometimes be physically capable of reproduction at approximately 18 months but in practice are rarely allowed to breed until a minimum age of 3 years, especially females. Horses four years old are considered mature, though the skeleton usually finishes developing at the age of six, and the precise time of completion of development also depends on the horse's size (therefore a connection to breed exists), gender, and the quality of care provided by its owner.

Also, if the horse is larger, its bones are larger; therefore, not only do the bones take longer to actually form bone tissue (bones are made of cartilage in earlier stages of bone formation), but the epiphyseal plates (plates that fuse a bone into one piece by connecting the bone shaft to the bone ends) are also larger and take longer to convert from cartilage to bone as well. These plates convert after the other parts of the bones do but are crucial to development. Depending on maturity, breed and the tasks expected, young horses are usually put under saddle and trained to be ridden between the ages of two and four.

Although Thoroughbred and American Quarter Horse race horses are put on the track at as young as two years old in some countries, horses specifically bred for sports such as show jumping and dressage are generally not entered into top-level competition until a minimum age of four years old, because their bones and muscles are not solidly developed, nor is their advanced training complete. For endurance riding competition, horses may not compete until they are a full 60 calendar months old. Horses have, on average, a skeleton of 205 bones.

A significant difference in the bones contained in the horse skeleton, as compared to that of a human, is the lack of a collarbone—their front limb system is attached to the spinal column by a powerful set of muscles, tendons and ligaments that attach the shoulder blade to the torso. The horse's legs and hooves are also unique, interesting structures.

Their leg bones are proportioned differently from those of a human. For example, the body part that is called a horse's "knee" is actually the carpal bones that correspond to the human wrist. Similarly, the hock, contains the bones equivalent to those in the human ankle and heel.

The lower leg bones of a horse correspond to the bones of the human hand or foot, and the fetlock (incorrectly called the "ankle") is actually the proximal sesamoid bones between the cannon bones (a single equivalent to the human metacarpal or metatarsal bones) and the proximal phalanges, located where one finds the "knuckles" of a human.

A horse also has no muscles in its legs below the knees and hocks, only skin and hair, bone, tendons, ligaments, cartilage, and the assorted specialized tissues that make up the hoof.

13

The Immunology of Pregnancy in Animals

FEMALE REPRODUCTIVE TRACT

The female reproductive tract is an immunologically competent set of organs in which immune reactions leading to inammation, humoral immunity and tissue graft rejection occur. Ever since the initial insights by Medawar on the immunological problem posed by viviparity, consequences of the presence of immune cells in the reproductive tract for the developing conceptus have been the subject of intensive study. Although immune responses can potentially lead to the destruction of what is a foetal allograft, and a variety of immuno-logical adjustments occur to limit maternal immunore-activity against the conceptus, it has also been suggested, originally by Wegmann, that some immunological events promote conceptus development.

In the mouse, T and B cells are not required for successful pregnancy. In contrast, genetic strains of mice without natural killer (NK) cells experience an increased rate of foetal loss beginning at midpregnancy that is associated with alterations in the structure of uterine arterioles and the decidua. Moreover, some roles of the immune system, or molecules commonly associated with the immune system, are indicated by the fact that many of the genes upregulated in the decidua in the second half of pregnancy are immune response genes. Evidence from other animal models is also indicative of immune recognition of pregnancy. As will be discussed, such an immune response has the potential to either promote or inhibit development and survival of the conceptus.

Historically, farm animal models were important for the development of the eld of pregnancy immunology. The purpose of this review is to address, in domestic ungulates, the importance of interactions between the cells and molecules of the immune system with the conceptus during early pregnancy, *i.e.* from the period of semen deposition through initial apposition and interdigitation of the trophoblast with the endome-trial epithelium. During this period, the immunological situation changes from the cleavage stages of develop-ment, when the conceptus apparently evades detection by the maternal immune system, to a time coincident with trophoblast elongation and initial placentation, when large-scale changes in endometrial function are brought about by conceptus cytokine secretion or alloantigen expression. Interactions between compo-nents of the maternal immune system and the conceptus can be either benecial or harmful. In particular, development and differentiation can be promoted by specic cytokines, but the activation of cell-mediated immunity against the conceptus or inammatory and immunological events in response to infectious disease can lead to the demise of the conceptus.

IMMUNOLOGICAL RECOGNITION OF THE CONCEPTUS

One can hypothesize two major ways in which the immune system could become activated to affect conceptus function. The immune system could detect the presence of alloantigens or receptor ligands on the conceptus. Alternatively, the immune system could be activated by chemokines and cytokines produced by the conceptus. In addition to those initiated by the conceptus, immune responses generated towards other cells or molecules could have consequences for the development of the conceptus. Examples discussed later include immunological responses to semen or microorganisms.

Of the two classes of major histocompatibility complex (MHC) antigens, only MHC class I antigens are expressed on the surface of the conceptus. Moreover, expression varies during development. In the cow, the best studied species, MHC class I molecules or transcripts can be detected throughout development to the blastocyst stage. Transcription, which is of paternally and maternally inherited genes, is low through the period of blastocyst hatching; transcript abundance declines after the zygote stage and remains low thereafter. Until hatching from the zona pellucida, it is likely that interactions between MHC class I molecules and CD8 on T cells are restricted because of the physical barrier posed by the zona pellucida. Following hatching, low expression of MHC class I may ensure that a tissue rejection response against the embryo is not invoked.

After hatching, little is known about MHC antigen expression through the period of placental attachment except in the horse. Available evidence would suggest downregulation of MHC antigen class I expression, as seen in the pig trophoblast from days 14 to 25 and in non-invasive horse trophoblast throughout most of gestation.

Low expression of MHC class I molecules makes the embryo susceptible to lysis by natural killer (NK) cells because MHC class I molecules ordinarily inhibit lytic activity of these cells through binding to inhibitory receptors. In the bovine embryo, at least, a non-classical MHC class I antigen (NC1) of limited genetic polymorphism is expressed beginning at the morula stage. This non-classical MHC class I antigen may non-classical MHC class I antigens in other species. Expression of NC1 by blastocysts can be increased with progesterone, inter-feron-c (IFNG), interleukin 3 (IL3) or IL4. Transcripts of another non-classical MHC class I molecule, NC2, remain low throughout develop-ment to the blastocyst stage.

Once the denitive placenta has formed, MHC class I antigen expression is largely downregulated on tropho-blast. Based on transcript abundance, non-classical MHC class I anti-gens are the most abundant MHC class I protein expressed on the trophoblast.

Some MHC class I genes may participate in the control of embryonic development. Fair *et al.* have identied a gene in cattle that is homologous to the Ped gene located in the Q region of the mouse that controls the rate of early embryonic development. Interestingly, bovine embryos that experienced rst cleavage division by 25–28 h after insemination had higher transcript abundance for bovine PED homologue than later-cleaving embryos.

The horse has a distinct pattern of expression of MHC class I molecules on trophoblast. At approxi-mately day 30 of pregnancy, invasive trophoblast begins to express paternally and maternally inherited MHC class I molecules. Expression continues through differen-tiation of the invasive trophoblast into endometrial cups and then becomes repressed by day 44 of pregnancy. During this period, expression of MHC class I molecules is non-detectable on the adjacent non-invasive trophoblast of the chorion and allantochorion membranes. Expression of MHC class I antigens is associated with a pronounced maternal cytotoxic antibody response against paternal MHC antigens and maternal leucocyte invasion at the endometrial sites adjacent to the endo-metrial cups.

It might be surmised that the leucocytes, which consist primarily of $CD4^+$ and $CD8^+$ lymphocytes, play a role in the regression of the endometrial cups from approximately days 75 to 150 of gestation. However, the time course of demise of the endometrial cups is similar in MHC class I–compatible and MHC class I–incompatible pregnancies and is not inuenced by skin allografts adminis-tered before pregnancy, even though such allografts heighten the antibody response to conceptus MHC class I antigens. Thus, activation of a leucocyte response to the endometrial cups is stimulated by molecules other than MHC class I antigens or, as will be discussed later, is associated with the inhibition of cell-mediated immunity against the conceptus so that effector functions of leucocytes adjacent to the cups are blunted.

EMBRYONIC SECRETION OF CHEMOKINES AND CYTOKINES

The conceptus can also signal its presence to the maternal immune system through the secretion of chemokines and cytokines that regulate leucocyte func-tion. Little is known about the secretion of such molecules during the preimplantation period. However, specic cytokines are produced during the periattach-ment period. Elongation of the pig conceptus from spherical to lamentous form on day 12 is associated with increased transcript abundance for the IL1b gene (IL1B). After day 13, transcript abundance decreases to low levels by day 15. Amounts of immunoreactive IL1B in the conceptus and uterine ushings follow a similar time course. The pig trophoblast also shows immunohistochemical staining for the proinammatory cytokine, macrophage migration inhibitory factor, as early as day 16 of gestation. Elongating cow, sheep and pig conceptuses also express IL6. Horse trophoblast at days 33–35 (both invasive and non-invasive) and endometrial cups from days 38 to 55 express the tumour necrosis factor-a gene (TNFA).

The most spectacular example of conceptus cytokine secretion is the production of interferon-s (IFNT) by the periattachment ruminant conceptus. It has been esti-mated that the sheep conceptus produces approximately 100 lg/day of IFNT at day 16 of pregnancy when secretion is maximal. The IFNT genes arose from the IFN-x gene approximately 36 million years ago, after pecoran ruminants diverged from other mammals. Thus, the gene is present in animals such as the cow, sheep, goat, deer and giraffe but is not present in other clades of mammals. Secretion of IFNT is restricted to trophoblast; it begins as early as the blastocyst stage, increases greatly when the embryo initiates trophoblast elongation and then declines to undetectable levels by the late periattachment period.

The prototypical function of IFNT is to inhibit uterine prostaglandin F2a release and prevent luteolysis. Inhibition involves reduction in oxytocin receptor con-tent in endometrial cells, either by blocking expression of the oestrogen receptors necessary for oxytocin receptor synthesis, as indicated in sheep, or through actions independent of oestrogen receptor expression, as indicated in cow. There is also evidence that IFNT inhibits expression of genes encoding for PGH synthase (PGHS) and PGF synthase in the sheep and can cause degradation of PGHS in the cow.

In addition, IFNT has other biological actions that alter endometrial function. It possesses antiviral activ-ity and is inhibitory to lym-phocyte proliferation and stimulatory to activity of NK-like cells. Gene expression in endometrial epithelial cells is under broad control by IFNT. Chen *et al.* found that treatment of an immortalized luminal epithelial cell from sheep with IFNT caused changes in transcript abundance for 8 per cent of 15 634 genes examined. Among the processes affected were antiviral activity, apoptosis, prostaglandin metabolism, growth factors and their receptors, the nuclear factor-jB cascade, extracellular matrix accretion, angiogenesis, blood coagulation, and inammation. Interferon-s enhances induction by progesterone of specic endometrial genes *in vivo* and may therefore act with progesterone to prepare the endometrium to support placental attachment and development.

The pig conceptus also secretes interferons during the periattachment period. In contrast to ruminants, how-ever, the molecules involved are the type I interferon, IFN-d, and the type II interferon, IFN-c (IFNG), with the latter predominating. Unlike the ruminant, conceptus interferons are not involved in the regulation of luteolysis; rather, oestrogen is the major conceptus signal prevent-ing luteolysis.

Production of interferons during the periattachment period is probably not a general characteristic of mammalian pregnancy. While there is some evidence for trophoblast production of interferons in mice and humans, the timing of gene expression and the depen-dence upon viral infection for expression make the situation much different than what is seen in ruminants and pigs. Roberts *et al.* have argued that the presence of genes typically induced by interferons in uterine tissues of pregnant females in a wide range of species including rodents and the human may mean that species-specic conceptus signalling systems induce a common set of uterine genes and that many of these are interferon-regulated genes.

ACTIONS OF CELLS AND MOLECULES OF THE IMMUNE SYSTEM THAT PROMOTE EARLY EMBRYONIC DEVELOPMENT

CYTOKINES

There is evidence that products of the immune system can enhance embryonic development and survival. In the cow, transfer of autologous peripheral blood mononuclear cells on day 4 after oestrus increased pregnancy rate when embryos were transferred to the uterus at day 7. Pregnancy rates were 60 per cent for controls and 79 per cent for cows receiving peripheral mononuclear cells (n = 72–73 cows/group). This effect of mononuclear leucocytes could involve increased capacity for the embryo to undergo trophoblast elongation. Conceptus length at day 15 was longer for embryos transferred at day 7 into the uterus of cows receiving peripheral blood mononuclear cells on day 4 than for embryos transferred into control cows.

One possible mechanism by which lymphocyte trans-fusion could increase embryonic development is through increasing concentrations of pro-developmental cyto-kines in the reproductive tract. Among the cytokines that can increase the percentage of embryos that develop to the blastocyst stage *in vitro* in the cow are IL1B, leukaemia inhibitory factor and colony-stimulating factor 2 (CSF2).

The most well studied of these cytokines with respect to actions on the embryo is CSF2. In addition to its effect in cattle, CSF2 improves development to the blastocyst stage in the human, pig and mouse. Additional reported effects of CSF2 are inhibition of embryo apoptosis, shown in mice and cattle, and stimulation of embryo cell number, shown in humans and cattle. In cattle, CSF2 affects transcription in the preimplantation period in a way that could alter the pattern of gastrulation. In partic-ular, treatment of bovine morulae with CSF2 on day 5 resulted in alterations in the transcriptome at day 6 that could lead to the inhibition of neurogenesis and stimu-lation of mesoderm formation.

Exposure of bovine embryos to CSF2 from days 5 to 7 of development has profound effects on the subse-quent developmental fate of the embryo after transfer into recipients. In particular, a greater percentage of embryos result in pregnancies at days 30–35 of pregnancy and fewer of the pregnancies established at that point are lost thereafter. A similar effect of CSF2 on embryonic survival after transfer is seen in mice.

Recently, it was tested whether the actions of CSF2 to increase embryonic survival at days 30–35 of pregnancy involve increased embryonic survival before the embryo blocks luteolysis or enhanced trophoblast development and IFNT secretion. Embryos produced *in vitro* in the presence or absence of 10 ng/mlCSF2 from days 5 to 7 after insemination were trans-ferred into cows and ushed from the uterus at day 15 of pregnancy. There was a non-signicant tendency for the proportion of cows with a recovered embryo to be greater for those receiving a CSF2-treated embryo (7/20, 35 per cent for control vs/20, 66 per cent for CSF2) as well as a non-signicant tendency for cows receiving CSF2-treated embryos to have longer embryos at day 15. As determined by qPCR, expression of IFNT in trophoblast was 22.4-fold greater for embryos treated with CSF2, while expression of another trophoblast gene, keratin 18 (KRT18) was 297.4-fold higher in the trophoblast of embryos treated with CSF2 when com-pared to controls.

As summarized in Fig. 4, a model can be constructed to explain actions of CSF2 on the preimplantation embryo to improve calving rate. The increased survival of conceptuses at days 30–35 caused by exposure to CSF2 from days 5 to 7 of development is the result of increased embryonic survival before day 15 (probably, effects of CSF2 were not signicant) and a greater capacity of the conceptus to elongate and secrete IFNT.

Increased embryonic survival to day 15 could be due, at least in part, to an increased cell number in the inner cell mass and resistance to pro-apoptotic signals. The mechanism by which CSF2 improves conceptus survival after pregnancy diagnosis at days 30–35 is not known. There was no difference in the global transcriptome between CSF2 and control elongated conceptuses at day 15. However, the alterations in expression of genes involved in gastrulation at day 6 leads to the speculation that CSF2 affects the pattern of organ and tissue development and that such effects improve survival of the conceptus later in development.

It should be kept in mind that the regulation of embryonic development by cytokines does not neces-sarily indicate a role of the immune system in pregnancy.

Indeed, cytokines are produced by a plethora of tissues. In the cow, for example, CSF2 is present in both oviduct and endometrium throughout the oestrous cycle and staining is greatest in epithelial cells. Immunoreactive IL1B can also be found in epithelial cells and stroma of the bovine oviduct and endometrium.

Angiogenesis

There is some evidence from the pig that endometrial lymphocytes contribute to the vascular remodeling required for pregnancy. In particular, Tayade *et al.* observed that endometrial lymphocytes from pregnant gilts had higher expression of vascular endo-thelial growth factor (VEGF) (days 19–23 of gestation) and hypoxia-induced factor-a (days 15–23 of gestation) than endometrial lymphocytes from virgin gilts. More-over, transcript abundance in sites with healthy concep-tuses increased progressively during the times of pregnancy examined and was higher than for lympho-cytes isolated from sites where conceptuses were classi-ed as arresting. Another source of VEGF in the pig is the endometrial DC-SIGN$^+$ dendritic cell; expression of VEGF in these cells is greater at day 20 of gestation than at day 50.

Semen as a potential regulator of immune responses in utero that affect embryo survival Sperm cells are antigenic in females, and immuni-zation against sperm can lead to infertility. Deposition of semen in the reproductive tract leads to an inammatory response characterized by inux of polymorphonuclear leucocytes, macrophages, dendritic cells and T cells as well as increased local production of cytokines such as CSF2, IL6 and mono-cyte chemotactic protein-1. It is likely that the inammatory response to semen contrib-utes to the removal of sperm by the innate immune system and thereby prevents acquired immune responses against sperm.

A case has been made in the mouse that components of semen, particularly transforming growth factor-b (TGFB), cause important changes in immune function in the female that facilitate establishment and maintenance of pregnancy. The evidence is equivocal as to whether semen enhances the probability of pregnancy in farm animals. If seminal plasma is important for pregnancy, one would expect that pregnancy rates following articial insemination (AI) would be lower than following natural mating, unless the fraction of seminal plasma deposited during AI is sufficient to trigger an appropri-ate immune response.

Other differences between mating schemes, including damage to semen during freezing for AI, sire differences in fertility and the possible positive effect of the presence of the male, make interpretations of differences between AI and natural mating difficult. Nonetheless, there is little evidence for a decline in fertility when a well-designed AI scheme is implemented. Pregnancy rates to AI similar to natural mating have been observed for pigs, beef cattle, dairy cattle and mares.

Additional evidence against a role for seminal plasma is the nding that removal of seminal vesicles had no effect on fertility of boars. Similarly, there was no signicant effect of addition of TGFB to semen extender on total or live foetuses per litter, implantation rate or foetal survival in gilts. There was also no effect of addition of seminal plasma to sperm used for AI on farrowing rates in pigs or addition of seminal plasma or TGFB on pregnancy rates in beef and dairy cattle. In this last study, there was a tendency for TGFb to improve pregnancy rates of beef cattle when herd fertility was low, however.

In contrast to these studies, O'Leary *et al.*, working with a small number (n = 4–7 per treatment) of prepubertal gilts induced to ovulate with equine and human chorionic gonadotropin, reported that intrauter-ine infusion of seminal plasma 2 h before AI increased the number of viable embryos at days 5 and 9 after mating as well as embryo size at day 9. This effect of seminal plasma was associated with increased corpus luteum size and circulating progesterone concentrations.

Benecial effects may depend upon immune status of the uterus at the time of insemination. Rozeboom *et al.* found that the addition of seminal plasma to extended sperm improved conception and farrowing rates in pigs when animals were treated with a proin-ammatory signal [lipopolysaccharide (LPS) or killed semen] 12–18 h earlier. In the absence of such inam-matory signals, there was no improvement in conception or farrowing rates using seminal plasma.

Addition of seminal plasma to extended semen also improved fertility in mares in which inammation was induced 12 h earlier by intrauterine deposition of killed sperm. Thus, immunosuppressive or antiphagocytic molecules in semen may improve fertility when inam-mation makes pregnancy establishment problematic. Spermatozoa themselves may dampen immune re-sponses in utero. In pigs, deposition of spermatozoa into the uterus reduced endometrial mRNA for IL8, IL10, TGFB, TNFA and PGHS.

IMMUNOLOGICAL CAUSES OF EARLY PREGNANCY LOSS

While certain immune responses may facilitate preg-nancy, inappropriate inactivation of the immune system can result in infertility. An obvious case is acquired immunity against conceptus antigens. In fact, immuni-zation against conceptus material caused a reduction in fertility in heifers.

A series of studies in the pig comparing immune status in the endometrium adjacent to healthy concep-tuses with endometrium adjacent to conceptuses under-going developmental arrest illustrate some of the adjustments of endometrial lymphocytes to pregnancy and the possible role of lymphocyte dysregulation for pregnancy loss. At days 21 and 23 of pregnancy, sites adjacent to arresting conceptuses had higher transcript abundance for IFNG, FAS, Fas ligand, TNFA, IL1B and IL1 receptor in endometrium and IFNG in endo-metrial lymphocytes and trophoblast (day 23 only) than for sites adjacent to healthy conceptuses.

Similar results were observed for the expression of IFNG in endometrial lymphocytes and trophoblast at day 20. In contrast, there was no change in transcript abundance in endometrium or trophoblast between arresting and healthy sites at day 20 for IFNG, TNFA, IL5, IL6, IL10 and TGFB or protein levels for IFNG, TNFA, IL2, IL4, IL6 or 1L10. One possibility is that differences between healthy and arresting sites are not a cause of conceptus loss but rather reect endometrial responses to a dying conceptus.

Inammatory responses in the reproductive tract can also reduce fertility, as has already been described for the induction of inammation by administration of LPS or killed sperm. Endometritis in cattle is another example of inammation-associated infertility. At least three molecules produced during inammation can compromise embryonic development. Prostaglandin F2a reduces competence of preimplanta-tion bovine embryos to develop to the blastocyst stage and to hatch from the zona pellucida and lowers pregnancy rates after embryo transfer.

Tumour necrosis factor-a induces apoptosis in bovine embryos, and nitric oxide blocks the development of preimplantation bovine embryos. Bovine embryos that did not go to term had higher expression of TNFA at the time of transfer than embryos that did develop to a live calf. The trophoblast is also susceptible, most prob-ably, to phagocytes and their products and has been shown to be lysed by NK cells and lymphokine-activated killer cells.

Infection of the reproductive tract can also result in damage to endometrial cells caused by infectious organisms. Moreover, endometritis can cause ovarian changes detrimental to fertility such as reduced growth of the dominant follicle and circulating concentrations of progesterone. Extrauterine effects of uterine infection are attributable to release of bioactive molecules from the reproductive tract such as LPS and prostaglandins.

Immune responses generated outside the reproductive tract can also compromise fertility. The best studied example is mastitis in dairy cattle. Several studies in which cows have been classied based on the presence of clinical or subclinical mastitis indicate that occurrence of mastitis is associated with reduced probability of estab-lishment of pregnancy and increased probability of pregnancy loss. Experimental injection of killed Streptococcus pyogenes or the pepti-doglycan and polysaccharide component of the organism reduced pregnancy rate in ewes.

The mechanism by which an immune response in one region of the body (for mastitis, the mammary gland and associated draining lymph nodes) causes changes in the reproductive tract is likely to involve release of bacterial products, cytokines and chemokines from the site of infection that affect the hypothalamus, pituitary or reproductive tract.

REGULATION OF UTERINE IMMUNE FUNCTION DURING EARLY PREGNANCY

Given the risk to the conceptus posed by tissue graft rejection responses, NK cells and lymphokine-activated killer cells, it is not surprising that the immune function in the reproductive tract is regulated during early pregnancy. Semen itself is immunosuppressive and contains molecules that limit phagocytosis. Both the conceptus and the reproductive tract produce prostaglandins, and one of these, prostaglandin E2 can inhibit lympho-cyte proliferation. Transition of the reproductive tract from oestrogen domination at oestrus to progesterone domination beginning a few days later is accompanied by largely undescribed processes regulated by progesterone that make the uterus more susceptible to uterine infection.

Treatment of ovariectomized animals with progesterone decreases ability to clear uterine infections in the cow, horse, sheep and pig. Progesterone also reduces tissue graft rejection re-sponses in the uterus, at least in the sheep, so that skin grafts placed in utero have prolonged survival.

One of the molecules mediating effects of progester-one on uterine immune function is SERPINA14, a product of endometrial epithelial cells in a limited group of animals including ruminants, the pig, horse and some carnivores. In the sheep, this member of the serine proteinase inhibitor family can block lymphocyte proliferation *in vitro*, NK cell activity *in vitro* and *in vivo* and T-cell-dependent antibody production *in vivo*. It is unlikely that SERPINA14 is the only molecule responsible for the effects of progesterone on uterine immunity, particularly during early pregnancy, because the protein does not appear in uterine ushings until approximately days 13–16 of pregnancy.

Immune suppression is reinforced at the time of conceptus elongation by IFNT secretion. In addition to increasing gene expression for SERPINA14, many of the endometrial genes upregulated by IFNT are immunosuppressive. Walker *et al.* identied canonical pathways that were regulated in the endometrium of the cow at day 17 of pregnancy. Analysis of functional properties of individual genes was consistent with the idea that the conceptus pro-motes a locally immunosuppressive environment at this time while also enhancing innate immunity to protect from viral and bacterial pathogens.

Thus, IFNT induces expression of genes for the immunosuppressive proteins interferon-induced transmembrane protein 1 (IFITM1), transporter 1, ATP-binding cassette, sub-family B (TAP1) and indoleamine 2,3-dioxygenase as well as genes involved in antiviral activity [MX1, MX2 and 2,5¢ oligoadenylate synthase 1 and 2], several components of the complement system and antibacterial proteins (lipopolysaccharide binding protein and lyso-zyme 1).

Two of the genes that were found by Walker *et al.* to be higher in pregnant cows at day 17 or pregnancy, IL7 and IL15, are involved in proliferation and survival of Treg cells. This subpopulation of T cells is becoming increasingly recognized as playing an important role in the inhibition of maternal immune responses against the conceptus. There is also evidence for the involvement of Treg cells in the maintenance of endometrial cups in the horse because there was accumulation of lymphocytes positive for the Treg marker, FOXP3, in the endometrium adjacent to endometrial cups. Pregnancy in the mare is also associated with a reduction in the ability to induce cytotoxic T lymphocytes against paternal antigens. It is not known whether, as in the mouse, reduced cellular immune responses are specic to paternal antigens.

Based on the available literature, we can gain insight into the changing nature of the immunological relation-ship between the conceptus and maternal system during early pregnancy. Prior to hatching, the conceptus largely evades detection by the maternal immune system. Transcript abundance for MHC class I antigens, both classical and non-classical, is low, and the zona pellucida may serve as a physical barrier between the conceptus and lymphocyte. Cytokines produced by lymphocytes resident in the reproductive tract or by stromal or epithelial cells of the oviduct and endome-trium may participate in promoting and directing embryonic development, but activation of cytokine secretion is not apparently induced by the presence of the conceptus.

The situation changes when the conceptus prepares to initiate placentation with the endometrium. In species where the trophoblast secretes an interferon molecule, that cytokine causes large-scale remodelling of the endometrial transcriptome to inhibit lymphocyte func-tion and enhances the antibacterial and antiviral status of the uterus. The role of other changes in the endometrial transcriptome directed by trophoblast interferon remains to be determined, but it is possible that these genes are involved in placentation. Indeed, activation of immune response genes may be a common feature of pregnancy in mammals. In the horse, the maternal immune system is also activated although as a result of upregulated expression of MHC class I molecules on the invasive trophoblast.

While beneting from certain aspects of signalling pathways characteristically active in the immune system, the conceptus executes its developmental programme in an organism that recognizes it as foreign and in an organ that is continuous with the extracorporeal environment. Immunological recognition of the conceptus by mater-nal antipaternal lymphocytes or NK cells can lead to embryonic death. So too can activation of immune responses against infectious agents in the reproductive tract, or even in other organs. Accordingly, the mother and conceptus act in an endocrine and paracrine manner to control maternal immune function during pregnancy to prevent an immune response that could be cata-strophic to the conceptus.

14

Animal Cloning

Attempts to clone animals were on since a fairly long time. However, many of the initial attempts were unsuccessful and resulted in nothing. Partial success in animal cloning was achieved when frog embryonic cells were used to clone tadpoles, by the process of nuclear transfer. However, the tadpoles could not survive for long and died before growing into mature frogs. Nevertheless, the creation of cloned tadpoles was a breakthrough step for cloning scientists. Further, clones of mammals were also created through the same process of nuclear transfer of embryonic cells. Even this time, the cloned mammals could not survive for long.

The first actual success in the field of animal cloning was seen when the cloned sheep, Dolly, was created in 1997 in Scotland, which could survive and also naturally reproduced itself. Ian Wilmut, and his team at the Roslyn Institute in Edinburgh, is credited with the creation of Dolly. Unlike the previous animal cloning attempts, Dolly, was not created through a developing embryonic cell.

Rather, a developed mammary gland cell taken from a full grown sheep was used to produce the cloned Dolly. Since the successful creation of Dolly, scientists have also succeeded in cloning many other animals, such as rats, cats, horses, bullocks, pigs, deer, etc.

Animal cloning has come a long way since that first tadpole more than 50 years ago. The U.S. Food and Drug Administration's (FDA) declaration in early 2008 that food products derived from the clones -of cows, pigs and goats are safe for human consumption intensified an already growing interest in the process.

Cloning has additional uses besides its ability to help farmers breed consistently top-notch burgers and bacon. Other potential applications include the preservation of species, biomedical research, drug and organ production and even commercial ventures that aim to keep little Fido (or at least a convincing substitute) in the family forever.

The possibility of having carbon copies of man's best friend bounding around the house leaves some people giddy and others understandably edgy.

It may also leave you wondering just how many of these walking photocopies already exist. Or perhap-s more importantly, did the hamburger you just finished eating get its start in a petri dish?

DEVELOPMENT OF ANIMAL CLONING

Scientists have been attempting to clone animals for a very long time. Many of the early attempts came to nothing. The first fairly successful results in animal cloning were seen when tadpoles were cloned from frog embryonic cells. This was done by the process of nuclear transfer. The tadpoles so created did not survive to grown into mature frogs, but it was a major breakthrough nevertheless. After this, using the process of nuclear transfer on embryonic cells, scientists managed to produce clones of mammals.

Again the cloned animals did not live very long. The first successful instance of animal cloning was that of Dolly the Sheep, who not only lived but went on to reproduce herself and naturally. Dolly was created by Ian Wilmut and his team at the Roslyn Institute in Edinburgh, Scotland, in 1997. Unlike previous instances, she was not created out of a developing embryonic cell, but from a developed mammary gland cell taken from a full-grown sheep.

Since then Scientists have been successful in producing a variety of other animals like rats, cats, horses, bullocks, pigs, deer, etc. You can even clone human beings now and that has given rise to a whole new ethical debate. Is it okay to duplicate nature to this extent? Is it okay to produce human clones? What would that do to the fabric of our society?

CLONING IN NATURE

Cloning has been going on in the natural world for thousands of years. A clone is simply one living thing made from another, leading to two organisms with the same set of genes. In that sense, identical twins are clones, because they have identical DNA. Sometimes, plants are self-pollinated, producing seeds and eventually more plants with the same genetic code.

Some forests are made entirely of trees originating from one single plant; the original tree spread its roots, which later sprouted new trees. When earthworms are cut in half, they regenerate the missing parts of their bodies, leading to two worms with the same set of genes. However, the ability to intentionally create a clone in the animal kingdom by working on the cellular level is a very recent development.

EARLY PROGRESS

The first cloned animals were created by Hans Dreisch in the late 1800's. Dreich's original goal was not to create identical animals, but to prove that genetic material is not lost during cell division. Dreich's experiments involved sea urchins, which he picked because they have large embryo cells, and grow independently of their mothers. Dreich took a 2 celled embryo of a sea urchin and shook it in a beaker full of sea water until the two cells separated.

Each grew independently, and formed a separate, whole sea urchin. In 1902, another scientist, embryologist Hans Spemman, used a hair from his infant son as a knife to separate a 2-celled embryo of a salamander, which also grow externally. He later separated a single cell from a 16-celled embryo. In these experiments, both the large and the small embryos developed into identical adult salamanders. Spemman went on to propose what he called a "fantastical experiment" -- to remove the genetic material from an adult cell, and use it to grow another adult. In this way, he theorized, he would be able to prove that no genetic material was lost as cells grew and divided.

New Advances

There were no major advances in cloning until November of 1951, when a team of scientists in Philadelphia working at the lab of Robert Briggs cloned a frog embryo. This team did not simply break off a cell from an embryo, however. They took the nucleus out of a frog embryo cell and used it to replace the nucleus of an unfertilized frog egg cell, completing the "fantastical experiment" of nearly 50 years before. Once the egg cell detected that it had a full set of chromosomes, it began to divide and grow. This was the first time that this process, called nuclear transplant, was ever used, and it continues to be used today, although the method has changed slightly.

False Hopes

In 1977, a German scientist shocked the world, claiming to have cloned three mice from embryos. Although embryos had been cloned before, no one had been able to do the experiment with mice because the cells were so small and the tools so large that the cells were traumatized and would eventually die after a few divisions. He instantly became famous, telling the world how he cloned his mice. However, he refused to actually demonstrate any of his techniques, and when other scientists couldn't replicate his work, he came under suspicion. He was challenged -- repeat his work or be discredited. He accepted.

He claimed to work nights and mornings when no one was around, but the equipment was never disturbed. He showed off his mouse embryos' growth daily, even though a malfunction in the water purification system left other scientists at his lab unable to grow other embryos. Later, in his cabinet, test tubes were found with mouse embryos in them, each at a different stage of development. Most scientists do not believe that this scientist was ever able to clone adult mice.

In 1978, a science fiction writer published a book claiming that a millionaire (known to the readers only as Max) had come to him because of his connections as a writer, and asked the him to arrange for Max to be cloned. The author eventually agreed, as the story goes, and Max was cloned. The book was ranked in the Top 10 list of popular books. Scientists who read his book, however, noticed discrepancies between the book and scientific data. One man who was quoted in the book was angry enough to sue. The publisher admitted that the book was a hoax, but the author maintains his claim to this day.

Within these two years, two front-page advances in cloning were discovered to be, most likely, frauds. As a direct result, many scientists began to claim that cloning of mammals was impossible. Funding and interest dropped, and cloning returned to the realm of science fiction for several years.

First Cloned Mammals

A breakthrough came in 1986. Two teams, working independently but using nearly the same method, each on opposites side of the Atlantic, announced that they had cloned a mammal. One team was led by Steen Willadsen in England, which cloned a sheep's embryo. The other team was led by Neal First in America, which cloned a cow's embryo. Many advances were made during the course of these experiments, including progress in keeping tissue alive in lab conditions. However, neither team believed that it was possible to clone from an adult's differentiated cells. With no progress in sight, the prospect of cloning fell by the wayside, and little research was done on the matter.

Dolly

Ian Wilmut at the Roslin Institute in Scotland was assigned to a project in 1986. His goal was to create a sheep that produced a certain chemical in its milk. He chose to alter adult cells, which held up well in laboratory conditions, and then clone them, producing animals with the altered gene all throughout their bodies. He began the paperwork in 1987, and began research in 1990.

One of Wilmut's colleagues, who had experience with cloning from early embryo cells, suggested that the reason so many cloning attempts failed was that the cells were in incompatible stages of life. In one stage, the cells are adding to the DNA, in another, they are proofreading it, and in another, splitting it. The cells, he theorized, could not always start over. Wilmut's team learned that by starving the cells, they could be forced into what is called the G0 phase, similar to cellular hibernation. This advance increased the survival rate of the cloned cells; Megan and Morag, two lambs, were cloned from sheep embryos.

Wilmut's team now realized that differentiation did not matter in cloning. More work was done, and on July 5, 1996, a lamb was born, cloned from a frozen mammary cell from another adult sheep. Wilmut, who names his animals very creatively, named her Dolly after Dolly Parton.

Although Dolly was just a step in a long experiment, the press descended upon the first animal cloned from an adult. The Roslin Institute was overrun with journalists and reporters. However, other scientists were critical -- Dolly took 277 tries to create, and other labs were unable to reproduce the results. In addition, it took over a year for the institute to test Dolly's DNA to make sure that it was indeed the same as that of the frozen mammary cells. Science, although temporarily impressed, demanded a better way.

Herd of Mice

Oct 3, 1997, the Honolulu Technique created Cumulina the cloned mouse. She was cloned from cumulus cells (cells which surround developing egg cells) using traditional nuclear transfer. The nucleus was taken from the cumulus cell and implanted in an egg cell from another mouse. The new cell was then treated with a chemical to make it grow and divide. The scientists repeated the process for three generations, yielding over fifty mice that are virtually identical by the end of July, 1998. The Honolulu Technique's success rate of 50:1 is almost six times better than that of the Roslin Institute's success rate, 277:1. As cloning technology improves, more and more applications will be seen in everyday life.

Mainstream Cloning

How much do you love your dog? Is your dog so perfect that you would pay over $2.3 million dollars to have another just like it? One couple thinks their 11-year-old dog is just such an animal. Wishing to remain anonymous to avoid run-ins with the press, this couple has contracted Texas A&M University to clone their dog, Missy.

Scientists are hailing this for its scientific achievement; no dogs have been cloned before because their reproductive system is rather complicated. If the cloning of dogs can be achieved, perhaps exceptional animals like rescue animals can be reproduced.

In addition to the pure scientific appeal of cloning a dog, the attempt to clone Missy has another interesting addition to make to the history of cloning. A private couple wants their dog cloned. They are, of course, spending millions to have her cloned, but consider the possibilities. Could cloning the family pet one day become a normal alternative to buying a new one?

ANIMAL CLONING PROS AND CONS

When the first cloned sheep Dolly arrived in this world, the world media was taken aback by the medical breakthrough scientists had achieved. Cloning has been since then regarded to be one of the most debated topics in the media and amidst erudite biologists, religious priests and animal lovers. The debate on animal cloning pros and cons, mind you, is endless. Since we all agree to disagree and each one of us has a right to opine, it seems logical to take a neutral stand and study both facets of cloning. That will, for sure, not solve the ethical issues related to animal or even human cloning, but it is surely a more wiser step.

PROS AND CONS OF ANIMAL CLONING

With the concept of cloning gaining appreciable success in the last 10 years, it is said that if human beings succeed in getting total control over cloning, they will be able to 'create life'. The power to create life is a territory that separates the creator from the creation; humans from God (for those who believe in existence of God). So is man on the way to become God? With this intriguing question in our minds, let's discuss on numerous animal cloning pros and cons.

PROS OF ANIMAL CLONING

Cloning in human beings can prove to be a solution to infertility. Cloning has the potential of serving as an option for producing children. Cloning may make it possible to reproduce a certain trait in human beings. We will be able to produce people with certain qualities, human beings with particular desirable traits, thus making human beings a man-made being!

Cloning technologies can prove helpful for the researchers in genetics. They might be able to understand the composition of genes and the effects of genetic constituents on human traits, in a better manner. They will be able to alter genetic constituents in cloned human beings, thus simplifying their analysis of genes. Cloning may also help us combat a wide range of genetic diseases. Cloning can make it possible for us to obtain customized organisms and harness them for health benefits of society. Cloning can serve as the best means to replicate animals that can be used for research purposes.

Some of the potential benefits of cloning are certainly thought provoking. Improvement in animal breeding, for instance, is one of the most beneficial aspects of cloning animals. During the process of animal breeding, when two species of same or different breeds are crossed, the probability of healthy offspring, with desired traits can't be predicted with mathematical accuracy. Hence, in many animal breeding cases, there are unhealthy, diseased and weak offspring. Cloning eliminates this threat as it helps in production of exact replica of the animal that is required. So in essence, we can breed cattle as per our desire with no sick or deformed animals. It can eventually boost cattle production business all across the world. Moreover, healthy domesticated animals can be produced in large number for food sources. This will further help in alleviating problems of world hunger.

One of the other pros of animal cloning is that it will help in saving endangered species who're facing threats of extinction. This is apparently a very beneficial aspect of animal cloning. Similarly, proponents of animal cloning support that cloning will help in protection of animals from constant risks of animal testing. It has to be understood that there are numerous animal testing cons that innocent animals have to face during experiments. Due to cloning, once if any laboratory test in done on an animal, say a rat, it will be standardized and fixed for rats with same genetic features. This will also lead to better results and accuracy in predicting outcome of any medicine or drug.

Otherwise, till now results of laboratory tests are said not be immaculate as a cat × may not respond in a same fashion to a drug as another cat Y owing to differences in individual entities. Further, animal cloning pros and cons debate enthusiasts argue that cloning animals is beneficial in a way that it helps in creation of new organs. Applied on the same principles, if that process is successful in humans, an individual in requirement of a kidney, leg, liver or heart will be able to get it by the help of cloning!

CONS OF ANIMAL CLONING

Cloning created identical genes. It is a process of replicating a genetic constitution, thus hampering the diversity in genes. While lessening the diversity in genes, we weaken our ability of adaptation. Cloning is also detrimental to the beauty that lies in diversity. While cloning allows man to tamper with genetics in human beings, it also makes deliberate reproduction of undesirable traits, a probability. Cloning of body organs might invite malpractices in society.

In cloning human organs and using them for transplant, or in cloning human beings themselves, technical and economic barriers will have to be considered. Will cloned organs be cost-effective? Will cloning techniques really reach the common man? Moreover, cloning will put human and animal rights at stake. Will cloning fit into our ethical and moral principles? Cloning will leave man just another man-made being. Won't it devalue mankind? Won't it undermine the value of human life?

Just like animal cloning pros, there are several animal cloning cons. High cost of research and whopping amount of money spend on cloning process makes it as a very expensive procedure. Making cloning a mainstream part of social life still seems to be an impractical option. Financial feasibility is very important for any new medical breakthrough to succeed. Hence, when it comes to economics, animal cloning fails. Results of cloning have also not been amazingly beneficial as many experiments on cloning have failed with poor results.

There hasn't been any major scientific evidence on health and well being of cloned animals for domestication purposes. Although, FDA has been studying risks of eating foods derived from cloned animals and it has even said in 2008 that meats and dairy products of cloned animals are not harmful, Americans are still not very comfortable in accepting foods from such cloned animals. Also, risks of alterations at microscopic levels in the cells of such cloned animals hasn't been denied completely by medical fraternity.

Definitely, the FDA needs to conduct more research and studies. However, it is not unlikely that foods sourced from cloned animals will be in the markets within four to five years from now.

Amongst scholars, the most frightening aspect of animal cloning pros and cons is the argument that what if human beings with nefarious pursuits use animal and human cloning as a weapon to wipe out peace and humanity in various nations? Threats of biological and chemical terrorism have advanced to alarming proportions in this cyber era. Is there any guarantee that extremists won't use such a advanced concept to achieve their objectives? We all have seen in war movies, dangers of any invention or discovery if it goes in the wrong hands.

This was all about some of the most important animal cloning pros and cons. So what of animal cloning? Should it be allowed or must it be limited? But then, who will define the limits? Poor and developing countries can't invest eye popping money in R&D of animal cloning as they are grappling with their own problems. Developed countries can think of it but then what about numerous threats cloning brings with it? As I said earlier in this article, this debate continues. Join us in this debate on pros and cons of cloning by giving your valuable views in the 'comments column' below. We will ensure that your views reach millions of readers spread all across the globe.

PROCESS OF ANIMAL CLONING

The initial attempts to clone animals made use of developing embryonic cells from which the DNA nucleus was extracted. The DNA nucleus was then implanted into an unfertilized egg, from which the existing nucleus had already been removed. An electric shock or chemical shock treatment was given to the egg, in order to simulate the process of fertilization. This artificially induced union led to the development of cells, which were then implanted into host mothers. The resultant cloned animal came out to be genetically identical to the original cell. After the creation of Dolly, clones are now possible to be created by non-embryonic cells.

The technique of animal cloning can be used both for reproductive and non-reproductive or therapeutic purposes. Cloning for therapeutic purposes is done for producing cells or other such cells. Without duplicating the whole organism, these cells can be used for therapeutic purposes, such as healing or recreating damaged organs. However, even as animal cloning opens the way for a lot of beneficial possibilities, there are some who see cloning as unethical and an outrageous attempt to go against nature. Some countries also allow for animal cloning, though cloning humans is not allowed anywhere.

Animal clones are genetically identical. Natural clones occur in the form of identical twins but it is also possible to produce artificial clones by nuclear transfer. The nucleus is removed from a somatic (body) cell and placed in an egg whose own nucleus has been removed. The egg is then implanted in a surrogate mother and develops to term.

NUCLEAR TRANSFER

Nuclear transfer is carried out by fusing the donor somatic cell to an egg whose own nucleus has been removed. Fusion is achieved in a culture dish by applying an electric current. The change in electrical potential also mimics the normal events of fertilisation and initiates development.

A key aspect in the success of nuclear transfer is synchronisation of the cell cycles between the donor nucleus and the egg. Before fertilisation, the egg's nucleus is quite inactive. The nucleus of the donor cell must also be made inactive otherwise it will not be reprogrammed and development will fail. Inactivation is achieved by culturing the cell but starving it of essential nutrients. The cell stops dividing and enters a quiescent state compatible with nuclear transfer.

Fifty years of animal cloning

- *1952:* Cloning by nuclear transfer first demonstrated in animals. Source of nuclei was the very early embryo of the frog Rana pipens
- *1956:* Animal cloning in toads (Xenopus laevis) achieved by nuclear transfer from tadpoles.
- *1989-90:* Cloning first achieved in mammals (rabbits, sheep, cows) by nuclear transfer from very early embryos.
- *1995:* Cloning first achieved by nuclear transfer from cultured mammalian cell line, resulting in the sheep Megan and Morag.
- *1997:* Cloning first achieved using adult sheep cell, resulting in Dolly.
- *1997:* Cloning first achieved using a transgenic sheep, Polly.
- *1998-2000:* Cloning achieved using adult cells in mice, cows, pigs, goats and monkeys.
- *2001:* Cloning first achieved following gene knockout in sheep.

Animal cloning has the potential to overcome the limitations of the normal breeding cycle. In the future, it may be used to produce elite herds by cloning the superior animals, or to rapidly produce herds of transgenic or otherwise modified animals. Transgenic farm animals make useful bioreactors, producing valuable proteins in their milk. Another application is the use of genetically-modified pigs as a source of organs suitable for transfer to humans (xenotransplantation).

THE PROCESS OF ANIMAL CLONING

Initial attempts at artificially induced Animal Cloning were done using developing embryonic cells. The DNA nucleus was extracted from an embryonic cell and implanted into an unfertilized egg, from which the existing nucleus had already been removed. The process of fertilization was simulated by giving an electric shock or by some chemical treatment method. The cells that developed from this artificially induced union were then implanted into host mothers. The cloned animal that resulted had a genetic make-up exactly identical to the genetic make-up of the original cell.

Since Dolly, of course, it is now possible to create clones from non-embryonic cells.Now animal cloning can be done both for reproductive and non-reproductive or therapeutic purposes. In the second case, cloning is done to produce stem cells or other such cells that can be used for therapeutic purposes, for example, for healing or recreating damaged organs; the intention is not to duplicate the whole organism.

ETHICS OF ANIMAL CLONING

While most scientists consider the process of animal cloning as a major break through and see many beneficial possibilities in it, many people are uncomfortable with the idea, considering it to be 'against nature' and ethically damning, particularly in the instance of cloning human beings.The truth is that most of the general public are not aware of the exact details involved in cloning and as a result there are a lot of misconceptions about the entire matter.

In recent times, there have been a spurt of new laws banning or regulating cloning around the world. In some countries, animal cloning is allowed, but not human cloning. Some advocacy groups are seeking to ban therapeutic cloning, even if this could potentially save people from many debilitating illnesses. In a large percentage of cases, the cloning process fails in the course of pregnancy or some sort of birth defects occur, for example, as in a recent case, a calf born with two faces. Sometimes the defects manifest themselves later and kill the clone.

On the favourable side with successful animal cloning-particularly cloning from an adult animal-you know exactly how your clone is going to turn out. This becomes especially useful when the whole intention behind cloning is to save a certain endangered species from becoming totally extinct. That this is possible was shown by cloning an Indian Gaur in 2001. The cloned Gaur, Noah, died of complications not related to the cloning procedure.

REASONS FOR CLONING

Cloning is often performed for medical reasons. Experiments are carried out on animals that carry a disease which causes mutations in their genes. Farm animals are cloned to produce drugs and other substances that are useful in medicine. Cloning is a way to produce large numbers of genetically engineered animals.

THERAPEUTIC CLONING

In therapeutic cloning stem cells are reproduced in order to create new organs and tissue. New, healthy tissue can help a person get a new heart or a new liver to replace his ill one. Such a method could also create stem cells that you could use for patients who suffer Alzheimer's or Parkinson's disease.

TECHNIQUES OF ANIMAL CLONING

What are cloning techniques? Cloning refers to the development of offspring that are genetically identical to their parent. Animals which reproduce asexuallyare examples of clones that are produced naturally. Thanks to advances in genetics however, cloning can also occur artificially by using certain cloning techniques. Cloning techniques are laboratory processes used to produce offspring that are genetically identical to the donor parent. Clones of adult animals are created by a process called somatic cell nuclear transfer. There are two variations of this method.

They are the Roslin Technique and the Honolulu Technique. It is important to note that in all of these techniques the resulting offspring will be genetically identical to the donor and not the surrogate, unless the donated nucleus is taken from a somatic cell of the surrogate.

THE ROSLIN TECHNIQUE

The Roslin Technique is a variation of somatic cell nuclear transfer that was developed by researchers at the Roslin Institute. The researchers used this method to create Dolly. In this process, somatic cells (with nuclei in tact) are allowed to grow and divide and are then deprived of nutrients to induce the cells into a suspended or dormant stage. An egg cell that has had its nucleus removed is then placed in close proximity to a somatic cell and both cells are shocked with an electrical pulse. The cells fuse and the egg is allow to develop into an embryo. The embryo is then implanted into a surrogate.

The Honolulu Technique was developed by Dr. Teruhiko Wakayama at the University of Hawaii. In this method, the nucleus from a somatic cell is removed and injected into an egg that has had its nucleus removed. The egg is bathed in a chemical solution and cultured. The developing embryo is then implanted into a surrogate and allowed to develop.

SOMATIC CELL NUCLEAR TRANSFER

The term somatic cell nuclear transfer refers to the transfer of the nucleus from a somatic cell to an egg cell. A somatic cell is any cell of the body other than a germ (sex) cell. An example of a somatic cell would be a blood cell, heart cell, skin cell, etc.. In this process, the nucleus of a somatic cell is removed and inserted into an unfertilized egg that has had its nucleus removed. The egg with its donated nucleus is then nurtured and divides until it becomes an embryo. The embryo is then placed inside a surrogate mother and develops inside the surrogate.

Researchers hope that these techniques can be used in researching and treating human diseases and genetically altering animals for the production of human transplant organs.

Animal Cloning is the process by which an entire organism is reproduced from a single cell taken from the parent organism and in a genetically identical manner. This means the cloned animal is an exact duplicate in every way of its parent; it has the same exact DNA. Cloning happens quite frequently in nature. Asexual reproduction in certain organisms and the development of twins from a single fertilized egg are both instances of Cloning. With the advancement of biological technology, it is now possible to artificially recreate the process of Animal Cloning.

ANIMAL CLONING PROCESS EXPLAINED

Animal cloning process produced the first animal 'clone', that is an exact genetic duplicate of an animal in the form of 'Dolly', a sheep, who was born on 5th of July 1996. Since then, the animal cloning process has been refined and has produced many animal clones. This article will give a brief outline of the animal cloning process and the benefits of animal cloning.

There are many types of cloning procedures. The process of creating an exact genetic replica of an animal, in the form of another organism is 'Reproductive Cloning'. The basic idea behind reproductive cloning of animals is to transfer the ready made DNA (Deoxy Ribose Nuclei Acid-the genetic material which is the blue print of life) into an egg and create an identical organism! The DNA of every animal is unique and it holds all the unique information of creating an exactly same copy of that animal. The animal cloning process is called 'somatic cell nuclear transfer'.

Let us see the steps in which the animal cloning process is carried out.

- *Nucleus Transfer:* The first step is the transfer of genetic information from a cell of the animal to be cloned, to an egg which has been stripped of its cell nucleus! That is, the genetic information of the egg is supplanted with the genetic information of the animal to be cloned.
- *Stimulate Cell Division:* Now the egg has been transplanted with complete information of the object to be cloned. This implanted egg is now totipotent like embryonic cells. That is, it holds the ability to create an entire organism through cell division. Next the egg is stimulated to divide by treatment with some chemicals or electric current.
- *Embryo Transplant in Host:* With stimulation, the 'asexually' produced zygote starts dividing into a multi cellular embryo! When this embryo is sufficiently developed, it is planted into the uterus of a female host, who acts as its surrogate mother! The rest of the development of the embryo happens just like a normal organism.

So, this was the animal cloning process in brief. Every stage of this operation is a very delicate job and is not as simple as I made it sound here! Read more on 'DNA Research'. The mitochondrial genetic material of the egg is not replaced and it is inherited by the cloned organism, leading to some unpredictable complications.

So truly speaking, the clone is not an exact replica, as it contains different mitochondrial DNA material. This was a pitifully brief overview of the animal cloning process but it covers the basics. So, reproductive cloning is an asexual means of producing an exact replica of an organism, still being perfected over time. Hope these animal cloning facts have stimulated your curiosity to know more about animal cloning process. Read more on 'Pros and Cons of Cloning'.

People might ask what are the benefits of animal cloning? What is the use of creating identical copies of an animal? There are many advantages of animal cloning process. Breeders of live stock have used the animal cloning process to breed purebred specimens from a herd. This way, they can guarantee superior performance traits in the next generation of their herd. Many pet owners have used the animal cloning process to create exact replicas of their dying or dead pets.

However, there are some inherent disadvantages of the animal cloning process. The cloned specimens have a low life expectancy rate due to inherent immune problems. Still, scientists are studying the reasons behind these cloning anomalies.The possibility of human cloning in this fashion has raised a storm of ethical controversy. Currently, human cloning is prohibited by law in most countries. Read more on 'Human Cloning Facts'. Animal cloning process holds a lot of promise for endangered species of animals, giving them a new lease of life. It holds the future possibility of bringing back long extinct animals, whose DNA material could still be found, as it holds the entire information of creating the organism! Hope this article about animal cloning process has given you an insight in to breakthrough research in biotechnology and the promise it holds for the future!

TRANSFORMATION-ANIMAL CELLS

GENERAL PROCEDURE FOR ISOLATION OF ANIMAL CELLS

- Dissected out tissues are Trypsinised
- Monitor the cell shape. When cells become spherical they are filtered through 4-layered cheeses cloth.
- Then the cells are washed with serum containing growth medium
- Plate them in growth medium and allow them to grow as single layers or what is called monolayer.
- The most common medium used is GIBC-BRL's Dulbecco's modified Eagle medium (DMEM). To this Glutamine is added as additive to 2mM concentration.

- In many cases fetal bovine serum (heat killed and filtered) is also added to 10 per cent(V/V). This supports growth of cells.
- Antibiotics such as Ampicillin or penicillin 100ug per ml are added to prevent bacterial contamination.
- The pH of the culture medium at 7.2 is maintained by adding bicarbonates (2.0 to 3.7gm per liter).
- During Transfection the cells have to be prepared in serum free state.

When cells are added to plates they adhere to the surface and divide and redivide and grow to density called confluence at which time cell-to-cell contact is maximum. This contact inhibits them further growth. In cancer cells contact inhibition is lost so cells pile up one another. The number of passage is limited to 8-10 times, and then the cells have to be extracted from fresh tissues and cultured.

During Transfection cells should be in 70-80 per cent confluence. Such cells are repeatedly sub cultured once in every 4-5 days. Cells at the density of $1\text{-}4 \times 10^4$ cells/cm^2 before the cells are used for Transfection. Viable cell concentration can be accounted by treating a sample of cells with Trypton blue stain. Stained cells are considered as dead cells and unstained are living cells. The cells used for the said purpose should be competent, whose efficiency can be estimated by using control experiments.

EMBRYONIC STEM CELLS

Cells are obtained from embryonic blastula stage. Blastocysts can be cultured in Petri plate with suitable culture media providing primary embryonic cells from fibroblast as feeder layer. When blastula embryos are grown on feeder layer of cells, the ectoderm spreads out and inner embryonic stem cells come out and now they are exposed to feeder layer of cells. Such stem cells can be expanded and maintained for a number of generations by reculturing. Precaution should be taken about the change in chromosomal number.

Such cells can be used for developmental studies for they have potentiality to develop into different types of tissues, which depends upon the kind of stimulants you provide. The feeder layer prevents stem cells from differentiating. Addition of Leukemia inhibitor factor (LIF) also prevents stem cells from differentiating. The number of passages for keeping stem cells in active state is possibly.

ANIMAL CELL CULTURE AND MEDIA

Animal cell culture and maintenance require expertise and experience. These cell lines cannot be maintained for a long time, in some cases fresh batch of cell cultures have to be initiated and some has to be transferred to fresh media for some period of time (8to 10 passage can be OK for some cell lines). Some of the cell lines are genetically transformed.

One has to use all his ingenuity to keep them intact and functional.

- Mouse connective tissue,
- M.fibroblast,
- M.embryonic stem cells,
- M.monocyte,
- M.macrophages,
- M.spleen cells,
- Mouse 3T3 NIH cell lines,
- Rat fibroblasts,
- Rat hepatomas,
- Human lymphomas,
- Human keratinocytes,
- H.small cell lung cancer cells,
- H.lymphocytes EBV transformed,
- H embryonic kidney cell HEK293 cell lines,
- Chinese hamster ovary cell lines (CHO),
- Cat kidney cell lines,
- African green monkey kidney cell lines,
- SV 40 transformed African monkey kidney cell lines (COS),
- Dog's primary hapatocytes,
- Chick embryonic fibroblast cell lines,
- Hela cells (Henrietta Lock),
- Meyloma cell lines,
- Bovine fetal heart cells,

Some of the egg cells and other cells cultured for Transgenic and animal cloning experiments:

- Human egg cells,
- Mouse eggs,
- Xenopus eggs,
- Cow eggs,
- Pig eggs,
- Sheep eggs,
- Sheep udder epithelial cells,
- Sheep embryonic epidermal cells,
- Mouse blastocysts,
- Many stem cells from variety sources have been ultured.

Index

H

I

L

M

N

P

Q

R

S

T

U

V